에스라 느헤미야의 결혼 개혁

THE MARRIAGE REFORMS OF EZRA-NEHEMIAH

에스라 느헤미야의 결혼 개혁

윤사무엘 지음

THE MARRIAGE REFORMS OF EZRA-NEHEMIAH

쿰란출판사

서언　　Foreword

　　오늘날 현대사회에서 타 인종과의 결혼은 별로 문제가 되지 않는다. 한국에서 다문화 가정이 해마다 증가하고 있다. 외국인 거주자 250만 명, 다문화 가정수가 40만으로 추산된다(2025년). 앞으로 다문화 가정은 계속 증가할 추세이다. 해외 동포 800만인 한인 공동체에서도 통혼은 꾸준히 늘고 있다. 미주 사회와 한국에서 필자는 한인과 다른 인종과의 결혼 주례를 한 해에 수십 번 집례하고 있다. 유대인, 아랍인, 동양인, 백인, 흑인 배우자와 결혼하는 한인이 계속 증가하고 있다. 내 딸들도 타 인종과 결혼을 했다.
　　성경에서 다문화 결혼에 대해 어떤 견해가 있는지 관심을 가지고 찾아보면 신앙문제가 아닌 한 허용하고 있다. "성경에서 타 인종과의 결혼에 대해 무엇이라 하느냐? What does the Bible say about interracial marriages?"에 대한 인터넷 자료[1]에서 다음 내용을 읽는다.

　　이 문제를 이해하기 위해서 중요한 구절은 고후 6:14이다. "너희는 믿지 않는 자와 멍에를 같이하지 말라"는 말씀에서 '믿지 않는 자'가 핵심 단어이다. 크리스천은 어떤 형태든 믿지 않는 자와 결혼하지 말아야 한다. 타 인종과의 결혼에 대해서는 신 7:1-6에서 "이스라엘

---
1) www.bibleinfo.com

사람들은 가나안 주민들을 멸망시켜야 하고 그들과 결혼하지 말아야 한다. 왜냐하면 이방 며느리가 네 아들을 유혹하여 그로 여호와를 떠나고 다른 신들을 섬기게 하므로 여호와께서 너희에게 진노하사 갑자기 너희를 멸하실 것이기 때문이다"라고 말씀하고 있다. 고후 6:14와 같은 핵심 단어가 여기서 나온다.

An important Scripture in understanding this subject is 2 Corinthians 6:14: "Do not be unequally yoked with unbelievers." That last word, "unbelievers" is of key importance. A Christian should not marry a non-Christian, no matter how kind and good they are. What about interracial marriage? Deuteronomy 7:1-6 tells the Israelites to destroy all the inhabitants of the Canaan land and not to intermarry with them, because they would "turn your sons away from following Me, that they may serve other gods." The same key concern of 2 Corinthians 6:14 is again expressed here.

모세의 아내 십보라는 다른 인종이었고 민 12:1-15에서 아론과 미리암이 이것을 비난하다가 하나님으로부터 벌을 받았다. 룻기에서는 그리스도의 육신의 조상이 된 한 이방 여인을 소개하고 있다. 기생 라합도 이방 여인인데 마 1장에 기록된 그리스도의 족보에 나온다. 골 3:11에 기록된 "거기는 헬라인과 유대인이나 할례당과 무할례당이나 야인이나 스구디아인이나 종이나 자유인이 분별이 있을 수 없나니 오직 그리스도는 만유시요 만유 안에 계시니라"의 말씀대로 하나님의 관점에서는 그리스도 안에서 모든 인류가 하나이다.

  Moses' wife(Zipporah) was of another race and in Numbers 12:1-15 Aaron and Miriam were punished for criticizing this interracial marriage. The book of Ruth tells a delightful story of a foreigner who became part of the lineage of Christ. The harlot, Rahab, also of another nation, is included in the lineage of Christ as recorded in Matthew 1. Colossians 3:11 makes it clear that from God's perspective all are one in Christ.

  성경은 믿는 자일 경우 인종이 다르더라도 결혼하는 것은 잘못이 아니라고 분명히 말씀한다. 결혼을 염두에 둔 크리스천 부부는 기도하고, 신중하게 가족 간의 문화적 상황을 고려하고, 가족 관계, 태어날 자녀, 그들이 사는 사회에 결혼이 어떤 영향을 미칠 것인지 고려해야 한다. 사랑하는 크리스천 부부는 그들 사이의 다른 점들에 대해 잘 적응할 수 있다. 그러나 타 인종 간의 결혼은 자녀들의 결혼을 수용하고, 태어날 후손을 받아들여야 하는 문화적 상황도 있다.

타 인종 간의 결혼은 오늘날 많은 사회에서 점차 보편화되고 있다. 결혼을 심각하게 고려하는 모든 신혼부부들은 실제 부닥치는 많은 문제들을 잘 생각할 필요가 있다. 성경은 이런 문제들까지 상세하게 다루고 있지는 않다.

The Bible is clear that when both parties are believers(equally yoked), interracial marriage is not wrong. A Christian couple contemplating marriage must prayerfully and carefully consider the impact their marriage will have within heir cultural context, their family relationships, future children and the society in which they live. A loving Christian couple may accommodate well to many kinds of differences between themselves. However, there are cultural contexts where interracial marriage poses significant barriers to acceptance of the marriage and/or the children of the marriage. Interracial marriages are becoming more common in many societies. All couples contemplating marriage need to give thoughtful consideration to a variety of practical issues, some of which may have no clear Biblical imperative.

본 서는 필자의 신학박사 학위논문인 "페르샤 시대에 있었던 유대인의 언약공동체 회복에 있어서 통혼 문제 The Problem of Intermarriage in the Restoration of Judean Covenant Community during the Persian Period"(Boston University School of Theology/Faith Theological Seminary and Christian College, Ph.D. 2006)를 개정한 것이다. 해당 본문(에 9-10장; 느 13:23-30)을 성경 내의 주석(inner Biblical exegesis)[2]을 통해 지식사회학적인 관점[3]에서 BC 6세기 말경의 유대 공동체에서 일어난 결혼 개혁 운동을 다루고 있다. 본 서를 통하여 성경 본문에 나타난 하나님 나라의 상징적 우주(symbolic universe)가 개혁주의적 세계관과 접목하고, 예배 회복을 통해 신정주의를 이룩하려던 에스라와 느헤미야의 역사적 인물을 만나게 될 것이다.

출판을 위해 수고해 주신 쿰란출판사 이형규 장로님께 진심으로 감사드린다. 필자를 지도해 주신 박준서 박사님(연세대), 장일선 박사님(한신대), Frank Benz(Warburg T. Seminary, Dubuque, IA), Frank M. Cross, Jr., Paul D. Hanson(Harvard Divinity School), Simon Parker(Boston University, School of Theology), Bernhard W. Anderson, Harold Beck(Boston University, School of Theology), Patrick D. Miller, Jr.(Princeton Theological Seminary), Peter L. Berger(Boston University), D.A.

---

2) Michael A. Fishbane, *Biblical Interpretation in Ancient Israel*, Clarendon Press, 1988.
3) Peter L. Berger & Thomas Luckmann, *The Social Construction of Reality: A Treatise of the Sociology of Knowledge*, The Penguin Books, 1967.

Waite(Dean Burgon Society, The Bible for Today Ministry), Gary Cohen & Paul Kang(강신권 박사님), Ronald Vandermey(Cohen University Theological Seminary), George Siemer, George Walters, Jr.(Faith Theological Seminary and Christian College) 교수님들께 감사를 드린다. 늘 기도와 내조로 연구에 동참하는 아내(오선화 박사)와 여섯 자녀들(3남 3녀) 및 손자, 손녀들(Dylan, Eliana, Judah, Jason, Jordan, new granddaughter in Sep. 2025), 바이블 아카데미(Bible Academy) 참석 목회자들, 페이스신학대학교대학원(Faith Christian University & Theological Seminary, 구 겟세마네 신학교) 가족들, 로이교회(구 겟세마네 장로교회) 성도 여러분들에게 늘 고마운 마음을 보낸다. 참고문헌은 본 서에 인용하지 않았어도 관련 문제들을 연구하는 데 도움이 되는 자료들을 정리한 것이다.

2025년 4월 20일
윤사무엘(윤삼열) 목사

약어표 Abbreviations

AJSL	American Journal for Semitic Languages and Literature
BA	Biblical Archeologist
BASOR	Bulletin of the American Schools of Oriental Research
BHS	Biblia Hebraica Stuttgartensia
BS	Bibliotheca Sacra
BT	The Bible Translator
BTB	Biblical Theology Bulletin
CBQ	Catholic Biblical Quarterly
EQ	Evangelical Quarterly
GJ	Grace Journal
HAR	Hebrew Annual Review
HJ	Heythrop Journal
HTR	Harvard Theological Review
HUCA	Hebrew Union College Annual
IB	Interpreter's Bible
IDB	Interpreter's Dictionary of the Bible
IDBS	The Interpreter's Dictionary of the Bible, Supplementary Volume
IEJ	Israel Exploration Journal
JANES	Journal of the Ancient Near Eastern Society
JAOS	Journal of the American Oriental Society
JBL	Journal of Biblical Literature
JETS	Journal of the Evangelical Theological Society
JHCS	Journal of Halacha and Contemporary Society
JJS	Journal of Jewish Studies

JNES	Journal of Near Eastern Studies
JNSL	Journal of Northwest Semitic Languages
JSJP	Journal for the Study of Judaism in the Persian
JSNT	Journal for the Study of the New Testament
JSOT	Journal for the Study of the Old Testament
JSS	Journal of Semitic Studies
JTS	Journal of Theological Studies
KJV	King James Version
NIDDOTTE	New International Dictionary of Old Testament Theology and Exegesis
PEQ	Palestine Exploration Quarterly
PJ	Palästina-Jahrbuchna-Jahrbuch
PTR	The Princeton Theological Review
RTR	Reformed Theological Review
SJOT	Scandinavian Journal of the Old Testament
TWOT	Theological Wordbook of the Old Testament
USQR	Union Seminary Quarterly Review
VT	Vetus Testamentum
VT	Sup Supplement to Vetus Testamentum
WTJ	Westminster Theological Journal
ZAW	Zeitschrift für die alttestamentliche Wissenschaft

차례 Contents

서언 Foreword · 4
약어표 Abbreviations · 10

I. 서론 Introduction · 15

1. 연구목적 및 과제 Problem of the Study · 16
2. 이론, 방법, 절차 Theory, Method and Procedure of the Study · 18
3. 연구사 Previous Research in the Field · 32
4. 연구의의 Significance of the Study · 51

II. 결혼개혁 배경 The Background of the marriage reforms · 57

1. 포수기 이후 유대 공동체 안에 있었던 통혼 현상 Phenomenon of intermarriage in the post-exilic Judean community · 59
2. 통혼에 대한 부정적인 태도 The Negative attitude towards intermarriage · 67
3. 포수기 이후 유대 공동체의 사회적 현실들 Social realities of the post-exilic Judean community · 95

III. 에스라와 느헤미야의 결혼 개혁들: 성경 주석 The marriage reforms under Ezra and Nehemiah: The Biblical Exegesis · 109

1. 본문의 역사적-사회적 배경 Historical-social background of the text · 111

2. 에스라 9-10장 주석 Exegesis of Ezra 9-10 · **122**
3. 느헤미야 13:23-30 주석 Exegesis of Nehemiah 13:23-30 · **199**
4. 요약 Summary · **217**

IV. 결혼개혁과 유대 공동체의 사회적 기반 회복 The marriage reform and the restoration of the social basis of Judean community · **221**

1. 유대 공동체 정체성의 위기 The crisis of Judean communal identity · **223**
2. 유대 공동체의 회복 Restoration of Judean community · **230**
3. 개혁 그룹의 상징적 세계 The Symbolic universe of the reform group · **245**
4. 요약 Summary · **261**

V. 결론 Conclusion · **269**

1. 전체 요약과 맺는말 General summary and concluding remark · **270**
2. 본 연구의 평가 Evaluation of the study · **277**
3. 연구과제로 남기는 문제들 Implications of the study · **279**

참고문헌 The Selective Bibliography · **287**

I

서론
Introduction

1. 연구목적 및 과제 Problem of the Study

본 서에서 다루는 연구의 목적은 에스라와 느헤미야가 수행한 결혼 개혁과 페르샤 시대에 포수기 후 유대 공동체가 재구성하는 데 끼친 영향을 살피기 위함이다.

The purpose of the present study is to examine the marriage reforms undertaken by Ezra and Nehemiah and their influence upon the reconstruction of the post-exilic Judean community during the Persian period.

핵심 질문은 "에스라와 느헤미야의 개혁운동이 규정한 결혼제도와 유대 예배 공동체의 세계관 사이의 관계는 무엇이었나?" 하는 것이다. 이 중심 질문은 다음과 같은 질문이 포함되어 있다. "왜 일부 유대인들이 그 당시 이방인 여인들과 결혼했는가? 이런 통혼이 개혁하던 포수기 후 유대 공동체에 어떤 영향을 미쳤는가? 에스라와 느헤미야가 이 통혼[4] 문제를 어떻게 해결했는가?" 하는 문제들을 본

---

[4] 통혼이란 히브리어는(The Hebrew equivalent of "intermarry" הִתְחַתֵּן인데 Hithpael of ḥtn, Aramaic, Hithpa'al에 전치사 בְּ가 붙은 with preposition (בְּ) 형태를 에스라 Ezra 9:14, 신명기 Deut. 7:3, 여호수아 Josh. 23:12에서 찾을 수 있다. 이 단어는 이스

서에서 다루고자 한다.

We will deal with one overarching question: "What was relationship between the institution of marriage as defined by the reforms of Ezra and Nehemiah and the world-view of the Judean worship community?" This major question includes the following questions: Why did some Judean men marry non-Judean women at that time? What effect might this kind of "intermarriage"[4] have on the reforming post-exilic Judean community? How did Ezra and Nehemiah solve the problem of intermarriage? These questions are to be the main issues in this study.

이방인과 결혼하는 일이 포수기 전에는 이스라엘 사회에서 일반적으로 수용되었던 것 같다.[5] 그러나 에스라와 느헤미야 시대에는 유대인과 이방인 사이의 통혼 문제는 사회적 위기가 되었다. 왜냐하

라엘인들이 이방인과 결혼한다는 뜻이다. This word generally means the Israelites' marriage-alliance with non-Israelites. Cf. F. Brown, S.R. Driver, & C.A. Briggs, *A Hebrew and English Lexicon of the Old Testament* (Oxford: Clarendon Press, 1906), 368; M. Jastrow (compiled), *A Dictionary of the Targumim, The Talmud Babli and Yerushalmi, and the Midrashic Literature* (New York: The Judaica Press, Inc., 1982), 514. 에스라와 느헤미야서에 다른 동사도 나온다. In the books of Ezra and Nehemiah, there is another verb meaning "intermarry"; Hiph'il of ישׁב with strange or foreign women נָשִׁים נָכְרִיּוֹת (Ezra 10:2, 10, 14, 17, 18; Neh. 13:23, 27).

5) 다음의 연구를 참고하라. See Morton Smith, *Palestinian Parties and Politics that Shaped the Old Testament* (London: SCM Press, LTD, 1987), 12-13: "이방인과 결혼하는 것에 대해 포로기 전 선지자들은 공격하지 아니하다. 신명기 사가는 통혼을 강하게 반대하지만 그 이유는 여호와 대신 다른 신들을 예배하는 것 때문이었다. 그런 예배의 위험이 없다면(예를 들면, 여자 포로들 경우) 신명기도 통혼을 허용한다. Marriage with aliens is not attacked by the pre-exilic prophets. The Deuteronomist is violently opposed to it, but their opposition seems to derive chiefly from their concern to prevent the worship of gods other than Yahweh. When there is no danger of such worship (for instance, in the case of a female captive), Deuteronomy permits the practice."

면 통혼으로 포로기 후 유대인 공동체의 사회적 정체성을 상실할 위험에 처했기 때문이었다. 에스라와 느헤미야의 결혼 개혁과정에서 일어난 합법화 구조를 분석할 것이다.

Marriage with non-Israelites seems to have been generally accepted in Israelite society during the pre-exilic period.[5] But the problem of intermarriage between Judean and non-Judean people became a social crisis at the time of Ezra and Nehemiah, for intermarriage threatened the loss of the social identity of the post-exilic Judean community. Our aim is to analyze the structures of legitimation actually operative in the marriage reforms of Ezra and Nehemiah.

2. 이론, 방법, 절차 Theory, Method and Procedure of the Study

1) 이론 Theory

위에 언급한 분석을 위하여 지식사회학을 방법론으로 택한다. 지식사회학은 종교적 이념과 사회적 배경의 관계를 조명한다. 이 이론은 포수기 후 유대 공동체의 사회적 위기를 이해하는 데 유용하다. 그 사회적 기반을 개혁하는 데 실제 작용하는 합법화 구조를 분석하는 데도 필요하다.

In order to undertake the above mentioned analysis, we will employ the sociology of knowledge, which investigates the relation of religious ideas to their social settings. This theory will be useful in understanding the social crisis of the post-exilic Judean community and in analyzing the structures of legitimation actually operative in reforming its social basis.

피터 버거와 토마스 러크만의 합법화 이론을 살펴보자. 이 이론은 본 연구에 적합하다. 이들의 저서에서 다음의 글을 인용하자.

We take the theory of legitimation of Peter L. Berger and Thomas Luckmann, for their theory is suitable for our task. Let us quote from their article:

> 어떤 인간 사회도 한 형태든 다른 형식으로든 합법화 과정 없이는 존재할 수 없다. 합법화는 합법화된 우주와 별개로 논의될 수 없다.…지식사회학의 과제는 지식의 사회적 형태, 개인이 이 지식을 획득하는 과정, 그리고 제도적인 조직과 지식의 사회적 분배를 분석하고 있는 것이다.…지식 사회학의 가장 중요한 과제는 사회적으로 구성된 세계(즉 그것에 대한 "지식")가 합법화되어지는 인식적이고 규범적인 장치를 분석하는 것이다.
>
> 지식사회학은 이념, 가치, 신념(신앙)의 사회적 위치에 관심을 가진다. 지식사회학은 특별한 이념(사상)들이 사회 구조의 특별한 유형들과 관련 있음을 보여주려고 한다. 사회적으로 구성된 이념이 어떤 공동체 안에서 합법화되어질 때, 당연시 되는 '객관화된' 지식이 될 수 있는 것이다.[6]
>
> No human society can exist without legitimation in one form or another…Legitimation cannot be discussed apart

---

6) Peter Berger and Thomas Luckmann, "Sociology of Religion and Sociology of Knowledge," *Sociology and Social Research* 47 (1963), 423-425.

from the universe that is being legitimated…The task of the sociology of knowledge is the analysis of the social forms of knowledge, of the processes by which individuals acquire this knowledge and, finally, of the institutional organization and social distribution of knowledge…And the most important task of the sociology of religion is to analyze the cognitive and normative apparatus by which a socially constituted universe(that is, "knowledge" about it) is legitimated…

The sociology of knowledge concerns itself with the social location of ideas, values, and beliefs. It seeks to demonstrate that specific ideas are related to specific types of social structure. When a socially constructed idea is legitimated in a community, it can become a taken-for-granted 'objectified' knowledge.[6]

이 두 학자들에 의하면 지식사회학은 종교사회학 없이는 불가능하다.[7] 막스 웨버(Maximilian Karl Emil Weber, 1864-1920)의 견해를 수용하면서, 버거는 광의적으로 "합법화"는 사회적으로 객관화된 "지식"으로 정의 내린다. 이 지식이 사회 질서를 설명하고 합리화시킨다. 모든 합법화 형태들은 객관적인 것과 주관적인 차원에서 실체를 유지하는 데 궁극적인 목적을 둔다.[8]

According to them, a sociology of knowledge is impossible

---

7) P. Berger and T. Luckmann, *The Social Construction of Reality*(Garden City, NY: Doubleday & Company, Inc., 1966), 185.
8) 버거의 합리화 개념에 대해서는 On Berger's notion of legitimation, see *ibid.*, 92-128; Cf. Peter L. Berger, *The Sacred Canopy*(Garden City, NY: Doubleday & Company, Inc., 1967), 29-51.

without a sociology of religion.[7] Following Max Weber, Berger defines "legitimation" in a broader sense as socially objectivated "knowledge" that serves to explain and justify the social order. All forms of legitimation are essentially intended to maintain reality, both on the objective and the subjective levels.[8]

버거는 인류사의 대부분 역사를 통해서 보면 사회를 유지하기 위해 중요한 합법화를 종교가 제시해 왔다고 주장한다. 사회적으로 구성된 모든 세계는 본질상 불안전하다. 인간의 활동을 지원받아, 이 세계들은 인간의 자기 이익과 무시로 말미암아 꾸준히 위협을 받게 되어 있다.[9]

Berger argues that through most of human history, the principal legitimations for the maintenance of society have been provided by religion. All the worlds socially constructed are inherently precarious. Supported by human activity, they are constantly threatened by the human facts of self-interest and ignorance.[9]

막스 웨버는 말하기를 사회적 관계의 가장 안정한 형태가 참석하는 개개인의 주관적인 태도들이 하나의 합법적인 질서를 굳게 믿는 신앙으로 나아갈 때라고 한다. 웨버는 "합법성이란 사람들의 위에 군림하는 권위가 단순한 사실뿐만 아니라 도덕적 만족을 충족하는 사실이라는 신념을 주는데 이 합법성이 이뤄지는 과정을 '합법화'이라 부른다"라고 정의 내린다.[10]

---

9) *The Sacred Canopy*, 29.
10) 웨버의 합법화 질서 개념에 대해: On Weber's notion of legitimation order, see *The*

M. Weber says that the most stable forms of social relationship are those in which the subjective attitudes of the participating individuals are directed towards the belief in a legitimate order. By legitimacy, that is, Weber means "the belief held by people that the authority over them is not only a simple fact but is a fact charged with moral content. And the process by which this legitimacy is acquired is called 'legitimation.'"[10]

버거와 러크만에 의하면, 합법화는 네 가지 단계가 있다는 것이다.[11] 그 합법화의 첫 단계는 아이들이 "왜 이렇게 되나요?"라고 묻는 질문에 대한 답변으로 하는 "모든 전통적이고 단순한 주장들"이 포함된다. 둘째 단계는 "원초적인 형태로 된 이론적 전제"인데 잠언, 격언, 속담, 이야기들이 이 단계에 해당한다. 셋째 단계는 "어떤 제도적 분야가 지식을 식별하는 체계의 관점에서 합법화되게 하는 명확한 이론들"을 포함하고 있다. 그리고 네 번째 합법화 단계는 "상징적 우주"를 포함한다. 본 서에서는 네 번째 단계에 관심을 가지는데, 성경 본문에 다른 단계에 대한 증거가 없기 때문이다.

According to Berger and Luckmann, there can be four levels in legitimation.[11] The first level of legitimation includes "all the simple traditional affirmations," such as answers to the child's question: Why are things done like this? The second level contains "theoretical propositions in a rudimentary form." Proverbs, moral maxims and wise sayings or narratives belong to this level. The third level contains "explicit theories by which an

---

Sociology of Religion, ET E. Fischoff (Boston: Beacon Press, 1963), 19-20, 284-287.
11) *The Social Construction of Reality*, 94-96.

institutional sector is legitimated in terms of a differentiated body of knowledge." And the fourth level of legitimation consists of "symbolic universes." In this study, we are interested in the fourth level, for we have no evidence of the other levels in our biblical text.

버거와 러크만에 의하면, "상징적 우주"란:[12]
  다른 의미 분야를 통합하는 이론적 전통 체계를 뜻한다. 또한 상징적 전체성 안에 있는 제도적 질서를 포함하고 있다; 상징적 과정들은 매일 하는 일상 체험과는 다른 실체를 언급하는 의미체계의 과정들이다. 제도적 질서의 모든 요소들은 모든 것을 포함하는 준거틀 속에서 통합되어 있다. 이제 이 준거틀이 단어의 문자적 의미로 한 우주를 형성하는 것이다. 모든 인간의 체험은 준거틀 안에서 일어난다고 인식할 수 있다. 상징적 우주는 "사회적으로 객관적이고 주관적인 진실한 의미들의 모체"로서 이해된다.
  비록 다른 상징적 우주가 인간 사회에 존재할 수 있더라도, 한 공동체는 그것에 의해 형성되고 합법화되는 한 상징적 우주가 있을 수 있다.

According to Berger and Luckmann, "symbolic universe" is:[12]
  a body of theoretical tradition that integrates different provinces of meaning and encompasses the institutional order in a symbolic totality; symbolic processes are processes of signification that

---

[12] *Ibid.*

refer to realities other than those of everyday experience. All the sectors of the institutional order are integrated in an all-embracing frame of reference, which now constitutes a universe in the literal sense of the word, because all human experience can now be conceived of as taking place within it. The symbolic universe is conceived of as "the matrix of all socially objectivated and subjectively real meanings."

Although different symbolic universes can exist in a human society, a community may have one symbolic universe under which the community is consolidated and legitimatized.

2) 방법론 Methodology

위에서 제기한 문제들을 해결하기 위해, 소위 사회적-주석적 방법을 사용한다. 이 방법론은 본문말씀(에스라 9-10장; 느헤미야 13:23-30)의 "성경 내적 주석"이며 이 본문에 나오는 결혼 개혁들을 사회학적으로 분석하는 것을 포함한다. 이 용어는 성경학에서 새로운 것은 아니다. 존 엘리엇이 베드로전서의 사회학적 주석에서 이미 사용한 것이다.[13] 엘리엇은 "사회학적 주석"을 다음과 같이 정의하고 있다:

> …사회학적 주석은 주석과 사회학적인 방법을 종합한 원리, 이론, 기술로서 주어진 본문을 분석적이면서 종합적인 해석을 하는 것이다. 이 방법론은 사회학으로부터 관점, 전제, 분석 방법, 비교 모델, 이론, 연구조사를 채택했기에 사회학적이다. 또한 이 방법론은 성경

---

13) *A Home for the Homeless : A Sociological Exegesis of I Peter, Its Situation and Strategy*(Philadelphia: Fortress Press, 1981).

본문을 연구하고 주석의 모든 분야를 사용하여 본문의 의미와 영향을 그 상황 속에서 살피기에 주석적이다.[14]

In order to solve the above mentioned problem, we will employ what we call "the socio-exegetical method." This method includes "inner biblical exegesis" of our main texts(Ezra 9-10 and Nehemiah 13:23-30) and sociological analysis of the marriage reforms in these texts. The terminology of this method is not new in biblical studies. John H. Elliott already applied sociological exegesis to The First Letter of Peter.[13] Herein Elliott defined a "sociological exegesis" :

> ⋯sociological exegesis is the analytic and synthetic interpretation of a text through the combined exercise of the exegetical and sociological disciplines, their principles, theories and techniques. The method is sociological in that it involves the employment of the perspectives, presuppositions, modes of analysis, comparative models, theories and research of the discipline of sociology. It is exegetical in that it focuses centrally upon a biblical document and through the employment of all the sub-disciplines of exegesis attempts to determine the meaning and impact of that text within its various contexts.[14]

---

14) *Ibid.*, 7-8.

본 서에서 '성경 내의 주석방법'으로 본문말씀을 주석할 것이다. 그리고 유대 공동체의 사회적 기반을 재구성하는 문제에 지식사회학의 합법화 이론을 적용할 것이다. 유대인 학자 피쉬베인(Michael A. Fishbane)[15]의 이론인 에스라 9-10장과 느헤미야 13:23-30은 오경에 기초한 "율법적 주석"(출 34:16; 신 7:3; 수 23:12-13; 삿 3:5-6)이라는 주장[16]에 동의를 하면서, 여기서는 사회적 도구 즉 지식사회학을 첨가해서 피쉬베인의 성경속의 주석방법을 발전시킬 것이다.

In this study, we will interpret our texts through "inner biblical exegesis," and we shall apply a legitimation theory of the sociology of knowledge to the reconstruction of the social basis of the Judean community. Accepting M. Fishbane[15]'s theory that Ezra 9-10 and Nehemiah 13:23-30 are "legal exegesis" based on the Pentateuch (Ex. 34:16 and Deut. 7:3; cf. Josh. 23:12-13; Judg. 3:5-6),[16] we will develop his "inner biblical exegesis" with sociological tools, especially, the sociology of knowledge.

성경 내의 주석 이론에 의하면, 어떤 훗날 성경 본문들은 앞에 기록된 성경 말씀의 주석적 개정이라는 것이다. 다른 말로 표현한다면 성경은 성경 속에서 자체의 주석을 한다는 것이다. 그래서 "성경 내의 주석"이란 히브리 성경 자체 내에서 이뤄진 주석을 말한다. 사르나(Nahum Mattathias Sarna)[17] 교수는 다음과 같이 주장한다. "주석의

---

15) 1943- , the Nathan Cummings Professor of Jewish Studies at the Divinity School, University of Chicago. Ph.D., Brandeis University.
16) M. Fishbane, *Biblical Interpretation in Ancient Israel*(Oxford: Clarendon Press, 1985), 115.
17) Nahum M. Sarna(1923-2005), 창세기와 출애굽기 연구에 집중했다. the study of Genesis and Exodus represented in his *Understanding Genesis*, 1966.

현상과 분문 강해는 어떤 특정한 태도로부터 씌여지거나 말로 된 말씀까지 발전되어야 한다. 이는 권위성, 불변성, 그리고 궁극적으로 신성한 것의 이념을 포함한다."[18]

According to the theory of inner biblical exegesis, some later biblical texts were the exegetical revisions of earlier biblical texts. In other words, the Bible has its own exegesis within the Bible itself. Thus we define "inner biblical exegesis" as the exegesis done within the Hebrew Bible itself. Sarna[17] insisted that "the phenomenon of exegesis and exposition of a text should evolve from a peculiar attitude to the written or oral word. It involves the idea of authority and immutability and ultimately of sanctity."[18]

이런 사르나 교수의 이론을 피쉬베인 교수는 더 발전시킨다. 그의 저서 《고대 이스라엘에서 성경해석》에서 피쉬베인은 초기 유대인의 성경 주석은 히브리 성경에서 그 원리를 찾았다고 주장한다. 전승의 내용(traditum)과 전승의 과정(traditio)를 구별하면서,[19] 고대 이스라엘에는 traditum과 traditio 사이에 역동적인 관계성이 있어왔다는 것이다. "전승 과정의 각 단계에서 전승 내용이 채택, 변형, 재해석되어졌다. 따라서 작은 구전(내부와 외부)로부터 시작해서 성경의 마지막 문서로 된 단계에 이르기까지 전승-형성의 과정뿐만 아니라 공동체-형성(Gemeindebildung)도 있다."[20] 여러 가지 증거를 들면서, 히브리 성

---

18) Nahum M. Sarna, "Psalm 89: A Study in Inner Biblical Exegesis," *Biblical and Other Studies*, ed. A. Altmann, Brandeis Texts and Studies(Cambridge, MA: Harvard University Press, 1963), 33.
19) Fishbane, *ibid.*, 6.
20) *Ibid.*, 7.

경 속에는 서기관, 율법, 하가다, 주술[21]의 주석이 있다. 이들 가운데 에스라 9-10장, 느헤미야 13:23-30은 율법적 주석에 해당한다는 것이다. 피쉬베인 교수의 저서를 통해 율법적 주석에 대해 알아보자.

Fishbane develops Sarna's theory further. In Biblical Interpretation in Ancient Israel, Fishbane claims that early Jewish biblical exegesis has antecedents in the Hebrew Bible. Distinguishing the content of tradition(=*traditum*) and the process of transmission(=*traditio*),[19] he observes that there has been a dynamic relationship between *traditum* and *traditio* in ancient Israel. "At each stage in the *traditio*, the *traditum* was adapted, transformed, or reinterpreted. Accordingly, the movement from the small oral traditions(native and foreign) to the final written stage of Scripture is not only a process of tradition-building but of *Gemeindebildung* as well".[20] With cumulative evidence, he presents the scribal, legal, aggadic and mantological exegesis within the Bible.[21] Among these, legal exegesis is relevant to the interpretation of Ezra 9-10 and Nehemiah 13:23-30. Here is a summary of the background of legal exegesis in Fishbane's book:

히브리 성경의 보존된 문서화된 율법은 보다 포괄적인 구전법의 표현일 뿐이다. 하나님의 계시로 제시된 성경의 율법 모음들과 언약적 생활의 근거는 포괄적인 법전들이라기보다는 법적이고 윤리적인 규범들의 원초적인 일람표로 간주될 수 있다. 히브리 성경 속에 나오는 여러 가지 법적 내용의 모음은 각자 반복된 율법적 개정으로

---

21) 영어의 mantology는 '점술'(the act or art of divination)을 말한다.

여길 수 있다: 후대에 편집될 때 많은 곳에서 부분적인 주석적 개정이나 초기 내용을 더 명확히 설명한 것이 있다. 성경의 법적 전승들은 법이 아닌 본문들 속에 보존된 법적 주석체로 발전했다…그래서 포수기 동안이나 그 후 주석이 전수된 전승들과 정확하고 충분한 이해력 사이의 간격을 메꾸었던 것이다.[22]

The preserved written law of the Hebrew Bible is but an expression of a much more comprehensive oral law. The biblical law collections which are presented as divine revelation and the basis for covenantal life may best be considered as prototypical compendia of legal and ethical norms rather than as comprehensive codes…The various legal collections in the Hebrew Bible were each subject to repeated exegetical revision : The later collections reflect (in many places) that they are(in part) exegetical revisions or clarifications of earlier ones. The biblical legal traditions developed a body of legal exegesis preserved in non-legal texts…Thus, whether during the exile or thereafter, exegesis filled the gap between inherited traditions and their accurate or adequate comprehension.[22]

피쉬베인에 의하면 에스라 9:1-2은 신명기 7:1-6과 23:4-9의 주석적 조화이다. 암몬 사람들, 모압 사람들 등과 통혼하는 것을 금지하는 신명기 7:1-3에 나오는 율법의 주석적 연장이었다. 이 본문은 신명기 23:4-9에 나오는 내용을 채택하고 사이에 삽입함으로 영향을 받은 것이다.[23]

---

22) Fishbane, *ibid.*, 95-97, 113.
23) *Ibid.*, 114-117.

그는 "느헤미야가 이방 여인들을 추방할 때 한 언급이 있는 느헤미야 13:23-27 속에 신명기 23:4-9를 암시하고 있음은 간접적으로 느헤미야 13:1-3에 있는 오경 자료를 분명히 사용하고 이를 이방인을 추방하는 것과 관련시킴으로 보아 이런 생각이 더 강화되었다"라고 말한다.[24]

According to Fishbane, Ezra 9:1-2 is an exegetical blend of Deut. 7:1-6 and 23:4-9. And the mechanism for prohibiting intermarriage with the Ammonites, Moabites, etc. was an exegetical extension of the law in Deut. 7:1-3 effected by means of an adaptation and interpolation of features from Deut. 23:4-9.[23] He insists, "The allusion to Deut. 23:4-9 in Nehemiah 13:23-27, in which Nehemiah refers to the expulsion of foreign women, is indirectly strengthened by the explicit use of that Pentateuchal source in Neh. 13:1-3, also in connection with the expulsion of foreigners."[24]

성경 속의 주석 방법은 오경 속에 나오는 옛 법적 수집들이 포수기나 포수기 후 사회 상황에서 어떻게 해석되었는지를 이해하는 데 매우 도움이 된다. 그러나 피쉬베인은 왜 귀환한 포로 공동체가 토라와 그의 주석을 그들의 생활 센터로 형성했는지를 설명하지 않는다.[25] 혹은 왜 에스라가 모든 이방 아내들과 그들의 아이들을 추방하자는 스가냐(Shechania)의 건의를 받아들였는지(에스라 10:2) 혹은 왜 요나단과 야스야(Jahzeiah)가 스가냐의 건의(에스라 10:15)를 반대했는지에 대해 설명하지 않았다. 그래서 에스라와 느헤미야가 규정한 결혼

---

24) Ibid. 126ff.
25) Ibid. 114.

제도와 개혁된 유대 공동체의 세계관 사이의 관계에 대한 질문을 답변하기 위해 지식사회학 방법이 적절하다.

This method of inner biblical exegesis is very helpful for understanding how the older legal collections in the Pentateuch were interpreted in the exilic or post-exilic social context. But Fishbane did not explain the reason why the returning community of the exile was formed with Torah and its exegesis at its living center or why Ezra accepted the proposal of Shechania to expel all foreign wives and their offsprings(Ezra 10:2)[25] or why Jonathan and Jahzeiah opposed the proposal of Shechania (Ezra 10:15).

Urgent is the sociology of knowledge method to answer the question of the relationship between the institution of marriage as defined by the reforms of Ezra and Nehemiah and the worldview of the reformed Judean community.

3) 절차 Procedure

본 서의 절차는 다음과 같다:

첫 번째 단계는 에스라와 느헤미야가 주도한 결혼 개혁의 배경을 살펴보는 것이다. 제2성전 봉헌 이후 포로기 후 유대 예배공동체의 사회적 성격을 동시적이며 통시적으로 살필 것이다. 그리고 그 당시 유대 공동체의 사회적 위기도 살펴볼 것이다.

The procedure of the present study is as follows:

The first step is to examine the background of the marriage reforms led by Ezra and Nehemiah. We will investigate the social character of the post-exilic Judean worship community after the dedication of the Second Temple synchronically as well as diachronically. And also we will explore the social crisis of the contemporary Jewish community.

두 번째 단계는 에스라 9:1-10:44과 느헤미야 13:23-30을 주석함으로 에스라와 느헤미야의 결혼 개혁을 살피는 것이다.

The second step is to examine the marriage reform of Ezra and Nehemiah through exegesis of Ezra 9:1-10:44, and Neh. 13:23-30.

세 번째이며 마지막 단계는 지식사회학적 관점에서부터 결혼 개혁의 합리화 구조, 즉 상징적 우주를 분석하는 것이다.

The third and last step is to analyze the structures of legitimation of the marriage reforms from the sociology of knowledge perspective, specifically, the symbolic universe.

3. 연구사 Previous Research in the Field

연구 조사 결과 지식사회학 관점에서 포수기 후 유대 예배공동체의 재구성 과정에서 이뤄진 결혼 개혁들에 대해 별로 연구된 바가 없다.[26] 다만, 본 서에서 다루는 주제를 취급하는 에스라-느헤미

---

[26] 몇 학자는 이 문제를 일반적으로 언급은 하지만 더 깊이 발전시키지 못했다. Some scholars mentioned this task in general, but they do not develop it further. 예를 들

야에 나타난 결혼 개혁들에 관한 연구들 몇 개를 살필 가치가 있다. 출판 연대의 순대로 살펴보자.

As far as we know, only a few studies were done on the marriage reforms in the reconstruction of the post-exilic Judean worship community from the sociology of knowledge perspective which this study employs.[26] However, it is worth examining some recent studies concerning the marriage reforms in Ezra-Nehemiah which bear on the subject treated in this study. Let us review these studies in the order of publication year.

1) 보스만 David Bossmann

보스만(David Bossmann)[27]은 에스라의 결혼 개혁은 이스라엘 백성들을 예배 공동체로 분리시키는 것이라고 지적했다.[28] 그의 논지는 "에스라의 결혼 개혁은 제사장들이 모든 불결한 것으로부터 구별함에 따라 백성들의 성결이다. 이 주제가 에스라서의 중심 주제이며, 역대기 사가의 주제(leitmotiv)는 오페라나 교향시 등의 악곡 중에서 특정의 인물이나 상황 등과 결부되어, 반복해 사용되는 짧은 주제나

면 배튼은 주석에서 다음 한 문장을 인용한다. For example, Batten, in his ICC commentary, quotes one sentence from B. Stade, *Biblische Theologie des AT*, 2nd ed., 1905, III, pp. 30f.: "통혼의 악한 결과들은 공동체의 불완전하게 세워진 연대성과 종교 생활의 발전에 위협을 주었다. The evil consequences of the mixed marriages tended to threaten the imperfectly established solidarity of the community and the development of the religious life" (p. 351).
27) 그는 1985년부터 세톤 홀 대학 유대교-기독교학 교수로 재직하고 있다. Professor of Graduate Department of Jewish-Christian Studies, Seton Hall University since 1985.
28) D. Bossmann, "Ezra's Marriage Reform: Israel Redefined," in *BTB* 9 (1979), pp. 32-38; "Isaiah 56:1-8 and the Redefining of the Restoration Judean Community," BTB 30 (May 2000), 46-57.

동기를 가리킴이기도 하다"(37-38쪽)이다. 그는 에스라서 안에 있는 통혼 문제에 대한 문학적-신학적 해석을 제공한다.

David Bossmann[27] points out that the aim of Ezra's marriage reform was to separate the people Israel as a cultic community.[28] His thesis is that "Ezra's marriage reform as a purification of the people according to a priestly ideal of separation from all that is unclean follows a significant theme within the book of Ezra and serves as a *leitmotif* within the work of the Chronicler"(pp. 37-38). He provides a literary-theological interpretation of the problem of intermarriage in the book of Ezra.

보스만은 추측하기를 느헤미야는 BCE[29] 445년과 433년에 예루살렘에 도착했고 에스라는 428년에 도착했을 것이란다. 율법을 낭독한 후 에스라는 통혼 문제로 돌아왔다. 에스라 주도의 개혁 목표는 이스라엘을 모든 오염으로부터 분리하는 것이었다. 이스라엘 백성의 순결함이 다시 거룩한 하나님의 백성이 될 수 있게 할 것이라고 한다. 느헤미야서에서는 이스라엘의 후손은 모든 이방적인 것으로부터 자신들을 분리하는 것이다. 반면에, 에스라에서는 이스라엘 백성이 모든 이들의 정체성을 위협하는 결혼 문제에 덫이 걸려들어 있다(스 9:11). 그 지방 사람들과 결혼한다는 것은 이런 상황 속에서는 배교(背敎)(스 9:4), 수치와 죄의식(스 9:6), 그리고 절교(스 9:7)이다. 그래서 이스라엘은 더 이상 하나님 앞에 설 수 없게 되었다(스 9:15). 이스라엘이 순결하게 살라고 가르치는 하나님의 말씀이 토라가 이제 불결한 이방으로부터 분리하지 않는 이스라엘을 정죄하고 있다(36-37쪽).

---

[29] 유대인 학자들은 BC(Before Christ) 대신 BCE(Before Common Era)로 사용한다.

보스만은 다음과 같이 결론을 내린다(37-38쪽):

He assumes Ezra would have arrived at Jerusalem in 428 BCE[29] after Nehemiah returned in 445 and 433. Following the reading of the law, Ezra turned to the question of mixed marriages. The goal of the reform under Ezra was the separation of Israel from all contamination; the purification of the people Israel would render them again the people of the holy God. In Nehemiah the people of Israelite descent separate themselves from all who are of foreign extraction. In Ezra, on the contrary, the people of Israel are enmeshed in marriages which threaten the identity of all (Ezra 9:11). Such marriages with the people of the land are in this context apostasy(9:4), the cause of shame and guilt(9:6), and repudiation(9:7). Thus Israel can no longer stand in God's presence(9:15). Torah, as God's word to Israel instructing Israel in the ways of purity, now stands to condemn Israel for failure in keeping separate from the unclean nations(pp. 36-37). Bossman concludes as follows(pp. 37-38) :

…예배 정결의 제사장적 이념이 공동체에도 적용된다. 새로운 대제사장으로서 부임한 에스라의 목표는 이스라엘을 제사장적인 정결 이념 위에 세우는 것이다. 사마리아인들이 이스라엘의 새로운 제사장적 정의로부터 추방되었다는 상식적인 이해와는 반대로, 에스라는 사마리아인과의 결혼을 파기하라고 하는 의도는 없었다. 사마리아는 재통일의 대상이 된 북 이스라엘의 수도였다.…이제 불결로부터 청결함을 받아야 할 대상이 제사장뿐만 아니라 모든 백성들이 모든 혈육으로부터 오염된 것으로부터 분리되어야 한다. 그래서 9:2에서 거룩한 씨를 언급한 것이다. 그러므로 백성의 연합이 거룩한

백성들로 그들을 불러주시는 이스라엘의 하나님 면전에서 단결을 이룰 수 있는 것이다. 보스만이 정결의 제사장적 이념이 새로운 이스라엘을 이룩한다고 주장하는 것은 옳지만(37-38쪽), 그는 사회학적인 관점에서 이 제사장적 순결 이념을 분석하지 않았다.

···the priestly ideal of a cultic purity is brought to bear upon the community. It is said that the goal of Ezra as a new high priest was to establish one Israel under the priestly ideal of purity. Contrary to the commonly held understanding that the Samaritans were to be excluded from the new priestly definition of Israel, Ezra indicates no intention to break up marriages with Samaritan women; Samaritans were members of the northern tribes of Israel which Ezra hoped to reunite···Now it is not only the priests who must be free of contamination, but all the people must be separated from all forms of blood-contamination; hence the appeal to the holy seed in 9:2. Therefore, the unity of the people would be a fulfillment of their solidarity before the God of Israel who called them to be his holy people. He is right in saying that the priestly ideal of purity is to re-establish a new Israel(pp. 37-38), but he does not analyze the priestly ideal of purity from the sociological perspective.

2) 코헨 Shaye J. D. Cohen

코헨 교수(Shaye J. D. Cohen)[30]는 세 군데의 본문 말씀(신 7:3-4, 23:2-

---

30) 그는 하버드대 고대근동학과 교수이다(the Littauer Professor of Hebrew Literature and Philosophy in the Department of Near Eastern Languages and Civilizations of

9; 레 18:21)을 유대적 주석을 통해 유대인과 이방인 사이의 통혼에 대한 역사적 유대인들의 부정적인 태도에 대한 이유를 탐구한다.[31] 그에 따르면, "모든 나라와의 통혼이 금지된 것은 아니다. 출 34:15이나 신 7:3-4, 23:2-9의 말씀도 이스라엘 사람 이외의 모든 이방인과의 통혼을 금지하고 있지 않다. 또한 통혼 금지에 어떤 특별한 중요성이나 중심적 문제를 두지 않는다"(23쪽). 유대 예배공동체 사이에 통혼을 금지하는 역사적인 이유는 다음과 같다(36쪽):

Cohen[30] explores the reason for the historical Judean negative attitude towards intermarriage between Judeans and non-Judeans through the Jewish exegesis of three Biblical passages (Deut. 7:3-4, 23:2-9; Lev. 18:21).[31] According to him, "the prohibition of intermarriage with all gentiles is not biblical. Neither Exodus 34:15 nor Deuteronomy 7:3-4, 23:2-9 prohibits intermarriage with all non-Israelites, and neither accords any centrality or unusual importance to the prohibitions which it does contain."(p. 23). He explains the historical reason for the prohibition against intermarriage among the Judean worship community as follows(p. 36):

제2성전 시기에, 국가적인 품위를 잃고 이방인과의 접촉이 빈번함

Harvard University).

31) "From the Bible to the Talmud: the prohibition of intermarriage," *HAR* 7 (1983), 23-39. 그는 랍비이며 1975년 콜롬비아 대학에서 고대 역사분야에서 박사학위를 받았다. 2001년부터 하버드에서 유대인과 이방인 사이의 경계에 대한 강의를 하고 있다. He received his Ph.D. in Ancient History, with distinction, from Columbia University in 1975. He is also an ordained rabbi, and for many years was the Dean of the Graduate School and Shenkman Professor of Jewish History at the Jewish Theological Seminary in New York. Before arriving at Harvard in July 2001, he was for ten years the Samuel Ungerleider Professor of Judaic Studies and Professor of Religious Studies at Brown University. The focus of Professor Cohen's research is the boundary between Jews and gentiles and between Judaism and its surrounding cultures. He is also a published authority on Jewish reactions to Hellenism and to Christianity.

에 따라 유대인들은 그들이 살아남을 수 있는 길은 이방 문화로부터 그들의 이념적(혹 "종교적")이고 사회적인 분리에 의존했다고 느꼈다. 모세 법은 그들의 요구에 불충분해서, 그들은 이방인들과 자신들 사이에 새로운 벽을 쌓기 시작했다. 특히 마카비 시대와 랍비 시대에 더욱 그러했다.

During the period of the Second Temple, however, with the loss of national sovereignty and the increased interaction with gentiles, the Jews sensed that their survival depended upon their ideological(or "religious") and social separation from the outside world. Since the Mosaic legislation was inadequate for their needs, they erected new barriers between themselves and the gentiles, especially during the Maccabean and rabbinic periods.

코헨은 다음과 같이 결론을 내린다. "이방인과 성적 교제나 통혼을 금지시킨 사람은 모세가 아니라 후대 유대교 지도자들이었다"(36쪽). 그의 율법 주석(신 7:3-4, 23:2-9; 레 18:21)은 성경 속의 주석을 사용하고 있으며, 유대인의 통혼 문제에 대한 태도를 이해하는 데 매우 도움이 된다. 그러나 에스라의 결혼 개혁의 사회적인 차원을 고려하지 않는다.

He concludes that "it was not Moses but later authorities who forbade sexual intercourse as well as intermarriage with all foreigners"(p. 36). His exegesis of legal texts(Deut. 7:3-4, 23:2-9 and Lev. 18:21) uses inner Biblical exegesis and is very helpful for understanding a Jewish attitude toward intermarriage. However, he does not consider the social dimensions of Ezra's marriage reform.

코헨은 다른 논문에서[32] 솔로몬의 통혼 문제를 다루면서 신명기 사가의 평가를 살핀다(왕상 3:1, 7:8, 9:16, 24, 11:1-2). 그리고 역대 사가의 역사적 관점도 다룬다(대하 8:11). 신명기적 평가에 따르면 솔로몬은 가장 악한 악들의 하나로 간주된다. 성전을 건축하고 위대한 영웅담의 주인공인 솔로몬이 어떻게 금지법을 극악무도하게 어겼을까? 수수께끼 같은 생각이 들게 한다. 그러나 역대기 사가는 솔로몬의 결혼도 어떤 행위도 정죄하지 않는다. "솔로몬이 이집트 공주를 다루는 것은 왕과 남편으로부터 경건의 교훈으로 나온다"(37쪽). 코헨도 이 연구에서 유대 공동체에 있어서 통혼에 대한 사회적 조건을 간과하고 있다.

In another paper,[32] Cohen deals with the problem of Solomon's marriage to foreign women by a comparison of the Deuteronomic-historical evaluation(1 Kings 3:1, 7:8, 9:16, 24, 11:1-2) and the Chronicler's historical point of view(2 Chr. 8:11). According to the Deuteronomic evaluation, Solomon was looked upon as one of the most notorious kings. One might puzzle over how Solomon, the builder of the temple and the great sage, could have violated the prohibition so flagrantly. However, the author of Chronicles does not condemn either the marriage or any other act of Solomon. In his account, "Solomon's treatment of his Egyptian wife is a lesson in piety from a model king and husband"(p. 37). This study also overlooks the social conditions of intermarriage in the Israelite community.

---

32) "Solomon and the Daughter of Pharaoh: Intermarriage, Conversion, and the Impurity of Women," *JANES* 16-17 (1984-85), 23-37.

코헨 교수의 두 편의 글에서 개혁으로 규정된 결혼 제도와 포로기 후 유대 공동체의 개혁, 재구성, 유지하는 문제 사이의 연관성을 취급하지 않는다.[33]

Cohen's two papers do not deal with the relationship between the institution of marriage as defined by the reforms and the reconstruction and maintenance of the post-exilic Judean community.[33]

3) 클라인즈 David J. A. Clines

클라인즈(David J. A. Clines)의 주석에서,[34] 결혼 개혁의 문학적-역사적 차원들을 다루고 있다. 그에 의하면 역대 사가는 고의적으로 결혼 개혁을 에스라의 주요 활동으로 선택하였다(116쪽). 에스라는 자신이 임명 받은 개혁자도 아니었고 또한 다른 백성들의 군기를 잡는 이도 아니었다. 그는 페르샤 왕의 명에 의해서 유대 속국에게 오경

---

33) 코헨의 유대인의 통혼 문제를 다룬 글 이외에도, 현대 유대인 사회의 인종적-종교적 위기에 직면한 역사적-랍비적 해석에 초점을 맞춘 글들이 몇 편 있다. Besides the essays of Cohen concerning the problem of Judean intermarriage, there are a few studies on this subject which focus on the historical-rabbinical interpretation confronted with the ethnic-religious crisis of modern Jewish society. For example, J. David Bleich, "The Prohibition Against Intermarriage," Journal of Halacha and Contemporary Society , Vol. I, No. 1 (1981), 5-27 ; D. R. Mace, Hebrew Marriage : A Sociological Study(New York: Philosophical Library, Inc., 1953); E. Feldman, "Intermarriage Historically Considered," Yearbook of the Central Conference of American Rabbis 19 (1909), 271-301 ; Carol Diament(ed.), "Jewish Marital Status," A Hadassah Study, esp. ch. VI(Northvale, NJ: The Jewish Book Club, 1989).

34) David J. A. Clines, Ezra, Nehemiah, Esther, The New Century Bible Commentary (London: Marshall, Morgan & Scott Pub. LTD., 1984); The Bible and the Modern World. Corr. ed. (Sheffield: Sheffield Phoenix Press, 2005). 클라인즈는 쉐필드 대학의 성경학 원로교수이다(David J. A. Clines emeritus professor of biblical studies at the University of Sheffield).

의 법이 국법임을 가르치도록(스 7:25f) 위임받아서 예루살렘으로 온 것이었다. 이 같은 국법을 다니엘서에서는 "메데와 바사의 법"(단 6:8)이라고 표현한다.

In his commentary,[34] Clines treats the literary-historical dimensions of the marriage reforms. According to him, the Chronicler has deliberately chosen the marriage reform as a prime illustration of the work of Ezra(p. 116). Ezra was neither some self-appointed reformer nor custodian of other people's morals. He came to Jerusalem as a commissioner of the Persian king, with instruction, to insist that in the sub-province of Judea the Pentateuchal law was state law(Ezra 7:25f), "the law of the Medes and Persians"(cf. Dan. 6:8).

에스라는 법적 권력을 쓰지 않고, 백성의 지도자들에게 스스로 책임을 질 것을 설득한다(10:7f, 10:14). 느헤미야가 더 관용의 견해를 가졌는지 분명하지 않다. 느헤미야는 에스라보다 더 강하게 자기의 권위를 행사하였다(117쪽). 클라인즈는 에스라와 느헤미야를 페르샤 정부의 정치적 지도자들로 간주한다. 그러나 그는 에스라와 느헤미야의 결혼 개혁의 사회학적인 분석은 하지 않는다.

Far from using the force of his authority, Ezra persuades the leaders of the people to take the responsibility upon themselves (10:7f, 10:14). And it is not clear that Nehemiah took a more tolerant view, and certain moreover that he exerted his authority more forcibly than Ezra(p. 117). Clines considers Ezra and Nehemiah political leaders under alien rule. But he does not undertake a sociological analysis of the marriage reforms of Ezra and

Nehemiah.

4) 브렌킨소프 Joseph Blenkinsopp

브렌킨소프 교수(Joseph Blenkinsopp)는 그의 주석에서[35] 결혼 개혁의 정치적이고 사회적 정황을 기술하고 있다. 그러나 결혼 개혁 문제를 사회학적으로는 다루고 있지 않다. 몇 학자들(S. Japhat, H. Williamson)의 의견을 반대하면서, 에스라-느헤미야서는 "본질적으로 역대기서의 연속"으로(개인이든 학파든) 역대기 사가의 저술이라는 주장을 고수한다.[36] 결혼 개혁은 역대기 사가의 편집상 손질된 것으로 이해한다(176쪽).

In his commentary, Blenkinsopp[35] describes the political and social context of the marriage reform. But he does not deal with the marriage reform itself with any sociological method. As against some scholars(S. Japhat, H. Williamson), he defends the position that Ezra-Nehemiah is "essentially a continuation of 1-2 Chronicles," authored by the Chronicler(whether conceived as an individual or a school).[36] According to him, the marriage reform is

---

35) Joseph Blenkinsopp, *Ezra-Nehemiah,* The Old Testament Library(Philadelphia: The Westminster Press, 1988). Blenkinsopp는 Notre Dame 교수임. John A O'Brien Professor of the Hebrew Bible. 그의 저서로는 Publications: *The Promise to David,* 1964; *From Adam to Abraham,* 1965; *Jesus is Lord,* 1967; *Celibacy, Ministry, Church,* 1969; *Sexuality and the Christian Tradition,* 1969; *Gibeon and Israel,* 1972; *Prophecy and Canon: A Contribution to the Study of Jewish Origins,* 1978; *Wisdom and Law in the Old Testament,* 1983; *A History of Prophecy in Israel,* 1984; *Ezekiel,* 1990; *The Pentateuch: Introduction to the First Five Books of the Bible,* 1992; *Sage, Priest, Prophet: Religious and Intellectual Leadership in Ancient Israel,* 1996.
36) S. Japhet, "The Supposed Common Authorship of Chronicles and Ezra-Nehemiah Investigated Anew," VT 18 (1969), 330-371; H. G. M. Williamson, *Ezra, Nehemiah* (Waco, TX: Word Books, Pub., 1985).

described with the editorial hand of the Chronicler(p. 176).

5) 혹룬드 Kenneth G. Hoglund

고고학, 비문학, 문학적 증거를 사용하면서, 혹룬드 교수(Kenneth G. Hoglund)는 에스라와 느헤미야의 결혼 개혁의 사회적이고 정치적인 배경을 설명한다.[37] 사회와 신앙 개혁을 포함한 결혼 개혁들은 신학적인 관심에서가 아니라 당시 가나안 지역에 대한 페르샤 제국의 지배를 강화한 것이었다는 것이다. 에스라와 느헤미야는 이집트 혁명으로 인한 도전들에 직면하여 페르샤 제국이 유대 예배공동체에 대한 계속적인 통제를 확실히 할 필요 때문에 유대 예배공동체에 파견되었다.

Utilizing archaeological, epigraphic, and literary evidence, Hoglund establishes a social and political context for the marriage reforms of Ezra and Nehemiah.[37] The marriage reforms, including the social and religious reforms, were not motivated exclusively by theological concerns but reflected a concern to tighten imperial control over the Levant region. Ezra and Nehemiah were sent to the Judean worship community because of the need to insure continued control over the community in the face of the challenges resulting from the Egyptian revolt.

---

37) Kenneth G. Hoglund, *Achaemenid Imperial Administration in Syria-Palestine and the Missions of Ezra and Nehemiah*, SBL Dissertation Series 125(Atlanta: Scholars Press, 1992); Chronicler as Historian, Library Hebrew Bible/Old Testament Studies, by Patrick M. Graham, Steven L. McKenzie and Kenneth G. Hoglund, 1997. Kenneth G. Hoglund는 웨이크포레스트 대학의 종교학 교수임. Professor in the Department of Religion at Wake Forest University, Winston-Salem, North Carolina, USA.

결혼 개혁들은 인구를 인종별로 정리하며 오랫동안 지속할 수 있도록 지속할 필요성의 대표적 결단으로 보인다. 이런 운동은 앗시리아로부터 시작하여 페르샤 시대(Achaemenid)에 약간 수정되어 실행된 것이라고 한다. 에스라와 느헤미야의 사명은 공동체에 대한 새로운 자기 이해를 강요함으로 회복 공동체의 조직을 변형한 것 같다. 제국 행정의 목적에 대한 분명한 정체성을 유지할 필요성이 있어 그렇게 했다고 한다. 결혼 개혁들은 유대공동체와 그 후손들에게 동화와 정체성 상실이 비극적으로 될 상황 속에서 자기 보조의 수단을 제공했던 것이다(246쪽 이하).

이 연구는 결혼 개혁의 정치적 상황을 이해하는 데 매우 유익하나 개혁이 제국 상황 속에서 독립 운동을 하는 데 공헌한 점을 설명하지 않는다.

The marriage reforms stand as a further example of the long-standing imperial need to displace populations and define them in ethnic terms, a practice that began under the Assyrian empire and continued with slight modification into Achaemenid practice(p. 244). The missions of Ezra and Nehemiah appear to have transformed the fabric of the Restoration community by forcing a new self-understanding on the community, rooted in the need to maintain a clear identity for the purposes of imperial administration. The marriage reforms provided the Judean worship community and its subsequent generations with the means for self-preservation in a setting where assimilation and the loss of identity would have been disastrous(pp. 246f). This study is very helpful to understand the political context of the marriage reforms, but the author does not explain how the reforms served imperial context as against independence.

6) 문학적-신학적 연구들 Literary-Theological Research

솔궤(Felisi Sorgwe)는 에스라-느헤미야 개혁에 대해 역사비평적, 정경적, 마소라적 해석을 하고 있다. 에스라와 느헤미야서의 차이점과 공통점을 찾고 구약 정경과의 신학적 연관성을 연구했다.[38] 예배 공동체로서 이스라엘이 부름을 받고 지음을 받았다는 문제를 신학적으로 잘 다루고 있다.[39] 유대 백성들이 열국의 축복의 도구가 되기 위해 에스라-느헤미야의 메시지의 선언을 연구했으나, 에스라-느헤미야가 이스라엘이 우주적 축복의 도구임을 제시하는 자료는 제공하지 못했다. 그의 간결함과 에스라-느헤미야를 종합해서 다루고 있어서 에스라의 신학적 분석을 잘 하고 있다.

F. Sorgwe discusses historical-critical, canonical, and Masoretic approaches to interpretation, the authorship of Ezra-Nehemiah, similarities and dissimilarities between the canonical shapes of Ezra-Nehemiah and Chronicles,[38] and the theological interrelations between Ezra-Nehemiah and the rest of the OT canon. However, he devotes only one chapter to the isolation of nine theological themes whose composite message is "the calling and molding of Israel by God to be a worshiping community." The author's abstract expands his statement of Ezra-Nehemiah'

---

[38] Felisi Sorgwe, "The Canonical Shape of Ezra-Nehemiah and its Theological and Hermeneutical Implications."(Ph.D. diss., Baylor University, 1991), 133-176. 솔궤는 휴스턴 침례대학 교수임. Professor in the Religion department at Houston Baptist University, Houston, TX.

[39] Ibid., 175.

s message, adding the phrase "so that the people might become an instrument of blessing to all the nations." He fails, however, to provide any data to substantiate his claim that Ezra-Nehemiah presents Israel as an agent of universal blessing. His brevity and combined treatment of Ezra and Nehemiah limit this chapter's value as a theological analysis of Ezra.

타마라 에스케나지 교수(Tamara Cohen Eskenazi)는 학위 논문에서(2년 후 출판됨), 에스라의 개혁문제를 문학적으로 잘 분석하고 있다. 여기서 그녀는 반복, 특정화, 중심 이념의 관점 상호연결을 사용하여 에스라-느헤미야의 설화 구조를 분석하고 있다.[40] 그러나 에스라-느헤미야에 나오는 결혼 개혁들에 대한 사회학적인 분석은 하지 않는다. 에스라와 느헤미야가 동시대 사람이 아니라는 주장을 하면서 만약 동시대 사람이라면 자신의 견해를 재평가해야 한다고 가능성을 열어 둔다.[41]

At present the only full-length treatment of Ezra from a literary perspective is Tamara C. Eskenazi, "In An Age of Prose: A Literary Approach to Ezra-Nehemiah." She examines Ezra-Nehemiah's narrative structure, use of repetition, characterization, and interaction of viewpoints to locate its central ideology.[40] She does not, however, deal with any sociological analysis of the marriage

---

40) Tamara Eskenazi's Ph.D. dissertation, "An Age of Prose: A Literary Approach to Ezra-Nehemiah." Eskenazi's dissertation has been revised and published as *In An Age of Prose: A Literary Approach to Ezra-Nehemiah*(Atlanta: Scholars Press, 1988). 에스케나지는 히브리 유니언 대학의 성경학 교수임(The Effie Wise Ochs Professor of Biblical Literature and History, Hebrew Union College, LA, USA)
41) *In an Age of Prose*, 176-177.

reforms of these two books. Her work also suffers from the assumption that Ezra and Nehemiah were not contemporaries, thus skewing her analysis of perspective and characterization. "If it could be proven that Ezra and Nehemiah were, in fact, contemporaries, the significance of the pairing in the book would have to be reevaluated."[41]

또 다른 글에서 에스라의 신학과 문학적 특징에 대한 연구가 있으나 역시 사회학적인 분석은 없다. 예를 들면 니코라이센(Doug Nykolaishen)의 석사논문에서 에스라서에 나타난 예레미야 31장 인용 부분을 다루고 있으며, 레만(Timothy D. Lehman)은 에스라를 교육자적인 통찰력으로 분석함으로 포수기 후 이스라엘의 제사장의 교육적인 역할에 대하여 발표를 했다.[42]

Other theses discuss topics tangential to Ezra's theology and literary character, but none develop these aspects of Ezra proper. For example, Doug Nykolaishen examines "The Use of Jeremiah 31 in the Book of Ezra" and Timothy D. Lehman explores The Role of the Priest in the Education of Post-Exilic Israel: Educational Insights from the Life of Ezra.[42]

몇 학자들은 에스라의 신학에 대해 다루고 있다. 둠브렐(William Dumbrell)은 에스라와 느헤미야가 성전 회복, 제2출애굽으로 포로민들의 귀환 및 예루살렘 재건에 대한 포수기 후 종말적인 기대의 "신

---

42) Doug Nykolaishen examines "The Use of Jeremiah 31 in the Book of Ezra"(M.A. thesis, Trinity Evangelical Divinity School, 1991); Timothy D. Lehman explores "The Role of the Priest in the Education of Post-Exilic Israel: Educational Insights from the Life of Ezra"(M.Div. thesis, Grace Theological Seminary, 1984).

학적 테너"를 보존하고 있음을 보여준다.[43)]

William Dumbrell attempts to demonstrate how Ezra-Nehemiah preserves the "theological tenor" of post-exilic eschatological expectation in relation to the restoration of the temple, the return from captivity as a "second Exodus," and the rebuilding of Jerusalem.[43)]

팬샴(F. C. Fensham)은 역대 사가가 자기 자료들을 신학적으로 어떻게 사용하느냐를 이해하기 위한 방편으로 에스라와 느헤미야에 나오는 여러 주제들을 살피고 있다. 하나님의 이름들, 역사의 주로서의 하나님, 종교 훈련, 죄의식 그리고 하나님과 살아 있는 관계성에 대해 살피고 있다.[44)]

F. C. Fensham examines several themes in Ezra and Nehemiah as a means of understanding how the "Chronicler" uses his sources theologically. He examines five themes: the divine names, God as the Lord of history, religious discipline, a sense of guilt, and a living relationship with God.[44)]

또 다른 주석서들도[45)] 대개 에스라(혹 에스라-느헤미야)의 신학적이

---

43) William J. Dumbrell, "The Theological Intention of Ezra-Nehemiah," *RTR* 45 no. 3 (1986): 65-72.
44) F. C. Fensham, "Some Theological and Religious Aspects in Ezra and Nehemiah," *JNSL* 11 (1983): 59-68.
45) Edwin M. Yamauchi, "Ezra-Nehemiah," in *The Expositor's Bible Commentary*, ed. Frank E. Gaebelein(Grand Rapids: Zondervan Publishing House, 1985), 4: 565-598; F. Charles Fensham, *The Books of Ezra and Nehemiah*, The New International Commentary on the Old Testament, ed. R. K. Harrison(Grand Rapids: William B. Eerdmans Publishing Company, 1982), 16-19; Charles R. Wilson, "Joshua-Esther," vol. 1, pt. 2 of *The Wesleyan Bible Commentary*, ed. Charles W. Carter(Grand Rapids:

고 문학적인 논의를 하고 있으나, 사회학적인 분석은 거의 다루고 있지 않다. 에드윈 아마우치, 펜샴, 찰스 윌슨이 주석서를 쓰면서 제한적 토의를 제공한다.

More recently published commentaries often contain summary discussions of the theological and literary features of Ezra(or Ezra-Nehemiah). There are lack of the sociological analysis. Commentary authors who provide some limited discussion of these features include Edwin Yamauchi, F. C. Fensham, and Charles Wilson.[45]

7) 귀환과 거룩의 신학적인 해석: 필립 브라운 Philip Brown II[46]

필립 브라운(A. Philip Brown)[46]은 에스라는 거룩(holiness)의 마음으로 분리를 제시한다고 주장한다. 거룩의 분리는 필연적으로 긍정적인 면과 부정적인 면이 있다. 부정적으로는 거룩이 공통적이거나 불결한 모든 것으로부터 분리를 요구한다. 에스라가 여호와께 헌신된 거룩한 그릇들을 지키기 위해 열두 제사장들을 성별하는 의식이 바로 공통적이거나 불결한 것으로부터 분리하는 거룩의 예를 제시한다. 귀환자들이 혼합적인 이웃들이 제2성전을 재건하는 데 도와주겠다는 것을 거부했다. 개종자들이 "그 지방의 불결"로부터 자신들을 분리시켰다는 것은(스 6:22) 영적인 차원에서 거룩의 분리에 대한 두 가지 예로 든다.

William B. Eerdmans Publishing Company, 1967), 436.
46) A. Philip Brown II , "A Literary and Theological Analysis of the Book of Ezra," Ph.D. dissertation in Bob Jones University, 2002. Published as *Hope Amidst Ruin*(Bob Jones University Press, 2009). 브라운은 하나님의 성경학교 및 대학교의 성경학 교수임. A. Philip Brown, Professor of Bible & Theology, God's Bible School & College, Cincinnati, Ohio.

Brown argues that Ezra presents separation as the heart of holiness. Holiness' separation necessarily involves both positive and negative orientations. Negatively, holiness requires separation from all that is common or unclean. Ezra's hallowing of twelve priests to guard the holy vessels dedicated to Yahweh illustrates holiness's separation from the common or ordinary. The Returnees' refusal to permit their syncretistic neighbors to help rebuild the temple and the proselytes' separation of themselves from the "uncleanness of the lands"(6:22) provide two illustrations of holiness's separation in the spiritual realm.

긍정적으로 거룩은 자신을 여호와께 온전히 구별함을 포함한다. 이 긍정적 분리는 여호와를 찾는 마음의 분출이며 그분의 율법에 대한 순종함을 드러낸다. 에스라 8:22에서 설화의 청중에게 거룩이 귀환한 자들의 하나님과 관계가 중심이라는 주제에 맞는 내용을 묘사하고 있다. "이는 우리가 전에 왕에게 고하기를 우리 하나님의 손은 자기를 찾는 모든 자에게 선을 베푸시고 자기를 배반하는 모든 자에게는 권능과 진노를 베푸신다 하였으므로 길에서 적군을 막고 우리를 도울 보병과 마병을 왕에게 구하기를 부끄러워하였음이라." 거룩 없이는 하나님의 미래 축복을 받는다는 희망이 없다. 다른 말로 표현하면, 그들이 마음을 다하여 하나님을 찾고 이 땅의 모든 백성들의 불결로부터 자신들을 분리하면 선하신 하나님의 손길이 그들 위에 임한다는 것이다. 그러나 그의 연구는 신학적인 해석이며 사회학적 분석은 없다.

Positively, holiness involves separating oneself wholly unto the Lord. This positive separation is the outflow of a heart set to seek

Yahweh and manifests itself in obedience to His law. Ezra 8:22 enunciates the relevance of this theme to the narrative's audience: "The hand of our God is upon all those who are seeking Him for good and His strength and His wrath are against all those abandoning Him." The primary conclusion of this chapter is that Ezra 8:22 establishes the principle that holiness is the key to the Returnees' relationship to the Lord. Without holiness there is no hope of receiving His future blessings. If, on the other hand, they will set their hearts to seek Him and separate themselves from the uncleanness of the peoples of the lands, the good hand of God will again be upon them. His theological analysis lacks the sociological perspective.

4. 연구의의 Significance of the Study

에스라와 느헤미야 시대의 결혼 개혁에 대한 연관 연구들에 비교해서 본 연구의 중요성은 첫째, 성경 신학에 사회학적 연구방법을 도입하는 점에 공헌한다. 하워드 키 교수(Howard Clark Kee)[47]는 《진리를 알다: 신약해석에 대한 사회학적 연구》에서 기독교가 발생할 당시 변화하는 사회적 정황을 충분히 감안하여 신약성경 신학에 사회학적 방법론을 참고할 것을 제시하였다(vii 쪽). 신학적 개념들은 허

---

47) Howard Kee, *Knowing the Truth: A Sociological Approach to New Testament Interpretation*(Philadelphia: Fortress Press, 1989). 하워드 키 Howard Kee(1920-2017)는 보스턴대 신학부 신약학 교수였다. William Goodwin Aurelio Professor of Biblical Studies Emeritus at Boston University School of Theology, 1977-1988 and a visiting faculty member at the University of Pennsylvania.

공에서 생기는 것이 아니라 특별한 사회적 환경뿐만 아니라 역사적 환경과 사건들 가운데에서 생긴다. 위에서 언급했듯이 우리의 연구 문제에 대한 현존하는 연구물에는 결혼 개혁에 대한 사회학적 관점으로 본 연구는 없다.

In relationship to current studies concerning the marriage reforms at the time of Ezra and Nehemiah, the significance of our study is threefold. First, our investigation will make a contribution to a sociological approach to biblical theology. Howard C. Kee[47] published a book titled *Knowing the Truth: A Sociological Approach to New Testament Interpretation* in 1989. As the author wrote, this book is offered as a methodological prologue to a New Testament Theology on which he was at work, which seeks to take more fully into account the changing social contexts of nascent Christianity(p. vii). Theological conceptions arise not in a vacuum but in response to historical circumstances and events as well as in a specific social ethos. As we mentioned above, a survey of existing literature about our problem indicates that almost no research has been done on the marriage reform from a socio-logical perspective.

둘째, 본 연구가 히브리 성경연구에서 지식사회학을 연구 방법에 발전시키는데 공헌할 것이다. 신약학에서는 여러 학자들이 지식사회학을 다양하게 적용했다.[48] 그러나 히브리 성경연구에서는 지

---

48) John H. Elliott, A Home for the Homeless: A Sociological Exegesis of 1 Peter, Its Situation and Strategy(Philadelphia: Fortress Press, 1981); Gerd Theissen, Sociology of Early Palestinian Christianity, ET by J. Bowden(Philadelphia: Fortress Press, 1978);

식사회학을 사용한 학자는 거의 없다. 폴 핸슨(Paul Hanson, 1939- , Harvard Divinity School, Cambridge, MA에서 40년 강의 후 2009년 은퇴, Florence Corliss Lamont Research Professor of Divinity)[49] 교수는 그의 저서에서 인용 없이 "대체적인 상징적 세계", "합법화 기능", "의미의 세계" "확정하는 제도들" 등 지식사회학에서 사용하는 용어와 개념을 일부 사용했다(pp. 427-444). 그는 칼 마하나임의 지식사회학 방법인 두 가지 정신력들을 포수기 이후 유대 공동체의 두 제사장들의 집안의 내적 갈등을 분석하는 데 사용했다. 그래서 핸슨은 구약학 연구에 있어서 지식사회학을 사용한 선구자가 되었다.

또한 패트릭 밀러(Patrick D. Miller) 교수는 그의 "구약성경에 나오는 믿음과 이념"이라는 글에서[50] 히브리 성경에 나오는 믿음과 이념(이데올로기)의 관계성을 설명하면서 칼 만하임[51]의 지식사회학을 적용했다. 이들 지식사회학적 성경해석의 개척자의 노력들은 간과해서는 안 된다.

Secondly, this study will contribute to develop the use of the sociology of knowledge in Hebrew Bible studies. In the New

---

W. A. Meeks, The First Urban Christians: The Social World of the Apostle Paul(New Haven: Yale University Press, 1983); N. R. Petersen, Rediscovering Paul: Philemon and the Sociology of Paul's Narrative World (Fortress Press, 1985); Philip S. Esler, Community and Gospel in Luke-Acts: The Social and Political Motivations of Lucan Theory(New York:Cambrdige University Press, 1988); Joongsuk Suh, "Discipleship and Community in the Gospel of Mark," unpub. Ph. D. dissertation at Boston University, 1986; J. Andrew Overman, Matthew's Gospel and Formative Judaism: A Study in the Social World of the Matthew Community(Philadelphia: Fortress Press, 1989).

49) Paul D. Hanson, *The Dawn of Apocalyptic : The Historical and Sociological Roots of Jewish Apocalyptic Eschatology*(Philadelphia: Fortress Press, 1974).
50) Miller교수는 프린스톤 신학교의 구약학교수로 은퇴함 Charles T. Haley Professor of Old Testament Theology Emeritus at Princeton Theological Seminary.
51) *Ideology and Utopia : an Introduction to the Sociology of Knowledge*, ET by L. Wirth and E. Shils(New York: Harcourt, Brace and Co., 1936).

Testament studies, many scholars have already made provocative advances by their use of the sociology of knowledge.[48] In the Hebrew Bible studies, however, few scholars have employed the sociology of knowledge. In his apocalyptic study, Hanson[49] uses some terms of the sociology of knowledge such as "an alternative symbolic universe," "function of legitimizing," "universe of meaning," "reifying institutions," without any quotation(pp. 427-444). He used the sociology of knowledge of K. Mannheim in applying the two mentalities theory of K. Mannheim to the analysis of the inner conflict between the priestly houses of the post-exilic Judean community. Thus Hanson became a pioneer in the use of the sociology of knowledge in Old Testament studies. In his article "Faith and Ideology in the Old Testament,"[52] P. Miller also applied the sociology of knowledge of K. Mannheim in explicating the relationship between faith and ideology in the Hebrew Bible. These pioneering efforts in employing the insights and analytical tools of the sociology of knowledge in Biblical studies should not be overlooked.

셋째로, 본 연구는 포수기 이후의 유대인 공동체의 재건에 대한 이해를 증진시킬 것이다. 위에서 살펴본 대로 본 연구가 추구하는 포수기 이후 유대인 공동체의 결혼 개혁을 합법화하는 연구는 지금

---

52) Patrick D. Miller, "Faith and Ideology in the Old Testament," *Magnalia Dei : Essays on the Bible and Archaeology in Memory of G. Ernest Wright*, F. M. Cross, W. E. Lemke and P.D. Miller, Jr.(eds.)(Garden City, NY: Doubleday & Company, Inc., 1976), 464-479.

까지 없었다. 지식사회학을 통하여 우리는 페르샤 시대에 유대인 공동체의 개혁에 대한 합법화 구조들을 더욱 깊이 연구할 수 있다.

Thirdly, our study will enhance the understanding of the reconstruction of the post-exilic Judean community. As we examined above, little research has been done on the legitimation of the marriage reforms of the post-exilic Judean community which this study investigates. Through the sociology of knowledge, we can understand more deeply the structures of legitimation in the reforming of the Judean community during the Persian period.

II

결혼개혁 배경

THE BACKGROUND OF THE MARRIAGE REFORMS

　본 장에서는 에스라와 느헤미야가 주도한 결혼 개혁의 사회적, 종교적 배경을 살펴보려고 한다. 이 개혁의 핵심인 통혼 문제를 다루기 위해, 포수기 이후의 유대 공동체 안에 있었던 통혼 문제와 에스라와 느헤미야 이전의 문서들을 통해 통혼에 대한 부정적인 자세들을 살펴볼 것이다. 그런 후 결혼 개혁의 사회적-종교적 배경을 살펴볼 것이다.

　This chapter intends to examine the social and religious background of the marriage reforms undertaken by Ezra and Nehemiah. In order to deal with the problem of intermarriage which was the key to the reforms, we will investigate the phenomenon of intermarriage in the post-exilic Judean community and the negative attitude towards intermarriage in texts prior to Ezra and Nehemiah. Then we will examine the socio-religious background of the marriage reforms.

2-1. 포수기 이후 유대 공동체 안에 있었던 통혼 현상 Phenomenon of intermarriage in the post-exilic Judean community

에스라와 느헤미야가 주도한 결혼 개혁은 포수기 이후 공동체 안에 유대인[53]과 비유대인들 사이에 결혼이 있었음을 암시하고 있다. 본 항에서 포수기 이후 본문인 말라기 2:10-12과 느헤미야 6:17-19 두 본문을 통해 통혼 현상을 살필 것이다. 특별히 다른 언급이 없으면 필자는 본 연구에서 히브리 성경 마소라 본문, 타낙(MT, TaNaK)과 영어번역은 킹제임스 역을 사용하며, 한글 역은 개역, 개역개정을 사용하면서 부분적으로 사역(私譯)을 할 것이다.

The marriage reforms under Ezra and Nehemiah imply that there were still intermarriages between Judean[53] and non-Judean people in the post-exilic community. In this section, we will examine the phenomenon of intermarriage from two post-exilic biblical texts(Malachi 2:10-12, Neh. 6:17-19). Unless otherwise noted, I translate the biblical texts from the Masoretic Text based on the Hebrew Bible (MT, TaNak) in this study, using the reading of KJB and Korean Revised Version and my own translation.

---

53) 주전 588년 예루살렘이 멸망된 후 이스라엘은 정치적 독립을 상실했다. 코헨은 말하기를 "이 새로운 환경에서 이스라엘 종교는 점차적으로 유대교로 변해갔고 이스라엘 백성들도 점차로 유대인들이 되어 갔다." After the fall of Jerusalem in 588 BC, Israel lost its political independence. "In these new circumstances," Cohen insists, "Israelite religion gradually became Judaism, and Israelites gradually became Judeans."(S.J.D. Cohen, "From the Bible to the Talmud," *Hebrew Annual Review* 7(1983), 23.

2-1-1. 말라기(Malachi) 2:10-12

10 우리는 한 아버지를 가지지 아니하였느냐? 한 하나님의 지으신 바가 아니냐? 어찌하여 우리 각 사람이 자기 형제에게 신실하지 못하게 대하여 우리 조상들의 언약을 욕되게 하느냐? Have we not all one father? hath not one God created us? why do we deal treacherously every man against his brother, by profaning the covenant of our fathers? 11 유다는 신실하지 못하게 행하였고 이스라엘과 예루살렘 중에서는 가증한 일을 행하였으며 유다는 여호와의 사랑하시는 그 성결을 욕되게 하여 이방 신의 딸과 결혼하였으니 Judah hath dealt treacherously, and an abomination is committed in Israel and in Jerusalem; for Judah hath profaned the holiness of the LORD which he loved, and hath married the daughter of a strange god. 12 이 일을 행하는 사람에게 속한 자는 깨는 자나 응답하는 자는 물론이요 만군의 여호와께 제사를 드리는 자도 여호와께서 야곱의 장막 가운데서 끊어 버리시리라 The LORD will cut off the man that doeth this, the master and the scholar, out of the tabernacles of Jacob, and him that offereth an offering unto the LORD of hosts.

말라기 2:10-16은 제사장들을 포함하여 통혼한 유대인들을 공격하고 있다. 10절에 나오는 수사학적 질문들은 하나님으로부터 하나된 모든 유대인들에게 향하여 하나님께 얼마나 충성하는가에 대한 내용이다. 일부 유대인들이 이방 여인들과 통혼하며 그들의 이방신들을 따름으로 주님을 욕되게 하였다. 그들은 또한 이방 여인들과 결혼하기 위해 조강지처를 버렸다(스 2:13-16).⁵⁴⁾ 그래서 16절에서 이스라엘의 하나님이신 주님께서 말씀하시기를 이혼을 싫어하시는데 그 이유는 결혼이 하나의 계약이기 때문이다(말 2:14; 참고. 창 2:24-25; 겔 16:8; 호 2:19).

존스(D. Jones)는 "he hateth putting away"라고 번역하는 것은 신 24:1-4의 본문을 주석가들이 수정한 것으로 보아 바른 번역은 아니라고 주장한다. 오히려 그는 이 구절을 조건절로 읽는다: "만일 어떤 사람이 자기 아내를 미워하여 그녀와 이혼한다면."⁵⁵⁾ 토리(C. Torrey)는 말라기에서는 통혼이나 이혼에 대해 공격하는 것이 아니라 예루살렘에서 벌어지는 이방 종교에 대해 배교하는 것을 지적하고 있다

---

54) 말 2:14 그러나 너희들은 말하기를 "어떤 이유로?" 하는도다. 왜냐하면 너와 너의 젊어서 취한 아내 사이에 주님께서 일찍이 증거하셨기 때문이라. 그녀는 네 배우자요 너와 약속한 아내로되 네가 그에게 불신을 행하도다 Yet ye say, Wherefore? Because the LORD hath been witness between thee and the wife of thy youth, against whom thou hast dealt treacherously: yet is she thy companion, and the wife of thy covenant. 15 주님께서 하나로 만드시지 아니하셨느냐? 주님께서는 영으로 계시느니라. "어떤 이유로?" 그분께서는 경건한 자손을 찾으시느니라. 그러므로 너는 조심하여 젊어서 취한 아내에게 불신을 행하지 말지니라 And did not he make one? Yet had he the residue of the spirit. And wherefore one? That he might seek a godly seed. Therefore take heed to your spirit, and let none deal treacherously against the wife of his youth. 16 이스라엘의 하나님 주님께서 말씀하시기를 그분께서 이혼하는 것을 미워하시는데, 그 이유는 폭력으로 옷을 덮는 자를 미워하시기 때문이라. 만군의 주님의 말씀이니라. 그러므로 너희들은 조심하여 신실치 못하게 행하지 말지니라 For the LORD, the God of Israel, saith that he hateth putting away: for one covereth violence with his garment, saith the LORD of hosts: therefore take heed to your spirit, that ye deal not treacherously.

55) David Clyde Jones, "Malachi on Divorce," *Presbyterian* 15,(St. Louis, MO: Theological Seminary, 1989): 16-22.; "A Note on the LXX of Malachi 2:16," *JBL*, 109 (1990) : 683-85; William K. K. Kapahu, "Contrasting Canons: A Comparative Analysis of Malachi 2:10-16 in the Traditions of the Hebrew Leningradensis and the Greek Sinaiticus," MA thesis, 2013, McMaster Divinity College, Hamilton, Ontario, Canada; Ming Him Ko, "Be Faithful to the Covenant: A Technical Translation of and Commentary on Malachi 2.10-16" *The Bible Translator*, United Bible Society, March 26, 2014. Following A. van Hoonacker (1908), he insists that the pi'el infinitive שַׁלַּח should be repointed to a perfect form(שָׁלַח).

고 주장한다. 통혼을 통해서 다른 신들을 사랑하거나 예배하는 자(말 2:11-12)는 반드시 처벌을 받는다.[56] 이런 자들은 예루살렘 예배 공동체와 유대 계약 공동체로부터 축출되어져야 한다.

 Malachi 2:10-16 attacks intermarriage of some Judeans, including priests. The rhetorical questions in v. 10 reminds Judeans of the common derivation from and loyalty to the Lord. But some Judeans despised the Lord by intermarrying with foreign women and thereby following foreign gods. They were also faithless to the wives of their youth in order to marry foreign women(2:13-16). Thus in verse 16 The Lord, God of Israel, says that he hates divorce, for marriage is a covenant(Mal. 2:14; cf. Gen. 2:24-25, Ezek. 16:8, Hos. 2:19). Jones argues that the common English rendering of this verse("For I hate divorce") is inaccurate, as are commentators' attempts to emend the text in the direction of Deut. 24:1-4. Rather he reads the verse as a conditional sentence: "If [anyone] hating [his wife] divorces [her]." Torrey is right when he suggests that "Malachi's attack was not upon intermarriages and divorce at all, but upon apostasy to a foreign cult practiced in Jerusalem itself." The lover and worshipper of other gods through intermarriages(Mal. 2:11-12) can not go unpunished. Those intermarried Judeans are to be cut off from the Jerusalem worship community and from the Judean covenant community.

 그래져-맥도날드는 폰 불메린크, 후나커, 채리, 스미스, 젤린과 더

---

[56] C. C. Torrey, " The Prophecy of Malachi," *JBL* 17 (1898), 9f.

불어 말 2:11에 나오는 "이방신의 딸"을 문자적으로 번역하면 "외국 신의 딸"이라고 번역할 수 있다.57) 이 구절이 이방 종교를 믿는 여인을 말한다. 이 구절을 통해서 우리는 통혼이 예루살렘에서 심각한 문제가 되었는데, 이방 종교가 여호와를 믿는 신앙과 혼합주의 형태로 등장한 것을 보게 된다.58)

In her recent study, Glazier-McDonald agrees with some scholars like A. von Bulmerincq, A. can Hoonacker, T. Chary, J.M.P. Smith and E. Sellin that the phrase "the daughter of a strange god"(bat 'el nekar) in Mal. 2:11 can be translated literally, "the daughter of a foreign god". This phrase refers to heathen woman. From this verse, we see that intermarriage became a serious problem in Jerusalem, for it resulted in syncretistic phenomenon in Yahwism.58)

그래서 통혼하여 이방 신들을 따르는 자는 야곱의 택하신 장막에서 제거되어져야 한다는 것이다(말 2:12).59) 이것은 "출교"를 뜻한다(참고. 창 17:14; 민 9:13).60) 도이취(R. Deutsch)는 "외국 신의 딸"이란 단순히 외국 여인을 지칭하는 것이 아니라, 유다를 외국 신들을 섬기게 타락시키는 자(참고. 예. 신 13:6-11, 31:16)를 말하며, 렘 5:19, 8:19; 신 31:16-19; 왕하 17:7이하에 따르면 이런 여자는 처벌을 받아야 한다고

---

57) B. Glazier-McDonald, "Intermarriage, Divorce, and the *bat 'el nekar*," *JBL* 106 (1987), 603.
58) Ibid., 610.
59) "이 일을 행하는 사람에게 속한 자는 깨는 자나 응답하는 자는 물론이요 만군의 여호와께 제사를 드리는 자도 여호와께서 야곱의 장막 가운데서 끊어 버리시리라 The LORD will cut off the man that doeth this, the master and the scholar, out of the tabernacles of Jacob, and him that offereth an offering unto the LORD of hosts."
60) F. B. Huey, Jr., "An Exposition of Malachi," *Southwestern Journal of Theology* 30 (1987), 16.

주장한다.[61]

Thus those who intermarry and follow other gods should be cut off from the chosen tent of Jacob(v. 12).[59] This mean "excommunication"(cf. Gen. 17:14, Num. 9:13). Deutsch insists that the "daughter of a foreign god" is not just any foreign woman, but one who leads Judah astray to "serve foreign gods"(see, e.g. Deut. 13:6-11, 31:16), which should result in her punishment according to Jer. 5:19, 8:19, Deut. 31:16-19 and 2 Kings 17:7ff.[61]

말라기는 에스라와 느헤미야가 시작한 결혼 개혁을 재점검하고 완성하였다.[62] 그동안 학개와 스가랴의 대언들에 나타난 회복된 성전 시대와 연관된 높은 희망들이 산산이 부서져 왔다. 말라기서에서는 예배의 제물들에 관한 규정을 어기는 제의들로 타락된 제사장직을 묘사하고 있다. 통혼이 유대 공동체의 정체성에 대해 회의적으로 변하고 있었다.

Malachi renewed the marriage reform done by two great reformers Ezra and Nehemiah.[62] The high hopes connected with the era of the restored Temple reflected in the prophecies of Haggai and Zechariah clearly had been shattered. The book describes a priesthood that has degenerated into practices violating the laws regulating ritual sacrifices.; intermarriage is calling into question the identity of the Jewish community.

말라기서의 중심 주제는 주님의 계약에 대한 신실성과 유대 공동

---

(61) G. S. Ogden and R. R. Deutsch, *Joel & Malachi*, International Theological Commentary, (Grand Rapids, MI: WM. B. Eerdmans Pub. Co., 1987), 95.
(62) P. D. Hanson, " Malachi," *Harper's Bible Commentary*, 753-754.

체 안에서 만연된 도덕적 타락과 예배의 타락에 대한 경고이다.[63] 포수기 후기에 통혼은 유대인 공동체 내에서 급증했는데 그 이유는 그들이 어려운 사회적 환경에 처해있기 때문이었다. "경제적이고 사회적 신분이 더 나아지기를 바라면서,"[64] 많은 유대인 남편들이 자기들의 유대인 부인들을 버리고 부유하고 사회적 지위가 높은 이방 여인들과 결혼하기를 원했다. 제사장들의 집안조차 이웃 백성들과 통혼을 하였다.

One central theme of the book of Malachi is faithfulness to Yahweh's covenant and warning against moral degeneracy and cultic decay within the Judean community.[63] During the post-exilic period, intermarriage had been increasing within the Judean community, for they were in a depressed social condition. "Desirous of up-grading their economic and social status",[64] many Judean husbands were willing to abandon their Judean wives and wanted to marry wealthy and high class foreign women. Even the family of priests intermarried with the neighboring peoples.

2-1-2. 느헤미야(Nehemiah) 6:17-19

17 그때에 유다의 귀족들이 여러 번 도비야에게 편지하였고, 도비야의 편지도 그들에게 이르렀으니 Moreover in those days

---

[63] 핸슨은 말라기가 레위 제사장들이 현재 성전 예배를 장악하던 제사장들의 타락을 느꼈고 성전과 공동체에서 합법적인 제사장 권위를 주장하던 비도덕적 상태에 있는 것을 믿게 된다. Hanson believes Malachi belonged to "the levitical priests who felt that the present degraded state of the rival priesthood and the demoralized condition of the land substantiate their claims to legitimate priestly authority in the temple and community" (ibid., 753-754).

[64] Glazier-McDonald, "Intermarriage, Divorce, and the bat 'el nekar," 604-605.

the nobles of Judah sent many letters unto Tobiah, and the letters of Tobiah came unto them. 18 도비야는 아라의 아들 스가냐의 사위가 되었고 도비야의 아들 여호하난도 베레 갸의 아들 므술람의 딸을 취하였기 때문에, 유다에서 그와 동맹 한 자가 많았더라 For there were many in Judah sworn unto him, because he was the son in law of Shechaniah the son of Arah; and his son Johanan had taken the daughter of Meshullam the son of Berechiah. 19 그들이 그의 선행을 내 앞에 말하고, 또 나의 말도 그에게 전하였더라. 도비야가 내게 편 지하여 나를 두렵게 하고자 하였느니라 Also they reported his good deeds before me, and uttered my words to him. And Tobiah sent letters to put me in fear.

이 본문으로부터 우리는 느헤미야 당시에도 적어도 통혼한 사례를 두 건 볼 수 있다. 도비야는[65] 바벨론의 포로 생활에서 귀환한 아라의 아들 스가냐의 사위가 되었다(스 2:5; 느 7:10). 도비야의 아들 여호하난도 베레갸의 아들 므술람의 딸을 취하였는데, 많은 유대인 들이 도비야에게 동맹 약조를 맺었다(느 6:18). 므술람은 예루살렘의 성벽을 재건하는 데 동참했다(Neh. 3:4, 30). 확실히 므술람은 중요한 공무원이었고, 느헤미야의 성벽 재건 사업에 강력한 협조자였다.

From this text we can see at least two cases of intermarriage

---

(65) 도비야는 산발랏과 더불어 느헤미야의 주적들 중 한 명이었다. 그는 암몬사람으로 불리었다. Tobiah was one of the chief opponents(along with Sanballat) of Nehemiah. He was called "the Ammonite"(2:10, 19, 4:3, cf. 4:7, 6:1, 12). 그를 종이라 부르는 것은 아마도 페르샤 정부의 지방관료를 의미한다. The reference to him as "the servant" (2:10, 19) probably signifies his official title in the provincial government under the Persian rule.

in the time of Nehemiah. Tobiah[65] became the son-in-law of Shecaniah the son of Arah who had returned from exile(Ezra 2:5, Neh. 7:10), while his son Jehohanan had married the daughter of Meshullam son of Berechiah, so that many Judeans had sworn allegiance to Tobiah(Neh. 6:18). Meshullam joined in the rebuilding of the wall of Jerusalem(Neh. 3:4, 30). No doubt, Meshullam was an important official, a firm supporter of Nehemiah's building program.

19절은 포수기 이후 유대 공동체에서 도비야와 통혼하는 것에 대해 부정적인 입장을 보여준다. 이 사실 자체가 예루살렘에는 영향력이 많은 도비야 당이 있어서 느헤미야와 협상하는 데 어려움이 있었음이 분명해진다.

Verse 19 shows the negative attitude towards intermarriage with Tobiah in the post-exilic Judean community. This fact itself makes clear that there was an influential Tobiad party in Jerusalem with whom Nehemiah must have had difficulty in dealing.

2-2 통혼에 대한 부정적인 태도 The negative attitude towards intermarriage

이스라엘 사람들과 이방인들 사이에 통혼이 이스라엘 역사상(창 16:3-4, 25:1; 민 12:1; 삼하 3:3) 자주 있었음에도 불구하고 통혼은 보통 부정적인 결과로 인도하는 것으로 여겨졌다(삿 3:5-7, 14:1-20, 16:4-22; 왕상 11:1-5, 16:31). 창세기에서 이런 부정적인 태도의 주된 이유는 이스라엘 부족 사회가 족내혼(族內婚, 같은 부족 내의 결혼)을 실천했기 때문이었다. 같은 부족 내에서 혼인이 이루어져야 집안의 재산이 보존되었다. 민 36:6-7에 보니 "슬로브핫의 딸들에게 대한 여호와의 명이 이러하니라. 말씀하시기를 '슬로브핫의 딸들은 마음대로 시집가려니와 (민 27:1-11) 오직 그 조상 지파의 가족에게로만 시집갈지니 그리하면 이스라엘 자손의 기업이 이 지파에서 저 지파로 옮기지 않고 이스라엘 자손이 다 각기 조상 지파의 기업을 지킬 것이니라 하셨나니"라고 기록되어 있다. 신명기 사가들의 본문에서도 통혼에 대해 강력 규제하는 목적이 바로 배교를 방지하는 것이었다. 배교는 이스라엘 공동체의 사회적-종교적 구조를 해체하려고 위협했다.

Although intermarriage between Israelites and non-Israelites was popular through the Israel's history(Gen. 16:3-4, 25:1; Num. 12:1, 2 Sam. 3:3), intermarriage was usually portrayed as leading to negative results(Jud. 3:5-7, 14:1-20, 16:4-22, 1 Kgs. 11:1-5, 16:31). The main reason for negative attitude towards intermarriage in the Genesis narratives was that Israelite tribal society practiced endogamy. For tribal property must be maintained intact. According to Num. 36:6b-7, "Let them(=the daughters of Zelophehad, see Num. 27:1-11) marry whom they think best; only it must be into a clan of their father's tribe that they are married, so that no inheritance of the Israelites shall be transferred from one tribe to another; for all Israelites shall retain the inheritance of their ancestral tribes." The purpose of the strong interdiction against intermarriage in the deuteronomistic texts was to prevent apostasy, which threatened to disintegrate the social-religious structure of the Israelite community.

구약성경에서 통혼에 대한 강력한 부정적 태도들을 여섯 가지 본문들에서 살펴보자: 창세기에서 두 개 본문, 신명기 설교들에서 네 개의 본문들이다.

Let us explore the harsh attitude towards intermarriage in six biblical passages in the Hebrew Bible; two from Genesis narratives, four from the deuteronomistic homilies.

2-2-1. 창세기(Genesis) 24:1-4

1 아브라함이 나이 많아 늙었고 주님께서 그의 범사에 복을 주셨더라 And Abraham was old, advanced in years, and the Lord had blessed Abraham in all things. 2 아브라함이 자기 집 모든 소유를 맡은 늙은 종에게 이르되 청컨대 네 손을 내 환도뼈 밑에 넣으라 And Abraham said to his oldest servant of his house, who took charge of all that he owned, "Put, I pray thee, thy hand under my thigh: 3 내가 너로 하늘의 하나님, 땅의 하나님이신 주님을 가리켜 맹세하게 하노니 너는 나의 거하는 이 지방 가나안 족속의 딸 중에서 내 아들을 위하여 아내를 택하지 말고 And I will make thee swear by the Lord, the God of heaven, and the God of the earth, that thou shall not take a wife for my son from the daughters of the Canaanites, among whom I dwell, 4 내 고향 내 족속에게로 가서 내 아들 이삭을 위하여 아내를 택하라 but thou shall go to the country, and to my kindred, and take a wife for my son Isaac."

많은 후손들을 주시리라는 하나님의 약속(창 12:2, 15:5-6)을 믿고, 아브라함은 죽기 전에 그의 유일한 합법적인 아들인 이삭을 위하여 자기 집안에서 아내를 찾을 것을 확신했다. 2절에서 자기 환도뼈 밑에 손을 넣는 행위는 남성의 중요한 부분을 잡는 의식으로(참고. 창 24:9, 47:29) "생명을 건 맹세"를 말한다.[66] 3-4절에서 아브라함의 부탁은 엄격하다: "내 아들을 위하여 가나안의 딸들이 아닌 아내를 취하라." 그는 자기 종에게 가나안 여인 중에 아내를 취하는 것을 금지한다. 죽음을 앞두고 아브라함은 살아생전에 며느리를 보고 싶어 했다.[67]

Believing the divine promise of numerous offspring (Gen. 12:2, 15:5-6), Abraham made sure of finding a wife for Isaac, his only legitimate son, from his relatives, before he dies. The rite of touching the male generative organ in v. 2 [put, I pray thee, thy hand under my 'thigh'](cf. Gen. 24:9, 47:29) is considered an "oath at the source of life."[66] The apodictic command of Abraham in vv. 3b-4 is very strict: "Thou shall not take a wife for my son from the daughters of the Canaanites…" He forbade his servant to take a wife for his son from among Canaanite women. Anticipating his death, Abraham wanted to make sure this marriage while he was alive.[67]

---

66) C. Westermann, *Genesis 12-36, A Commentary*, ET by John J. Scullion, (Minneapolis: Augsburg Pub. House, 1985), 384.
67) 이 본문은 포수기 후기의 자료인 J의 일부로 족장 설화의 가장 긴 설화의 서론 부분이라고 문서설을 지지하는 학자들은 주장한다. Our text seems to be the post-exilic material, rather than a part of J. This is an introductory part of the longest narrative in the patriarchal stories. Although most scholars(M. Noth, Von Rad, W. Zimmerli, E.A. Speiser, W. Roth) attribute this text to J, Alexander Rof insists that Genesis 24 is a late composition, in terms of language forms, religious beliefs(prayer), and the moral imperatives. And J. Van Seters dates J to the exile("La composizione de Gen. 24," Bibblia e Oriente 129, 1981, 161-165).

비록 아브라함과 이삭이 가나안 원주민들과 평화롭게 살고 있었지만, 아브라함은 순수한 혈통을 유지하기를 원했다(4절). 이스마엘은 창 21:21에 보니 하갈이 주었던 이집트 여인과 결혼했다. 아브라함과 사라에게는 이스마엘이 누구와 결혼하든 중요하지 않았다. 아브라함은 자기의 합법적인 후손은 하란으로 돌아가서 그곳에 살던 자기 집안과 같은 혈통에서 태어나야 한다고 믿었다(참고, 창 24:7절). 또한 경제적인 이유로 그는 통혼을 엄금하였는데, 자기의 부동산을 이웃 민족들로부터 지키기 위함임을 부인하기 어렵다.[68] 무엇보다 더, 그는 여호와께서 자기 아들, 이삭에서 자기 혈족으로부터 배우자를 주실 것을 믿었다. 이 위임 설화는 확실히 그 당시의 족내혼(族內婚)의 관습을 반영하고 있다.

Although Abraham and Isaac were living peacefully with the native Canaanites, Abraham wanted to maintain pure blood (v. 4). Ishmael married an Egyptian wife in Gen. 21:21 whom Hagar gave him. For Abraham and Sarah, it did not matter whom Ishmael married. Abraham believed his legitimate descendent should be born through his clan back in Haran(cf. Gen. 24:7). Also, it is hard to deny that he forbade intermarriage for an economic reason, that is, to keep his estate from his neighboring peoples.[68] Above all things, he believed that the Lord will give a wife for his son Isaac from his relatives. This commission narrative surely reflects the custom of endogamy at that time.

---

68) Contra Von Rad, *Genesis*, ET by John Marks, rev. ed., Old Testament Library, (Philadelphia: Westminster Press, 1972), 255.

2-2-2. 창세기(Genesis) 27:46-28:4

창 27:46 리브가가 이삭에게 말하기를 "내가 헷 사람의 딸들 때문에 저의 생명을 싫어하거늘 야곱이 만일 이 땅의 딸들 곧 그들과 같은 헷 사람의 딸들 중에서 아내를 취하면 나의 생명이 내게 무슨 유익이 있으리이까?" And Rebekah said to Isaac, "I am disgusted with my life because of the Hittite daughters. If Jacob marries a Hittite daughter like these, from among the native daughters, what good shall my life do me?"

창 28:1 이삭이 야곱을 불러 그에게 축복하고 또 부탁하여 말하기를 "너는 가나안 사람의 딸들 중에서 아내를 취하지 말고 And Isaac called Jacob, and blessed him. He charged him, saying, "Thou shall not take a wife of the daughters of Canaan. 2 일어나 밧단 아람으로 가서 너의 외조부 브두엘 집에 이르러 거기서 너의 외삼촌 라반의 딸 중에서 아내를 취하라 Arise, go to Paddan-aram, to the house of Bethuel, thy mother's father, and take thee a wife from there of the daughters of Laban, thy mother's brother, 3 전능하신 하나님이 네게 복을 주어 너로 생육하고 번성하게 하시어 너로 여러 족속을 이루게 하시고 May El Shaddai bless thee, make thee fertile, and multiply thee, so that thou become a multitude of people, 4 아브라함에게 허락하신 복을 네게 주시되 너와, 너와 함께 네 자손에게 주사 너로 하나님이 아브라함에게 주신 땅 곧 너의 우거하는 땅을 유업으로 받게 하시기를 원하노라" May God grant the blessing of Abraham to thee and to thy offspring, that thou may possess the land where thou are a stranger, which God gave to Abraham."

창세기 27장에 의하면, 야곱은 아마도 이삭의 뜻과 반대하여 황급히 도망갈 수 있는데, 본문에서는 아버지 이삭이 아들 야곱을 축복하며 라반의 집이 있는 밧단 아람(창 28:5,7)으로 보내면서 성대한 의식을 치르는 기분이다.[69] 의도적이든, 무의식적이든, 이 본문은 오랜 편집 과정 속에서 제사장들의 정결예식이 반영된 듯하다.

Whereas according to ch. 27, Jacob flees in great haste (probably against Isaac's will), here [28:1-9] he is sent to Laban by Isaac with great ceremony(vv. 5, 7).[69] Consciously or unconsciously, the old tradition was unmistakably purified of everything objectionable sometime between the Yahwist and exilic and postexilic period.

이삭과 리브가가 에서가 가나안 여인들과 결혼한 것에 대한 반응은 매우 부정적이었다(창 26:35, 27:46, 28:8). 본문의 전후 문학적 상황은 에서의 이방인과의 결혼이다. 에서가 사십 세가 되었을 때 헷 족속 브에리의 딸 유딧과 엘론의 딸 바스맛과 결혼한 일이 이삭과 리브가의 근심이 되었다(창 26:34-35). 야곱이 엄마와 함께 아버지를 속여서까지 장자 축복을 받게 한 다음에도 리브가는 이삭에게 이 문제를 언급하면서 야곱이 원주민과 결혼하는 것을 금지하자고 제안한다(창 27:46). 문서 비평가들의 관점에서는 창 27:1-45 본문의 스타일, 구문론, 동기 등이 에서의 통혼과 야곱의 아람으로 도피하는 본문과 다름을 지적한다.[70] 창 28:8-9에 의하면, 에서 자신도 자기의

---

69) 폰 라트는 이 본문이 제사장 문서(P)에 속한 것으로 P문서에서 통혼에 대해 어떻게 생각하는지 살필 수 있는 좋은 예라고 주장한다. *Ibid.*, 281.
70) E. A. Speiser, *Genesis*, Anchor Bible, (New York: Doubleday, 1964), 215.

헷 족속 부인들이 부모의 마음을 불편하게 함을 깨닫고, 자기 아버지의 친족이 되는 여인인 이스마엘의 딸 느바욧의 누이 바스맛을 아내로 맞이했다(창 36:3). 그러나 그런 결혼도 부모의 마음을 위로하지 못했다. 그래서 이 본문의 삽입은 야곱이 유산을 이어 받을 권리를 합법화한 것이다. 창 27장과 달리, 이삭은 야곱을 자기 친족에게 보냈다. 에서의 결혼을 언급한 제사장 자료들(창 26:34-35, 28:8-9, 36:1-3)과 야곱이 밧단 아람으로 도피한 본문(창 27:46-28:9)은 통혼 문제가 대두되었던 포수기 이후 시대에 속한다.

The reaction of Isaac and Rebekah to the prospect of Esau's marriage with Canaanite women was strongly negative(Gen. 26:35, 27:46, 28:8). The literary context of this text is as follows: The final redactor of Genesis inserted the Yahwistic document(27:1-45) between two P pericopes: Esau's intermarriage with two Canaanite women(26:34-35) and Jacob's departure for Aram(27:46-28:22), for our text differs sharply from the preceding narrative(27:1-45) in style, phraseology, and motivation.[70] According to Gen. 28:8-9, even Esau himself recognized that his two Canaanite wives displeased his parents, and took a wife from his father's relatives; Mahalath(or Basemath 36:3), daughter of Ishmael. However, it does not cool down his parents' temper any longer. Thus this insertion is to legitimize Jacob's inheritance of clan leadership. Unlike in chapter 27, Isaac sent Jacob to his relatives in this text. The Priestly materials which mention the marriage of Esau(Gen. 26:34-35, 28:8-9, 36:1-3) and Jacob's departure for Paddan-aram(27:46-28:9) belong to the post-exilic period when intermarriage began to become an issue.

이 본문의 사회적 문맥은 무엇인가? 이 본문은 히브리 족장들이 족외혼 보다는 족내혼을 선호했다는 것을 말하고 있다(참고. 창 11:27-29, 20:12, 24:3-4, 28:2, 29:19 등). 족내혼의 습관은 이스라엘 공동체에서 항상 전통적으로 수용되어졌다. 포수기와 포수기 이후 시대에, 일부 유대인들은 비-유대인 여인들과 결혼하는 것이 그들의 공동체에서 허락이 되었다고 생각했다. 그러나 제사 문서 집필자들을 비롯해서 다른 유대인들은 통혼에 대해 부정적인 태도를 취했다. J 문서의 설화(Gen. 27:1-45)와는 달리 P 문서에서는 야곱이 족내혼을 위해 라반의 집으로 간 내용[도망간 것이 아님] 내용을 정당화하고 있다. 합법적인 아내는 자기 부모들의 친족이어야 한다. 폰 라트의 글을 인용하자:[71]

What is the social context of this text? This text indicates that the Hebrew patriarchs preferred endogamy to exogamy(cf. Gen. 11:27-29, 20:12, 24:3-4, 28:2, 29:19, etc.). The custom of endogamy was traditional accepted in the Israelite community at all times. During the exilic and post-exilic periods, some Judeans thought that marriage with non-Judean women was permitted in their community. But other Judeans, including the Priestly writers, took the negative attitude towards intermarriage. Unlike the Yahwistic narrative(J, Gen. 27:1-45), P justifies the departure[not flight] of Jacob from his hometown to Laban's house for the purpose of endogamy. The legitimate wife should be a relative of his parents. Let us quote von Rad.[71]

…고대 전승이 시대의 특별한 문제의 관심 속에 변형되었을 것으

---

71) G. von Rad, *ibid*., 282.

로 생각된다. 신명기는 결혼에서 믿음과 제의적 행위에는 관심이 없고(신 21:10-14) 통혼을 허락한다. 그러나 포수기 이후 초기에는 통혼 문제는 매우 중요했다. 왜냐하면 포로에서 귀환한 사람들은 우여곡절 끝에 고국으로 돌아오게 되었 는데 그때 원주민들이 결혼의 유혹을 해 와서 통혼하게 되었다(스 9:1f, 느 13:23이하). 그러므로 아내의 뿌리에 대한 관심은 특히 믿음의 관점에서 이해해야 하며 그들의 인종적 관점에서 보지 말아야 한다.

…and it is conceivable that the ancient tradition was transformed in the interest of a special problem of the time. Deuteronomy was still uninterested in the faith and cultic practice of the woman taken in marriage(Dt. 21:10-14), and permitted the intermarriage; but in the early post-exilic period the problem of mixed marriages became very important. For those who returned from the exile had to find their way to a home into which meanwhile some of the neighboring peoples had trickled(Ezra 9:1f; Neh. 13:23ff). The interest in the wife's origin, therefore, must be understood exclusively from the viewpoint of faith and not from a national or racial viewpoint.

통혼은 공동체의 순수성을 위협하기 때문에 제사장 문서는 신앙의 관점에서 통혼보다는 족내혼의 중요성을 강조하고 했다.

Since intermarriage threatened purity of their community, the Priestly writer(s) emphasized the importance of endogamy rather than intermarriage from the viewpoint of faith.

2-2-3. 출애굽기(Exodus) 34:11-16

11 너는 내가 오늘 네게 명하는 것을 지키라. 보라, 내가 네 앞에서 아모리 사람과 가나안 사람과 헷 사람과 브리스 사람과 히위 사람과 여부스 사람을 쫓아내리니 Observe thou that which I command thee this day: behold, I drive out before thee the Amorite, and the Canaanite, and the Hittite, and the Perizzite, and the Hivite, and the Jebusite. 12 너는 스스로 조심하여, 네가 들어가는 땅의 주민들과 계약을 맺지 말라. 그들이 너희 중에 올가미가 될까 하노라 Take heed to thyself, lest thou make a covenant with the inhabitants of the land whither thou goest, lest it be for a snare in the midst of thee: 13 너희는 도리어 그들의 제단들을 부수고, 그들의 우상들을 깨뜨리고 그들의 아세라 상을 찍을지어다 But ye shall destroy their altars, break their images, and cut down their groves(Asherim): 14 너는 다른 신에게 절하지 말라. 여호와는 질투라 이름하는 질투의 하나님임이니라 For thou shalt worship no other god: for the LORD, whose name is Jealous, is a jealous God: 15 너는 조심하여 그 땅의 주민들과 계약을 맺지 말지니, 왜냐하면 그들이 모든 신을 음란히 섬기며 그 신들에게 희생을 드리고 너를 청하면 네가 그 희생을 먹을까 함이라 Lest thou make a covenant with the inhabitants of the land, and they go a whoring after their gods, and do sacrifice unto their gods, and one call thee, and thou eat of his sacrifice; 16 또 네가 그들의 딸들로 네 아들들의 아내를 삼음으로 그들의 딸들이 그 신들을 음란히 섬기며 네 아들

로 그들의 신들을 음란히 섬기게 할까 함이니라 And thou take of their daughters unto thy sons, and their daughters go a whoring after their gods, and make thy sons go a whoring after their gods.

이 본문 안에 가나안 칠족들과 계약을 맺는 것은 금지되어 있다(참고. 출 23:22). 타민족들과 계약을 맺으면 통혼으로 인도하기 때문이며 통혼은 다음 세대들이 타 종교의 제의를 행하게 하기 때문이다.

In this text, to make a covenant(cf. Exo. 23:22) with six peoples in Canaan was prohibited. For making a covenant with other peoples would lead to intermarriage, and intermarriage would lead to the next generation practicing the other religions.

왜 통혼 금지가 모든 이방인들이 아니라 가나안 칠족에만 해당되는가? 이 여섯 이방족들과 통혼하는 일이 이스라엘의 종교적 정체성을 협박하여 이스라엘 백성들이 다른 신들을 예배함을 유혹했기 때문이다. 여호와께서 다른 민족들(아모리, 가나안, 헷, 브리스, 히위, 여부스)[72]을 몰아내치기로 약속을 하셨기에, 이스라엘 백성들은 여호와

---

[72] 출애굽에 나오는 가나안 칠족의 명단이 전승에 따라 다소 차이가 난다. 다음 명단을 비교해 보자. The list of the Canaanites varies from verse to verse in the book of Exodus for an unknown reason. Compare this list with others: Ex. 3:8,17 Canaanites, Hittites, Amorites, Perizzites, Hivites, Jebusites 13:5 Canaanites, Hittites, Amorites, Hivites, Jebusites 33:2 Canaanites, Amorites, Hittites, Perizzites, Hivites, Jebusites(LXX. Amorites, Hittites, Perizzites, Girgashites, Hivites, Jebusites, Canaanites) 34:11 Amorites, Canaanites, Hittites, Perizzites, Hivites, Jebusites(LXX. Amorites, Canaanites, Perizzites, Hittites, Hivites, Girgashites, Jebusites) *Samaritan* and LXX add the Girgashites after the Perizzites in 3:8, 17; *Samaritan* adds the Perizzites and the Girgashites after the Amorites but LXX and Syriac add the Perizzites and the Girgashites after the Jebusites in 13:5; *Samaritan* adds the Girgashites after the Hittites in 33:2 and 34:11. This comparison shows that there are some different literary traditions.

께서 그들에게 명령한 것을 지켰다(신 34:11, 참고. 신 23:27-31, 33:2). 여호와께서 그들에게 토착민 가나안 사람들과 어떤 계약을 맺지 말도록 권면하셨는데, 그 계약이 그들 가운데 위험한 올무가 되기 때문이다. 이스라엘 백성들은 가나안 땅에서 우상제단들, 신성한 기둥들, 가나인 백성들의 아세라 상들을 제거해야 했다. 여호와 하나님에 대한 예배에 방해되는 어떤 것이라도 제거해야 했다.[73] 가나안 족들의 이런 신성한 제의 물건들이 요시아의 종교 개혁 때 제거되었다(왕하 23:4-14).

Why did the prohibition against intermarriage apply not to all gentiles but only to the seven Canaanite nations? Because intermarriage with these six neighboring nations most likely threatened Israelite religious identity, tempting Israelites to worship other gods. The Lord promised to drive out other peoples(the Amorites, the Canaanites, the Hittites, the Perizzites, the Hivites, and the Jebusites),[72] so that the people of Israel may observe what the Lord commanded them to do(Deut. 34:11, cf. Deut. 23:27-31, 33:2). The Lord exhorted them not to make any covenant with the autochthonous Canaanite peoples, lest it could become a dangerous entrapment among them. The Israelites must extirpate from the land of Canaan the altars, the sacred pillars, and Asherim(or sacred poles) of the Canaanite peoples, thus removing even the slightest possibility of any compromise in their worship of Yahweh.[73] The destruction of these sacred things of the Canaanites came about as an accomplishment of Josiah's religious

---

73) John Durham, *Exodus* (Waco, TX: Word Books, Pub., 1987), 460.

reform(2 Kings 23:4-14).

여호와께서는 질투의 하나님이시니(엘 카나. 참고. 출 20:5; 신 4:24, 5:9, 6:15), 이스라엘 백성들은 다른 신들을 섬기지 말아야 한다(14-16절, 참고 신 23:21-23). 여호와께서 이스라엘이 헌신한 다른 경쟁자를 참지 못하신다. 만약 그들이 이 권면을 무시하고 가나안 원주민들과 계약을 체결하여, 통혼과 교제를 행하여 다른 신들에게 바친 제물을 먹게 될 것이다. 그러므로 16절에서 이스라엘 남자들과 가나안 여인들 사이의 통혼은 금지시켰다.

Since the Lord is a jealous God(אל קנא cf. Exo. 20:5, Deut. 4:24, 5:9, 6:15), the people of Israel should not worship other gods(vv.14-16, cf. 23:21-23). The Lord would not tolerate any rivals for Israel's devotion. If they would disregard this exhortation and make a covenant with the Canaanite inhabitants, such an action may lead to intermarriage and a fellowship, eating of sacrifices made to other gods. Therefore, in verse 16, intermarriage between Israelite men and Canaanite women was prohibited.

이제 본문의 문학적 배경을 살펴보자. 이 본문은 하나님과 언약이 깨어진 후(출 32장), 언약의 갱신으로 이해되는 출 34:10-26의 율법 조항에 속한다. 이 자료들이 하나님의 이름을 "여호와"로 사용하기에 (10, 14, 23, 24, 26절), 문서설을 옹호하는 학자들은 신명기적 언어를 가지고 J문서에 속하는 것으로 본다. 이 본문은 다음 절(18-26절)에 대한 서론적 설교라고 차일즈 교수(Brevard Springs Childs)[74]가 지적한다.

Let us examine the literary context of our text. This text belongs to the legal material of Exo. 34:10-26 which is understood

---

[74] B. Childs(1923-2007, 84세 별세), Yale 대학교 구약학 교수, 1958-1999년.

as a renewal of the covenant after it was broken(Ex. 32). Since this material used the divine name "the Lord"(vv. 10, 14, 23, 24, 26), this law seems to belong to J with some Deuteronomic language. This text is a homiletical introduction to the following verses(v. 18-26) as Childs points out :

문학 비평가들은 오랫동안 11-16절이 신명기에 의해 강하게 영향을 받은 후대 문학적 연장 자료에 속하는 것으로 관찰해 왔다. 현재 설화의 문맥에서 언약의 마지막 선포 후에 놓였고 실제 규정 전에 놓이게 된 것인데 이 항목은 언약을 해석하며 그 순종을 명하는 설교의 서론으로 보인다. 권면에서 강조하는 것은 이스라엘 백성들이 토착민들로부터 온전히 분리되어야 한다는 것이다. 경고의 근거는 질투하시는 하나님의 속성 때문이며 다른 신들의 예배를 용납하시지 않는 데(14절) 있으며, 가나안 사람들과의 접촉은 우상 숭배의 유혹을 가져온다는 것이다. 이 설교는 또한 비슷한 언어로 금송아지 숭배 설화를 연상시키는데, 예를 들면 예배 금지, 제물 금지, 먹는 것 금지, 창녀 금지 등이다(참고. 출 32:6 이하).[75]

Literary critics have long observed that vv.11-16 appear to reflect a later literary expansion which has been strongly influenced by Deuteronomy. In the context of the present narrative, placed after the final announcement of the covenant and before the actual stipulations, the section serves as a homilectical introduction which both interprets the covenant and commends its obedience. The whole emphasis of the admonition falls on Israel's complete separation from the inhabitants of the land. The warning is

---

75) B.S. Childs, *Exodus* (Philadelphia: Westminster Press, 1974), 613.

grounded in the nature of God who is a jealous God and will not tolerate the worship of another(v.14), and in the subtle temptation to idolatry which contact with the Canaanites inevitably brings. This homily also serves to remind of the golden calf episode by its similar language: not worship, nor sacrifice, nor eat, nor play the harlot(cf. 32:6 ff).75)

피쉬베인은 또한 이 본문은 고대 순례 달력과 규칙의 형태 위에 세워진 주석적 법적 자료(출 34:18-26, 무교절과 칠칠절)의 설교적, 훈계적 서언의 말씀으로 여겼다.76)

Fishbane also considered this text as the homiletical, hortatory prologue of the exegetical legal discourse(Ex. 34:18-26) which is built on the pattern of the old pilgrimage calendars and their rules.76)

요약을 하면 이 본문은 통혼을 계약 관계의 결과로 여기며, 통혼으로 인해 다음 세대가 이방 종교의 제의를 행하는 결과를 낳게 됨을 지적하고 있다.

In sum this text considers intermarriage the outcome of covenant relations, and the practicing of the other religion by the next generation as the outcome of intermarriage.

---

76) M. Fishbane, *Biblical Interpretation in Ancient Israel*, 195; cf. F. Langlemet, "Israël et ' l'habitant du pays'; vocabulaire et formules d'Ex. xxxiv 11-16," *Revue biblique* 76 (1969), 326.

2-2-4. 신명기(Deuteronomy) 7:1-4

7:1 네 하나님 여호와께서 너를 인도하사 네가 가서 차지할 땅으로 보내시고, 네 앞에서 여러 민족 헷 족속과 기르가스 족속과 아모리 족속과 가나안 족속과 브리스 족속과 히위 족속과 여부스 족속 곧 너보다 많고 힘이 있는 일곱 족속을 쫓아내실 때에 When the LORD thy God shall bring thee into the land whither thou goest to possess it, and hath cast out many nations before thee, the Hittites, and the Girgashites, and the Amorites, and the Canaanites, and the Perizzites, and the Hivites, and the Jebusites, seven nations greater and mightier than thou; 2 네 하나님 여호와께서 그들을 네게 인도하여 너로 치게 하시리니 그때에 너는 그들을 완전히 전멸할 것이라. 그들과 무슨 계약도 맺지 말 것이요 그들에게 자비를 보이지도 말 것이며 And when the LORD thy God shall deliver them before thee; thou shalt smite them, and utterly destroy them; thou shalt make no covenant with them, nor shew mercy unto them: 3 또 그들과 혼인하지 말지니 네 딸을 그 아들에게 주지 말 것이요 그 딸로 네 며느리를 삼지 말 것은 Neither shalt thou make marriages with them; thy daughter thou shalt not give unto his son(אל תתחתן בם), nor his daughter shalt thou take unto thy son. 4 그가 네 아들을 유혹하여 그로 여호와를 떠나고 다른 신들을 섬기게 하므로 여호와께서 너희에게 진노하사 갑자기 너희를 멸망하실 것이기 때문이라. For they will turn away thy son from following me, that they may serve other gods: so will the anger of the

LORD be kindled against you, and destroy thee suddenly.

이 본문은 바로 앞의 본문(출 34장)처럼 언약 통혼 배교의 순서와 같은 순서를 보여 준다. 이 현상은 이스라엘 백성들이 주변이 가나안 백성들과의 미래의 관계성을 다루고 있다. 이 법의 목적은 이스라엘 백성들을 주변의 백성들과 그들의 신들로부터 격려하는 것이다.[77] 이스라엘 백성들 가운데 많은 외국인들이 살기 때문에 많은 통혼들이 확실히 발생할 것이다. 이스라엘 백성들이 여호와께서 주실 땅에 들어갈 때 그들은 토착민 가나안 사람들과 결혼을 포함한 어떤 계약도 맺어서는 안 된다. 신명기의 기본 계명은 가나안 백성들을 금지하는 것이다(2절). 금지의 행위(ḥerem)는 세속적인 사용으로부터 배제하는 일종의 헌신이다. 폰 라트는 4절에서 이 "금지"와 연관하여 통혼을 금지하는 것을 설명하고 있다.

This text is to show same order as the previous text(covenant - intermarriage - apostasy). It deals with the future relationship of Israel with the surrounding Canaanite peoples. The purpose of this law is to alienate the Israelites from the surrounding peoples and from their gods.[77] The presence of many foreigners among the Israelites will doubtless result in numerous intermarriages. When the Israelites enter the land which the Lord will give them, they may not make any covenant, including that of marriage with the native Canaanite peoples. The Deuteronomic basic commandment, however, is to ban the Canaanite peoples(v.2). The act of banning(ḥérem) is a kind of dedication to exclusion

---

[77] Morton Smith, *Palestinian Parties and Politics that Shaped the Old Testament*(New York: Columbia University Press, 1971), 12-13.

from profane use. Von Rad explains the prohibition against intermarriage in v.4 by relating it to "the banning" as follows :

　금지(케렘 ḥerem)은 거룩한 전쟁의 제의적 마지막 의식인데, 전쟁포로들과 전리품을 여호와께 드리는 것이다. 신명기는 비교적 늦게 편집된 책인데, 신학적 관점의 결과로서 이스라엘 역사 초기보다 이 문제에 대해 훨씬 더욱 과격한 태도를 가지고 있다. 그래서 이스라엘과 토착민들 사이에 어떤 통혼이나 부부관계가 없었다. 이 규칙은 하나님의 성스러운 권리로부터 나왔기에 합리적인 설명이 더 이상 필요가 없다. 그럼에도 불구하고 한 가지 분명한 이유를 찾는다면, 이스라엘의 관련된 배우자는 여호와를 버리고 싶은 유혹에 빠지게 된다는 것이다(신 21:10이하에서는 통혼 문제에 대해 아직 염려하는 것이 없는 것 같음). 다른 이유는 보다 원시적인 것 같다; 이스라엘이 거룩한 국가 즉 여호와를 위하여 구별된 나라로 여호와의 주권의 종속에 편견이 있는 모든 것들로부터 금지해야 한다는 것이다.[78]

The banning(herem) is the final act in the ritual conduct of the Holy War, the handing over of the captive enemies and the booty to the Lord. Deuteronomy, being late, has, as a result of its theological viewpoint, a much more radical attitude on this matter than Israel had in the early days. Thus there may be no intermarriage, no *connubium* between Israel and the native population. This rule is derived from the sacral right of God and hence would need no reasoned explanation. Nevertheless, a clear reason is supplied: the Israelite spouse concerned might be tempted to forsake the Lord(on the rule in Dt. 21:10ff., which evidently

---

78) G. von Rad, *Deuteronomy*(London: SCM Press, 1966), 67.

did not yet worry about this). The other reason sounds much more primitive: Israel is a holy nation, that is, a nation set apart for the Lord, and must abstain from everything which might prejudice its subordination to the Lord's sole authority.[78]

신명기 사가에게 있어서, 다른 백성들과 통혼하는 일은 다른 신들을 예배하는 일에 유혹하기 때문에(3-4절) 명백하게 금지되어 있다. 그래서 이스라엘 백성들은 그들의 딸들을 가나안 아들들에게 주지 못하게 되어 있으며, 그들의 아들들은 가나안 딸들에게 결혼시켜서는 안 된다. 만약 그들이 이 법을 어겨서 이방 배우자들의 신들을 섬기게 되면 여호와께서 그들을 즉시 엄벌하실 것이다.

For the Deuteronomist, the intermarriages with other peoples were evidently prohibited because of its leading to worship of alien gods(vv. 3-4). Thus the Israelites were not supposed to give their daughters to Canaanite sons or their sons to Canaanite daughters. If they violate this law and worship the gods of their foreign spouses, the Lord will promptly punish them.

신명기 7장은 가나안 땅에서 배교에 대해 경고하고 있다. 이 장에서는 두 가지 주제들이 다뤄지고 있다: 첫째는, 이스라엘이 그 땅의 토착민들을 멸망시켜야 하는 것과 둘째는, 이스라엘이 그들의 신들을 예배하지 말 것을 가르치고 있다(4-5절, 7-15절, 25-26절).[79] 저자는 이방인 배우자들이 가져오는 우상으로 오염되기 때문에 통혼을 금지하고 있다(참고. 신 5:7, 6:14-15). "이스라엘 백성은 거룩해야 한다. 왜냐

---

79) A.D.H. Mayes, *Deuteronomy*, The New Century Bible Commentary,(Grand Rapids, Mich.:Wm. B. Eerdmans Pub. Co., 1981), 181.

하면 여호와께서 거룩하시기 때문이다"(레 19:2, 20:7). 이 말씀이 성결법전(레 16-26장)에 의하면 이스라엘의 종교 생활의 기초가 된다. 선민은 오직 여호와의 법령을 순종하며 여호와의 법도를 지켜 그 속에서 살아야 한다(Lev. 18:4-5, 24-26, 20:22 등)

Deut. 7 warns against apostasy in the land of Canaan. Two subjects are treated in this chapter: first, Israel is to destroy the older inhabitants of the land(vv. 1-3, 6, 17-24); second, she is not to worship their gods(vv. 4-5, 7-15, 25-26).[79] The lawgiver forbids intermarriages because of possible contamination of idolatry they bring with them(cf. Deut. 5:7, 6:14-15). "The people of Israel should be holy, for the Lord is holy"(Lev. 19:2, 20:7). This is the foundation of the Israelites' religious life according to the Holiness Code(Lev. 17-26). The chosen people should obey only the Lord's ordinances and keep the Lord's statutes and walk in them(Lev. 18:4-5, 24-26, 20:22, etc.).

이스라엘의 공동체는 혈통으로 정의를 내리지 않고(혈통 공동체, 출 12:38; 민 11:4), 종교(제의적 의무)로 정의를 내릴 수 있다. 통혼은 성결법전 혹은 신명기 본문에서 금지되어 있는데, 혈통의 순수성을 지키기 보다는 여호와 종교의 독특한 실천을 위해 동일성을 지키기 위함이다.

The community of Israel can not be defined by blood(a kinship community, Ex. 12:38, Num.11:4) but by religion(cultic observances). The intermarriages were prohibited in the Holiness Code or deuteronomistic texts in order to keep distinctiveness of identity based on distinctiveness of practice of faith of the Lord rather than to keep purity of blood.

2-2-5. 신명기(Deuteronomy) 23:3-8 [Hebrew Bible. Deut. 23:4-9]

3 암몬 사람 혹은 모압 사람은 여호와의 총회에 들어오지 못하리니; 그들에게 속한 자는 십대 뿐 아니라 무궁토록 여호와의 총회에 들어오지 못하리라. An Ammonite or Moabite shall not enter into the congregation of the LORD; even to their tenth generation shall they not enter into the congregation of the LORD for ever: 4 왜냐하면 그들은 너희들이 이집트에서 나올 때에 떡과 물로 너희를 길에서 영접하지 아니하였고, 메소보다미아의 브돌 사람 브올의 아들 발람에게 뇌물을 주어 너희들을 저주하게 하려 하였기 때문이라. Because they met you not with bread and with water in the way, when ye came forth out of Egypt; and because they hired against thee Balaam the son of Beor of Pethor of Mesopotamia, to curse thee. 5 그럼에도 불구하고 네 하나님 여호와께서 너를 사랑하시므로 발람의 말을 듣지 아니하시고 그 저주를 변하여 복이 되게 하셨나니 Nevertheless the LORD thy God would not hearken unto Balaam; but the LORD thy God turned the curse into a blessing unto thee, because the LORD thy God loved thee. 6 너의 평생에 그들의 평안과 형통을 무궁토록 구하지 말지니라 Thou shalt not seek their peace nor their prosperity all thy days for ever. 7 너는 에돔 사람을 미워하지 말라. 그는 너의 형제니라. 이집트 사람을 미워하지 말라. 네가 그의 땅에서 나그네가 되었음이니라. Thou shalt not abhor an Edomite; for he is thy brother:

thou shalt not abhor an Egyptian; because thou wast a stranger in his land. 8 그들의 삼대 후 자손은 여호와의 총회에 들어올 수 있느니라. 8 The children that are begotten of them shall enter into the congregation of the LORD in their third generation.

여호와의 총회에 출입을 금지시키는 의미는 무엇인가? 아마도 암몬 혹은 모압 자손과 통혼하는 것을 의미한다.[80] 이 두 민족은 고자된 사람처럼 비열한 이들이었다. 그러나 에돔 사람들과 이집트 사람들의 삼대는 총회의 정회원이 될 수 있었다.[81]

What was the meaning of the prohibition from entering the congregation of Yahweh? Probably it meant intermarriage with an Ammonite or Moabite.[80] These two nations were belittled as a man with mutilated genitalia and a bastard. But the third generation of Edomites and Egyptians may become full members of the congregation.[81]

3-6절의 설명은 발람 사건에서 암몬 사람들이 포함된다. 그러나 민수기 21-25장의 설명에서 모압 자손들만이 이스라엘의 원수라고

---

80) S.J.D. Cohen, "From the Bible to the Talmud," Hebrew Annual Review 7(1983), 31. Cf. Mishnah Qiddus 4:3. 코헨은 여호와의 회중에 들어온다는 의미는 이스라엘 사람과 결혼하는 것으로 적고 있다. Cohen writes that "to enter the congregation of Yahweh" is understood as "to marry an Israelite."
81) Morton Smith, *Palestinian Parties and Politics that Shaped the Old Testament*, 12-13: 이방인 영향의 위험이 있을 때 이 본문은 에돔인과 이집트인과 통혼하는 것을 기대한 것 같지만 전적으로 불인정하지는 않는다. "And even when there is danger of alien influence, this text seems to expect intermarriage with Edomites and Egyptians and, at least, does not wholly disapprove it."

언급한다. 모압의 왕 발락이 브올의 아들 발람을 고용하여 이스라엘 백성에게 저주를 하도록 했다. 그러나 모압과 암몬에 대한 적대감이 다른 성경 구절에 보면 전통적이었다(창 19:30-38; 삿 11:4-33; 삼상 11:1-11; 삼하 10). 그러므로 이 두 백성들은 이스라엘 공동체의 회원이 되는 것이 금지되었다.

The explanation in vv. 3-6 might include the Ammonites in the event of Balaam. But the account of Num. 21-25 mentions only Moabites' hostility against Israel: Balak, the king of the Moabites, hired Balaam, the son of Beor, to pronounce a curse on Israel. However, hostility against Moab and Ammon was traditional in other biblical passages(Gen. 19:30-38, Jud. 11:4-33, 1 Sam. 11:1-11, 2Sam. 10). Therefore, these two peoples were prohibited from becoming members of the Israelite community.

포수기 혹 포수기 이후의 성경 저자들은 에돔 자손들을 꾸짖었다(시 137:7-9; 사 63:1-6; 렘 49:7-22; 겔 25:12-14; 오바댜; 말 1:2-3). 왜냐하면 그들이 바벨론 군대가 예루살렘을 588년에 포위할 때 바벨론군을 도왔기 때문이다(왕하 25:8-12). 그러나 어떤 유대인들이 에스라와 느헤미야가 주도한 결혼 개혁(스 9:1; 느 13:23) 이전에 통혼한 명단에 보면, 암몬 사람들, 모압 사람들, 이집트 사람들이 있었지만 에돔 사람들은 없다. 이 명단에 의하면 유대인들이 에돔 사람들과 통혼한 사실은 없다.

Many exilic or post-exilic writers rebuke the Edomites(Ps. 137:7-9, Isa. 63:1-6, Jer. 49:7-22, Ezk.25:12-14, Obadiah, and Mal.1:2-3), for they helped the Babylonians to sack Jerusalem in 588 BC(2 Kings 25:8-12). However, in the list of peoples with whom some Judean people intermarried before the marriage reforms under Ezra and

Nehemiah(Ezra 9:1, Neh. 13:23), we find some Ammonites, Moabites, and Egyptians, but no Edomites. From this list, we find that no Judeans seemed to marry Edomites at all.

2-2-6. 여호수아(Joshua) 23:12-13

12 너희가 만일 돌이켜 너희 중에 남아 있는 이 민족들의 남은 자를 가까이하여 더불어 혼인하며 피차 왕래하면 Else if ye do in any wise go back, and cleave unto the remnant of these nations, even these that remain among you, and shall make marriages with them(מהב נתחתנתם), and go in unto them, and they to you: 13 확실히 알라. 너희 하나님 여호와께서 이 민족들을 너희 앞에서 다시는 쫓아내지 아니하시리니 그들이 너희에게 올무가 되며 덫이 되며 너희 옆구리에 채찍이 되며 너희 눈에 가시가 되어서 너희가 마침내 너희 하나님 여호와께서 너희에게 주신 이 아름다운 땅에서 멸망하리라 Know for a certainty that the LORD your God will no more drive out any of these nations from before you; but they shall be snares and traps unto you, and scourges in your sides, and thorns in your eyes, until ye perish from off this good land which the LORD your God hath given you.

여호수아 23장 전체는 가나안 땅 정복에 대한 신명기적 편집의 결론이면서 24장에 나오는 세겜 언약 갱신 예배에 참석을 준비하는 설교문이다.[82] 수 22:1에서 요단강 건너편의 세 지파 공동체들(르우벤 지파, 갓 지파, 므낫세 반지파)에게 권면을 한 후 그들을 돌려보낸 후, 여호수아는 나머지 지파들 전 이스라엘의 총회 앞에서 고별 설교를 하였다(23:1 이하). 신명기 사가의 이런 경고는 삿 3:1-6의 말씀에서[83] 상기시키며 확인하고 있다. 본문의 포수기 날짜를 예언자들의 위협과 이어지는 심판이 하나님께서 행하신 것을 저자가 미리 알고 있던 것을 예언하는 듯이 기록된 것이다.[84]

---

82) J. A. Soggin, *Joshua*, The Old Testament Library,(Philadelphia: The Westminster Press, 1972, 217 ; R. G. Boling, *Joshua*, Anchor Bible, 1982, 526.
83) 삿 3:1 여호와께서 가나안 전쟁을 알지 못한 이스라엘을 시험하려 하시며 Now these are the nations which the LORD left, to prove Israel by them, even as many of Israel as had not known all the wars of Canaan; 2 이스라엘 자손의 세대 중에 아직 전쟁을 알지 못하는 자에게 그것을 가르쳐 알게 하려하사 남겨 두신 열국은 Only that the generations of the children of Israel might know, to teach them war, at the least such as before knew nothing thereof; 3 블레셋 다섯 방백과 가나안 모든 사람과 시돈 사람과 바알 헤르몬산에서부터 하맛 입구까지 레바논 산에 거하는 히위 사람이라 Namely, five lords of the Philistines, and all the Canaanites, and the Sidonians, and the Hivites that dwelt in mount Lebanon, from mount Baalhermon unto the entering in of Hamath. 4 남겨두신 이 열국으로 이스라엘을 시험하사 여호와께서 모세의 손으로 그들의 조상들에게 명하신 명령들을 청종하나 알고자 하셨더라 And they were to prove Israel by them, to know whether they would hearken unto the commandments of the LORD, which he commanded their fathers by the hand of Moses. 5 이스라엘 자손은 마침내 가나안 사람과 헷 사람과 아모리 사람과 브리스 사람과 히위 사람과 여브스 사람 사이에 거하여 And the children of Israel dwelt among the Canaanites, Hittites, and Amorites, and Perizzites, and Hivites, and Jebusites: 6 그들의 딸들을 취하여 아내를 삼으며 자기 딸들을 그들의 아들에게 주며 또 그들의 신들을 섬겼더라 And they took their daughters to be their wives, and gave their daughters to their sons, and served their gods.
84) 이미 일어난 사건에 대해 필자가 마치 예언하는 것처럼 기록하는 것을 학술적으로 "사건으로부터의 예언"이라고 부른다. 일부 학자들은 단 7:2-11:39에서 특히 11장은 알렉산더의 사후에 벌어진 일을 미래에 있을 예언으로 기록한 것이 이런 실례라고 주장한다. 또한 복음서에 나오는 종말 예언도 AD 70년경 예루살렘 멸망 후에 씌여졌는데 이것도 사건 후 예언의 형식으로 씌여졌을 것이라고 일부 학자들은 주장한다. *Vaticinium ex ēventū* "prophecy from the event" is a technical theological or historiographical term referring to a prophecy written after the author already had information about the events being "foretold". Many modern scholars claim that in Daniel 7:2-11:39, especially Daniel 11, the Book of Daniel utilizes *vaticinium ex eventu*. Some scholars regard statements attributed to Jesus in the Gospels that foretell the destruction of

The entire chapter 23 gives the conclusion of the Deuteronomic edition of the narrative of the conquest and serves as hortatory preparation for participating in renewal of the covenant at Shechem in ch. 24.[82] After speaking to three tribes in Transjordan area(the Reubenites, the Gadites, and the Manasseh half-tribe) in ch. 22:1ff and sending them to their places, Joshua delivered a farewell sermon in front of all the Israelite assembly in this chapter(23:1). This warning of the Deuteronomist was to be reminded and confirmed in Judg. 3:1-6.[83] Given an exilic date for our text, it may be a *vaticinium ex eventu*[84] composed at a period when the threats of the prophets and the resultant judgments carried out by the Lord had been fulfilled.

이 고별 연설에서 여호수아는 강하게 통혼의 잘못을 고발하고 있다(참고. 7절 상반절). 만약 이스라엘 백성들이 이웃 백성들과 밀착하여 통혼을 한다면, 여호와께서 가나안 땅에서부터 다른 백성들을 몰아내시지 않아, 이방 민족들이 이스라엘에게 네 가지 위험이 될 것일 것이다: 올무(혹 낚시밥), 이스라엘에게 함정(혹은 새를 잡는 덫), 이스라엘 편에게 회초리, 그리고 이스라엘 백성들에게 가시(13절, 참고 신 33:55)이다. 이 단어들이 하나님의 심판의 비유적인 도구들로 상징된다.

In this speech, Joshua strongly pronounced an interdiction

Jerusalem and its temple as examples of *vaticinia ex eventu*; these scholars believe that the Gospels were all written after the siege of Jerusalem in AD 70, in which the temple was destroyed. However some Christian scholars reject this notion as the fulfillment of the acclaimed prophecy; the destruction of the temple is not recorded in the gospels or in the other letters and date the new testament scriptures before AD 70.

on intermarriage with the remnant of the alien peoples around Israel(cf. v. 7a). If the Israelites cling to(םתקבד cf. v.8 וקבדת) and intermarry(םתחתנתה) with other peoples, the Lord will refuse to drive other nations out from the land of Canaan and the nations shall become four dangers to Israel: a snare(or bait) and a trap(or bird-trap) for Israel, a whip to Israelite sides and thorns in Israelite eyes(v. 13, cf. Num. 33:55). All these words stand for the figurative tools of divine punishment.

요약하면, 여호와의 신앙에 대한 순수성을 지키기 위해 신명기 사가는 여호와께 충성을 강조하고 있다. 수 24:23(참고 24:2-3)에서, 여호수아는 "너희들 가운데 거하는 이방신들을 떠나라. 그리고 너희의 마음을 이스라엘의 하나님 여호와께 돌려라"(또한 삼상 7:3-4를 보라)고 말했다. 신명기 사가의 본문들은 이스라엘 공동체의 종교적 구조를 해체하기를 협박하는 배교를 금지하고 있다.

In sum to keep purity of faith in the Lord, the Deuteronomist emphasized loyalty to the Lord. In Josh. 24:23(cf. 24:2-3), Joshua said, "Then put away the foreign gods which are among you, and incline your heart to the Lord, the God of Israel"(also see 1 Samuel 7:3-4). The deuteronomistic texts prevent apostasy, which threatens to disintegrate the religious structure of the Israelite community.

2-3. 포수기 이후 유대 공동체의 사회적 현실들 Social realities of the post-exilic Judean community

이제 결혼 개혁들의 사회적이며 종교적 배경을 살펴봄으로써 팔레스타인의 포수기 이후 유대 공동체의 사회적 구조를 살펴보자.

BC 588년의 지각변동은 모든 이스라엘 백성들에게 매우 고통스러웠다. 솔로몬이 지은 성전이 파괴됨으로 이스라엘의 생활의 사회적 기반은 말할 것 없고 정체성이 상실되었다(참고. 왕하 24:18-25:21; 렘 52:1-34; 시 74:4-11, 79:1-4, 137:1-6; 사 64:11). 이스라엘 공동체의 사회적 질서는 완전히 붕괴되어 혼란에 빠졌다. 유다는 포수기 기간 동안 사마리아 주의 일부로 귀속되었다. 왕족 가족, 귀족들, 땅 소유주들, 군사 지도자들, 장로들, 기술자들, 제사장들, 대언자들 등 대부분 유대인들의 지도자들은 그들의 고국을 떠나 바벨론 세계로 포로로 잡혀갔다. 1차 포로 BC 599, 2차 588년, 3차 583년.[85]

---

85) 올브라이트(William Albright)의 성경 연대로는 BC 597, 587, 582이나 성경과학연구소의 연도를 따름. 우리는 구약성경에서 바벨론 포로로 잡혀간 유대인들의 수를 정확히 추산할 수 없다. 전 인구(왕하 24:14, 16, 25:21; 대하 36:20) 혹은 4,600명이라고 추산한다 (렘 52:28-30). 그러나 상당수의 유대인들이 고국에 머무르면서 지역 혹은 외부에서 영입한 백성들과 더불어 살았는데, 왕하 25:12에 의하면 이들은 가난한 사람들로 포도농사꾼 혹은 농부들이었다. We can not determine from the Hebrew Bible how many Judeans went into exile. The exiles might be almost the whole population(as in 2 Kings 24:14, 16, 25:21, 2 Chron. 36:20) or the small group of 4,600(as in Jer. 52:28-30). It is certain that the great majority of Judeans remained in their homeland, and mingled generally with the local and incoming peoples, even though 2 Kings 25:12 claims, "But the captain of the guard left of the poor of the land to be vinedressers and farmers." See P. R. Ackroyd, *Exile and Restoration: A Study of Hebrew Thought of the Sixth Century B.C.*, Philadelphia: The Westminster Press, 1968, 22-23, n. 24 ; W. F. Albright, *The Biblical Period from Abraham to Ezra*(New York: Harper & Row, 1965, 87-110. ; P.R. Ackroyd, "The History of Israel in the Exilic and Post-exilic Periods," in *Tradition and Interpretation*, ed. G.W. Anderson,(Oxford: Clarendon, 1979), 320-350. ; J. M. Miller & J. H. Hayes, *A History of Ancient Israel and Judah*,(Philadelphia: The Westminster Press, 1986), 417-420.

Now let us review the social structure of the post-exilic Judean community in Palestine by examining the social and religious background of the marriage reforms.

The catastrophe of 588 BC was very painful to all the Israelites. Destruction of the temple built by Solomon meant loss of the Israelites' identity as well as the social basis of their life(cf. 2 Kgs. 24:18-25:21, Jer. 52:1-34, Ps. 74:4-11, 79:1-4, 137:1-6, Is. 64:11). The social order of the Israelite community almost completely collapsed into chaos. Judah became part of the province of Samaria during the exilic period. Most the leading Judeans, including the royal family, nobles, landowners, military leaders, elders, craftsmen, priests, and prophets, were deported from their homeland to the centers of the Babylonian world in 599, 588, and 583 BC.[85]

유대인들의 원수들의 방해에도 불구하고(스 4:1-23), 성전 재건은 학개와 스가랴에 의해 부활되어 마침내 다리오 1세(BC 522-486)가 페르샤(혹 아케메니아) 제국을 통치하던 BC 516에 완공할 수 있었다. 성전 재건 후 성경의 자료들은 에스라와 느헤미야의 활동으로 초점을 옮긴다.

In spite of hindrance by the adversaries of Judah(Ezra 4:1-23), the temple reconstruction was revived under Haggai and Zechariah and was eventually completed by the group who returned from exile in 515 BC when Darius I(522-486) ruled the Persian(or Achaemenian) empire. After highlighting the reconstruction of the temple, the biblical materials move to focus on the activities of Ezra and Nehemiah.

에스라와 귀환(BC 515년)하고 느헤미야와 귀환(BC 502년)한 포로민들은 공동체에 섞여 있던 이방적인 요소들인 사회적이며 종교적 문제들에 관심을 가졌다(스 6:21; 느 9:2, 10:28, 13:3). 그들이 전수받았던 모세의 전통을 더욱 엄격하게 적용하는 종교법을 공고히 하였다(느 8:1-18). 이런 노력들 가운데 이방 여인들과 이혼하는 것이 에스라와 느헤미야의 핵심된 개혁이었다.

The returned exiles of Ezra and his followers(BC 515) and Nehemiah and his followers(BC 502) were concerned with social and religious problems, freeing the community of foreign elements(Ezra 6:21, Neh. 9:2, 10:28, 13:3) and establishing religious practice in stricter conformity to their understanding of the received Mosaic tradition(Neh. 8:1-18). Among these efforts, divorce from foreign women was the key reform of Ezra and Nehemiah.

유대를 재건하는 일은 페르샤 제국의 국제 정책의 결과였다. 그래서 유대가 계속 존속할 수 있었던 것은 더욱 큰 사회적-정치적 현실에 적응하는가에 달려 있었다.86) 페르샤 제국의 더욱 큰 세계는87) 성경 전통에서 큰 관심을 끌지는 못해서 페르샤 시대에 팔레스타인 유대 공동체의 생활 형태에 대해 많은 정보가 없다.

   The reconstituted Judah was the product of Persian international policy, hence her continued existence depended on accommodating to the larger socio-political reality.86) The larger world of the Persian empire87) receives little consideration in the biblical traditions and we are left to wonder about the course of life in the Palestinian Judean community during the Persian period.

---

86) See Hoglund, *Achaemenid Imperial Administration in Syria-Palestine*, 1-35.
87) The following political background is based on these sources: J. Bright, *A History of Israel*, 3rd Ed., Philadelphia: Westminster Press, 1981, 372 ff.; J. M. Miller & J. H. Hayes, *A History of Ancient Israel and Judah*, Philadelphia: Westminster Press, 1986, 437-473 ; H. Donner, *Geschichte des Volkes Israel und seiner Nachbarn in Grundz gen 2*, Göttingen: Vandenhoeck & Ruprecht, 1986, 391-432 ; E. Stern, "The Persian empire and the political and social history of Palestine in the Persian period," in *The Cambridge History of Judaism*, vol. I, W. D. Davies & L. Finkelstein(eds.), Cambridge: Cambridge U. Press, 1984, 70-87.

야벳 교수(Sara Japhet, 1934-)에 의하면,88) 회복 기간에 이스라엘 땅에는 아마도 세 유대인 공동체가 존재했을 것이다. ① 회복기 첫 세대로 유다에 정착포로로 갔던 귀환민 공동체 ② 포로로 가지 않고 고국에 남아서 살았던 유대 왕국의 시민들 ③ 북왕국 시민들로서 BC 723년에 앗시리아에 의해 북이스라엘이 멸망한 후 사마리아와 갈릴리에서 살았던 거주자들이다. 자연스럽게 이들 세 그룹들 사이에 긴장이 있었는데 특히 바벨론 포로 생활을 하고 돌아온 귀향민들과 팔레스타인에서 남아 살던 사람들 사이에 긴장이 있었다.89) 이 긴장은 종교적이라기보다는 사회적-정치적이었다.

According to Japhet,88) there were probably three Judean communities in the land of Israel during the period of restoration: ① the community of "returned exiles" established in Judah in the first generations of the Restoration, ② those inhabitants of the kingdom of Judah who were not exiled at all but remained in the land, and ③ the Israelite inhabitants of northern Israel who remained settled in Samaria and in Galilee after the Assyrian conquest(723 BC). Thus there was naturally tension among these communities, especially between the group that had returned from exile and other groups that had remained in the land of Judah.89) This tension was not primarily religious but rather

---

88) Sara Japhet, "People and Land in the Restoration Period," in G. Strecker(ed.), *Das Land Israel in biblischer Zeit*, Göttingen: Vanderhoeck & Ruprecht, 1983, 104-105.

89) C. Schültz, "The political Tensions Reflected in Ezra-Nehemiah," in *Scripture in Context*, eds. by C. D. Evans, W. W. Hallo, J. B. White, (Pittsburgh, PA: The Pickwick Press, 1980), 224, 228ff. : "According to the Chronicler, the identity of the opponents to the rebuilding of the temple is (1) adversaries of Judah and Benjamin (2) descendants of those whom Esarhaddon had settled in Palestine (3) the poor people (4) Samaritans and (5) neighboring governors."

essentially socio-political.

예를 들면, 폴 핸슨 교수가 주장한 대로 회복기의 유대 공동체 안에는 성전을 장악한 사독 계열의 제사장들과 성전 밖에서 활동한 "환상적인" 레위 지파 그룹들 사이에 투쟁이 있었다.[90] 후자 계층은 사독 계열로부터 떨어져 나와 당시 유대 사회의 변두리에 머물렀다(참고. 겔 44:9-14, 15-27). 이들 두 계층은 분명히 서로 다른 "상징적 세계" 혹은 세계관을 가지고 있었다. 핸슨 교수는 다음과 같이 저술하고 있다.[91]

For example, Paul Hanson maintained that there was a struggle between a Zadokite priestly group inside the temple and a "visionary" Levite group outside the temple among the Judean community during the restoration period.[90] The latter group, he believes, was disenfranchised by the Zadokites and remained at the margin of contemporary Judean society(cf. Ezek. 44:9-14, 15-27). These two groups apparently had each a different "symbolic universe" or world-view. Hanson writes as follows:[91]

---

90) P. Hanson, *The Dawn of Apocalyptic*, 9f, 29f, 211f.
91) P. Hanson, *The People Called: The Growth of Community in the Bible*(San Francisco : Harper & Row, Pub., 1986), 277.

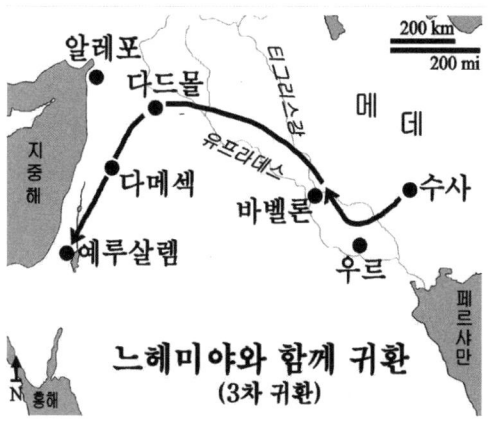

BC 538-515 사이에 사회와 예배의 회복 시기에 지도층 사이에 있었던 내적 갈등은 혼합된 신학적 유산을 낳아 매우 분명한 정치적 결과를 낳았다. 사독 계열의 제사장 계층은 예배적으로 사회적으로 재건한 공동체의 지도자로 등장했다. 비록 다윗 왕족 출신(스룹바벨 총독)과 사독 제사장 출신(여호수아 대제사장) 사이에 지도력이 공유되기는 했으나, 전자는 516년 성전 재건 이후 사라지고, 오직 사독계열 대제사장 지도자들만이 모든 국사의 일들을 장악했다.

The inner struggle for leadership in the restoration of the society and cult in the years BC 538-515, while producing a very mixed theological legacy, issued forth in a very clear political result: the Zadokite priestly party emerged as the head of the reconstituted community, both in cultic and civil matters. Although leadership was at first shared between Davidic prince and Zadokite high priest - that is, between Zerubbabel and Joshua- the former disappeared from the scene by the time of the temple's dedication in 515, leaving the Zadokite high priest as the sole head over the people in all domestic matters.

확실히 페르샤 제국과 귀환한 유대 공동체는 상호 다른 "상징적 우주관"을 가졌다. 그러나 유대의 종교 지도자들과 페르샤 제국의 외교 정책의 관심이 적절하게 융합되었다. 즉 유대는 토라에 기초한 예배의 갱신을 통해 페르샤의 주적인 이집트와 완충지대 역할을 하는 방향으로 강화되었다. 이런 방향은 사독계 지도자들에게 이상적으로 잘 어울렸다. 이들은 페르샤 제국이 추구하던 외교 정책의 방패막 역할을 추구하는 데 협조한 것이다.

Apparently, the Persian empire and the returned Judean community also each had a different "symbolic universe." However, the interests of the religious leaders of Judah and the established foreign policy of the Persian empire proportionally converged: Judah was to be strengthened as a buffer state bordering Persia's chief enemy Egypt by the renewal of the cult on the basis of the Torah. This state of affairs was ideally suited for a Zadokite leadership class willing to collaborate with the Persian authorities as a means of safeguarding its own position of pre-eminence.

BC 6세기 말까지 예루살렘 성전 주변에 모였던 종교적 공동체는 매우 취약했다. 말라기서(BC 약 450년)에 의하면 사독 제사장들과 레위 사람들은 그들의 종교적 의무를 무시했고, 귀족들의 최고 관심들은 서민들을 가난하게 하였고, 군주들은 서민들의 비용으로 호화롭게 살았다(말 1:6-2:9).

By the end-sixth century, the religious community which

gathered around the temple in Jerusalem was in a very vulnerable situation. As we learn from the book of Malachi(BC c. 450), both Zadokite priests and Levites neglected their religious duties, the nobility's high rates of interest were impoverishing the populace, and the governors were living lives of luxury at the expense of their destitute subjects(Mal. 1:6-2:9).

에스라가 페르샤로부터 예루살렘에 왔을 때 페르샤 왕의 허락으로 무너지고 있던 공동체를 회복하였을 때, 종교적인 죄를 행한 이 두 계층 사이에 어떤 갈등이 없었다. 그 대신에, 사독 제사장 집안과 레위 집안 사이에 통혼이 있었다(스 10:18-24). 에스라가 예루살렘에 도착하기 전에 많은 유대인들이 다른 백성들과 좋은 관계를 유지하고 있었던 것 같다.

When Ezra came to Jerusalem from Persia and with Persian royal permission conducted his work to restore the languishing community, there was no report of tension between these two groups which committed religious sin together. Instead, there was a report of intermarriage both the Zadokites and the Levites(Ezra 10:18-24). Just before Ezra arrived at Jerusalem, many Judeans seemed to enjoy good relation with other peoples.

요약하면, 본 장을 통해 우리는 에스라와 느헤미야가 수행한 결혼 개혁의 사회적-종교적 배경을 살펴보았다. 창세기에 나오는 기사들을 통해 통혼에 대한 부정적인 태도를 볼 수 있었다. 그 이유는 이스라엘 부족장 사회는 족내혼을 실천했기 때문이다(창 24:2이하, 27: 46-28:4). 이스라엘 사회에서 족내혼은 고대 유산 보존과 밀접하게 관계가 있었다. 족외혼은 땅의 부동산이 다른 지파에 넘어간다(민 36:6-9). 비록 이스라엘 사회가 족내혼을 더 선호했지만, 이스라엘 백성들과 비-이스라엘 백성들 사이의 통혼은 왕국 초기에는 종교적 문제가 되지 않았다. 대부분 포수기 이전의 대언자들은 통혼 문제에 대해 침묵을 지켰지만 왕국 후기 시대와 포수기 때에는 통혼에 대해 점점 비평적으로 발전된 것 같다.

In sum, through this chapter we examined the socio-religious background of the marriage reforms undertaken by Ezra and Nehemiah. The Genesis narratives show the negative attitude towards intermarriage, because Israelite Patriarchal society practiced endogamy(Gen. 24:2ff.; 27:46-28:4). In the Israelite society, endogamy closely related to preservation of the ancestral inheritance. Exogamy led to the transference of the land to the other tribes(Num. 36:6-9). Even though Israelite society preferred to endogamy, intermarriage between Israelites and non-Israelites was not a religious issue in the early monarchial period. Most pre-exilic prophets were silent on the problem of intermarriage, but a more critical view towards intermarriage developed during the late monarchial and exilic periods.

신명기 사관의 본문들에서 가나안 백성들과 통혼하는 것은 종교적 이유로 금지되었다(출 34:11-16; 신 7:2이하, 23:4이하; 수 23:7이하. 참고. 민 25:1이하; 삿 3:6). 그러나 암몬 백성과 모압 백성과의 통혼은 역사적 이유로 금지되었다(신 23:4이하). 신명기적 메시지는 특별히 포수기 생활한 이스라엘 백성들에게 향했다. 왜 이스라엘은 자기의 고국을 상실했으며 자기 조상들처럼 이방 땅에서 나그네 생활을 했는가? 그 이유는 그들이 다른 외국 신들을 따라가며 경배 드렸기 때문에, 그들은 여호와께서 주신 땅에서 추방되었다는 것이다. 그들이 긴 역사적 안목과 현재의 사회적 상황으로 볼 때, 포로 생활을 한 이스라엘 백성들은 우상 숭배의 비극적 결과에 대해 교훈을 배웠어야 했다. 신명기적 설교는 통혼이 이스라엘 공동체에서 부정적인 결과로 인도한다고 경고한다. 결혼한 이방 여인들이 이스라엘 남편들과 자녀들을 여호와로부터 멀어지도록 유혹을 한다는 것이다. 비록 이방인들은 그들의 외국 신들을 섬길지 몰라도 이스라엘 백성들은 여호와만을 섬겨야 한다(수 24:15). 이스라엘의 종교적 자부심은 주변의 열국의 종교들과 분리되는 데 있다. 그래서 이스라엘 백성들은 열국의 백성들과 어떤 계약이나 접촉을 피해야 하는데 그 이유는 그들의 종교의 순수성을 오염하기 때문이다. 그렇지 않으면 이스라엘은 자기의 땅 뿐 아니라 자기의 정체성을 상실할 수 있다.

In the deuteronomistic texts, intermarriage with Canaanites was banned for religious reasons(Ex. 34:11-16.; Deut. 7:2ff., 23:4ff.; Josh. 23:7ff.; cf. Num. 25:1ff.; Judg. 3:6). But the intermarriages with an Ammonite or Moabite were prohibited for historical reasons(Deut. 23:4ff.). The Deuteronomistic message was particularly aimed at the exiled Israelites. Why did Israel lose her land and wander into a foreign land as her patriarchs did? Because they followed and worshipped other alien gods, they were expelled from the good land which the Lord had given them. From their longer historical perspective and the present social situation, the exiled Israelites should have learned a lesson about the tragic results of idolatry. The deuteronomistic homilies warned that intermarriages led to negative results in the Israelite community, for foreign women lure their Israelite husbands and children away from the Lord. Although the other peoples may serve many foreign gods, Israel must serve the Lord only(Josh. 24:15). Israel's religion prided itself on its separateness from those of the surrounding nations. Thus the Israelites should avoid any contact or covenant with the nations, for that could contaminate the purity of her religion. Otherwise, Israel might lose her unique identity as well as her own land.

포수기 이후의 유대 공동체 사이에서 유대인 정체성을 세울 세계관의 합일이 없었다. 어떤 유대인들 가정들은 그들이 포로 생활에서 돌아와 통혼을 허용하였지만 대부분 유대인들은 통혼의 현상에 대해 심각하게 생각했다. 후자는 생각하기를 통혼이 퍼지면 그들의 민족 정체성에 위기가 온다는 것이다. 그들의 종교적 정체성을 세우는 데 전통적인 세계관을 강화할 필요성을 느꼈다.

다음 장에서 우리는 에스라와 느헤미야가 주도한 결혼 개혁들을 에스라 9-10장, 느헤미야 13:23-30의 주석을 통하여 분석할 것이다.

There was no consensus of world-view which could establish the Judean identity among the post-exilic Judean community. Some Judean families accepted intermarriage after they returned from the exile, but most Judeans were quite serious about the phenomenon of intermarriage. The latter thought the spread of intermarriage might lead to the crisis of their identity. Urgent was the reform to reinforce the traditional world-view which constructs their religious identity.

In the next chapter, we will analyze the marriage reforms that were carried out under Ezra and Nehemiah through an exegesis of Ezra 9-10 and Neh. 13:23-30.

III

에스라와 느헤미야의 결혼 개혁들: 성경 주석

THE MARRIAGE REFORMS UNDER EZRA AND NEHEMIAH : THE BIBLICAL EXEGESIS

본 장에서는 에스라 9-10장과 느헤미야 13:23-30을 주석함으로 에스라와 느헤미야가 주도한 결혼 개혁들을 살펴보고자 한다. 결혼 개혁들의 역사적-사회적 배경을 살핀 후 이 두 본문들을 문학적-사회학적 관점에서 분석할 것이다.

This chapter intends to examine the marriage reforms led by Ezra and Nehemiah through exegesis of Ezra 9-10 and Nehemiah 13:23-30. We will investigate historical-social background of the marriage reforms, then analyze these two texts with a literary-sociological outlook.

제2성전을 완공한 후 바벨론 포로로부터 귀환한 유대인들 사이 [앞으로 "유대 공동체"라 부름]에는 공동체 일원과 타 백성들 사이에 여전히 통혼들이 있었다. 에스라는 이 통혼의 현상에 대해 어떻게 반응을 했는가? 에스라의 지지자들은 누구였는가? 에스라가 행한 결혼 개혁은 어떤 것이었는가? 에스라의 결혼 개혁에 반대하는 자들은 누구였는가? 느헤미야는 나중에 도착하여 그때도 있었던 통혼 문제를 어떻게 다루었는가? 본 장에서 이런 문제들을 다룰 것이다. 우리가 사용하는 역사적 자료들은 포수기 이후 것이며 어느 정도 통일성을 이룬다는 동의하에 에스라서와 느헤미야서를 다룰 것이다.

Since the dedication of the second temple (BC 515), there had been intermarriages between insiders and outsiders of the group that returned from exile[hereafter, Judean community]. How did Ezra react against this phenomenon of intermarriage? Who was his support group? What was the marriage reform done under Ezra? Which group made a protest against Ezra's marriage reform? How did Nehemiah deal with some intermarried families later on? We will deal with these questions in this chapter. We treat the books of Ezra and Nehemiah, starting from the consensus that the historical materials which we use were postexilic and constituted some sort of unity as a position.

3-1. 본문의 역사적-사회적 배경 Historical-social background of the text

본 항의 목적은 팔레스타인에 있던 포수기 후의 유대 공동체의 사회적 배경을 살피는 것이다. 공동 현실을 반영하는 구절들을 살핌으로 당시 유대 공동체의 사회적, 문화적, 종교적 현상을 살필 것이다.

The purpose of the present section is to review the social ethos of the post-exilic Judean community in Palestine. By dealing with a set of passages which reflect a common reality, we can examine the social, cultural, and religious phenomenon of the contemporary Judean community.

3-1-1. 제2성전 봉헌 후 After the dedication of the Second Temple

BC 588년의 참사는 이스라엘 백성 모두에게 매우 아픈 일이었다. 솔로몬이 지었던 성전의 파괴는 이스라엘의 사회적 기반뿐만 아니라 자기 정체성을 잃는 것을 뜻했다(참고. 왕하 24:18-25:21; 렘 52:1-34; 시 74:4-11, 79:1-4, 137:1-6; 사 64:11). 이전에 이스라엘 세계의 사회적 질서와 더불어 존재한 것들이 이제는 말로 표현할 수 없는 무법상태가 되어 버렸다. 이스라엘은 세스바살이 페르샤 제국으로부터 임명되기 전까지(BC 538년) 사마리아의 주의 일부가 되어버렸다. 왕족 가족, 귀족들, 부동산 소유자들, 군사 지도자들, 장로들, 기술자들, 제사장들, 대언자들을 포함한 대부분 유대인들의 지도자들은 고국 땅에서 바벨론의 땅으로 세 차례에 걸쳐(BC 599년, 588년, 583년) 이주되었다.

The catastrophe of 588 BC was very painful to all the Israelites. Destruction of the temple built by Solomon meant loss of the Israelites' identity as well as their social basis(cf. 2 Kgs. 24:18-25:21; Jer. 52:1-34, Ps. 74:4-11, 79:1-4, 137:1-6; Is. 64:11). What had previously been in existence with social order of the Israelite world now became unspeakable anomie. Judah became part of the province of Samaria until Sheshbazzar was appointed by the Persians(BC 538). Most leading Judeans, including the royal family, nobles, landowners, military leaders, elders, craftsmen, priests, and prophets, were deported from their homeland to the fringes of the Babylonian world in BC 599, 588, and 583.

구약성경에서는 얼마나 많은 유대인들이 포로생활에 끌려갔는지

알 수 없다. 전 인구가 포로로 끌려갔을 수 있고(왕하 24:14, 16, 25:21; 대하 36:20) 혹은 4600명의 적은 숫자가 포로 생활을 한 것 같다(렘 52:28-30). 최근 고고학적 증거에 의하면 포로 생활을 한 유대인 숫자는 어린이와 여인들을 포함해서 2만 내지 3만 명으로 추정한다.[92] 왕하 25:12에 보면 "빈천한 국민을 그 땅에 남겨두어 포도원을 다스리는 자와 농부가 되게 하였더라"고 되어 있어 대부분의 유대인들이 고국에 머물렀던 것 같다.

We can not figure out exactly how many Judeans went into exile from the Hebrew Bible. The exiles might be almost the whole population(as in 2 Kings 24:14, 16, 25:21; 2 Chron. 36:20) or the small group of 4,600(as in Jer. 52:28-30). From recent archeological evidences, we assume that the size of the exile was at the most 20,000-30,000 Judeans including women and children.[92] Thus, it is certain that the great majority of Judeans remained in their homeland, while 2 Kings 25:12 writes, "But the captain of the guard left of the poor of the land to be vinedressers and husbandmen."

포로민들에게는 여호와 신앙이 사회적 통일성을 이루는 강력한 끈이었다. 반면에 팔레스타인에 남은 백성들은 토착민들과 유입한 백성들과 섞여 살게 되었다. 여호와의 종교는 별 의미가 없었다. 포

---

92) See P. R. Ackroyd, *Exile and Restoration: A Study of Hebrew Thought of the Sixth Century B.C.*, Philadelphia: The Westminster Press, 1968, 22-23, n. 24 ; W. F. Albright, *The Biblical Period from Abraham to Ezra*, New York: Harper & Row, 1965, 87-110; P.R. Ackroyd, "The History of Israel in the Exilic and Post-exilic Periods," in *Tradition and Interpretation*, ed. G.W. Anderson, Oxford, 1979, 320-350.; J. M. Miller & J. H. Hayes, *A History of Ancient Israel and Judah*, Philadelphia: The Westminster Press, 1986, 417-420.

로생활 중, 유대인들의 종교적 관심은 특히 모세의 이름과 관련된 법들에 있어서 랍비적 유대교의 특징이 된 배타성이 자라고 있었다.

For the exiles, the faith for the Lord was their strong bond of social unity; whereas for those who remained in Palestine mingled largely with the local and incoming peoples, the religion of the Lord made little sense. During the life of exile, the Judeans' religious interest had particularly concentrated on the laws associated with the name of Moses, and had fostered the exclusiveness which later became so characteristic of the rabbinical Judaism.

그래서 귀환한 포로민들은 예루살렘에서 제단, 성전, 도시를 재건하는 데 뿐만 아니라, 또한 공동체에서 이방적 요소들로부터 자유하게 하는 사회적, 종교적 문제들에도 관심을 가졌다. 그리고 모세의 법을 이해하는 데 더욱 엄격한 적용으로 종교적 제도를 세워나갔다. 포수기 이후 유대 공동체의 종교적 세계는 객관적이면서 주관적인 현실이었는데, 왜냐하면 그들이 귀환한 후 그 공동체의 취약한 구조를 재건해야 하기 때문이었다. 객관적으로 정치적 도움으로 종교적 합법화가 공동체 안에서 과정에 있었다. 주관적으로는 개인의식으로 공동체가 어떤 굳은 바탕 위에 실재적으로 설 수 있었다.

Thus the returned exiles were concerned not only with reconstruction of altar, temple, wall and city in Jerusalem, but also with social and religious problems, freeing the community of foreign elements, and establishing religious practice in stricter conformity to their understanding of Mosaic law. The religious world of the post-exilic Judean community was objective and subjective reality, for it began to reconstruct its plausibility structure after the return. Objectively, the religious legitimation was on the process in the community with the political support. Subjectively, it was real to the individual consciousness with which the community could stand on the firm basis.

성전은 스룹바벨 총독(정치 지도자)과 여호수아 대제사장(종교적 지도자)가 다리우스 1세(BC 522-486)가 페르샤(혹 아케메니아) 제국을 다스리고 있을 때인 BC 515년에 완공되었다. 재건된 성전은 자기들 스스로 종교적 사명을 가진 경건한 남은 자로 생각하는 귀환한 포로민들에게 사회적 돌파구를 제공했다.

The temple reconstruction under the Governor Zerubbabel (political leader) and the High Priest Jeshua (religious leader) had been completed in 515 BC when Darius I(522-486) ruled the Persian (or Achaemenian) empire. The rebuilt temple provided a social breakthrough for the returned exiles who considered themselves as the godly remnant with a religious mission.

다리우스 1세는 BC 512년에[93] 자기 제국을 소아시아의 보스퍼

---

93) 정치적인 배경은 다음 자료들을 요약한 것이다. The following political background is the summary from these sources: Herodotus IV, 88-144; J. Bright, *A History of Israel*, 3rd Ed., Philadelphia: Westminster Press, 1981, 372ff.; J. M. Miller & J. H. Hayes, *A History of Ancient Israel and Judah*, Philadelphia: Westminster Press, 1986, 437-473 ; J. A. Garraty & P. Gay (eds.), *The Columbia History of the World*, Harper & Row Pub., 1972, 163ff.; H. Donner, *Geschichte des Volkes Israel und seiner Nachbarn in Grundz gen 2*, G ttingen: Vandenhoeck & Ruprecht, 1986, 391-432 ; E. Stern, "The Persian empire and the political and social history of Palestine in the Persian period," in *The Cambridge History of Judaism*, vol. I, W. D. Davies & L. Finkelstein (eds.), Cambridge U. Press, 1984, 70-87.

러스(Bosphorus)를 넘어, 트레이스(Thrace)를 정복하고, 스구디아인 (Scythians)들을 추격하여 다누브 (Danube) 입구까지 진격했다. 동쪽과 서쪽, 아시아와 유럽은 이제 수 세대 동안 이어진 전투장으로 휩쓸려 들어갔다. 이런 국제적인 긴장 후, 소아시아와 키프러스(구브로)에 있던 그리스 도시들이 아테네에 의해 격려와 지원을 받아 BC 499년에 페르샤인들에게 반란을 일으켰다. 이들을 진압한 다리우스 왕은 아테네 군대를 향해 보복을 시작했다. 그는 그리스를 침공했지만 마라톤 해전(BC 490년)에서 참패를 하여 창피를 당했다. 다리우스는 아테네에 대해 다른 전쟁을 기획했지만 전쟁 준비 도중 BC 486년 초에 이집트의 반란을 당했다. 그래서 그해 후반에 죽고 그의 아들(고레스의 딸 아톳사와 사이에 낳은 아들)인 후계자 크세르크세스 1세(BC 486-465)가 이집트를 3년 후에 진압하였고 그리스를 침공했다.

In BC 512,[93] Darius I extended his empire westward into Europe, crossing the Bosphorus of Asia Minor, conquering Thrace, and pursing the Scythians to the mouth of the Danube. East and West, Asia and Europe became embroiled in a struggle that would last for generations. After a period of increasing international tensions, Greek cities in Asia Minor as well as Cyprus rebelled against the Persians in BC 499, being encouraged and supported in their endeavor by Athenes. After suppressing the uprising, Darius set out to retaliate against the Athenians. He invaded Greece but was humiliated especially at the battle of Marathon(BC 490). Darius wanted to wage another war against Athens, but during the course of making preparations he was confronted with a rebellion in Egypt early in BC 486. His death later in the year left the subjugation of Egypt and invasion of

Greece to his successor, Xerxes I(486-465), Darius' son by Atossa, the daughter of Cyrus. The Egyptian revolt was suppressed three years later, but only after heavy fighting.

크세르크세스가 그리스를 향하여 진군하기 전 바벨론에서 다시 반란이 일어났으나 심하게 진압되었다. BC 481년까지 크세르크세스는 자신을 바벨론의 왕이라고 부르는 것을 중단했다. 이 뜻은 바벨론 지역에 정부가 다시 재건되었다는 것을 의미했다. 그리스를 향한 그의 대 원정은 그해(481년)에 시작되었다. 그러나 여러 전투에서 그리스가 승리를 거두었다. 크세르크세스는 그리스와 전쟁하는 것을 포기하고 자기의 참모 대재상(vizier)인 아르타바누스에 의해 살해를 당했다. 크세르크세스의 막내 아들인 아닥사스사 1세(Artaxerxes I, 465-424)가 페르샤 통치를 위해 투쟁했다. 이집트는 삼메티쿠스 3세(Psammetichus III)의 아들 이나로스(Inaros)가 반란을 일으켜 왕위를 찬탈했다. 아테네는 그 반란을 격려할 뿐만 아니라 해군을 파견하여 측면 지원을 하였다. 455년 페르샤인들은 이집트와 아테네를 오랜 전쟁 끝에 점령하였다. 결국 페르샤와 아네테는 갈리아스 평화협정(449년)을 체결하게 되었는데 아테네가 이집트와 키프러스의 내정에 참여하지 못하게 했고, 페르샤 왕이 소아시아이 남부와 서부 해안에 있던 그리스 도시들의 내정을 간섭하지 못하게 한 것이었다.

Before Xerxes could move against Greece, revolt erupted again in Babylon but was severely repressed. By 481, Xerxes ceased calling himself king of Babylon, which suggested governmental restructuring in the area. His great expedition against Greece began in BC 481. But in several battles, the Greek won significant victories. Xerxes gave up the struggle with the Greeks and was subsequently murdered by his vizier Artabanus. Xerxes' youngest son, Artaxerxes I(465-424), fought his way to dominance at the Persian court. The Egyptian Inaros, a son of Psammetichus III, took the occasion of the struggle over the throne to organize a revolt. Athens not only encouraged the uprising but also dispatched naval forces to aid the effort. In 455 the Persians took over Egyptians and Athenians after a lengthy war. After all, Persia and Athens agreed in the Peace of Callias(449) that the Athens would not intervene in affairs of Egypt and Cyprus and that the Persian king would keep hands off the Greek cities along the southern and western coasts of Asia Minor.

아닥사스사가 죽은 후(BC 424), 왕자의 난이 있었는데 자기의 합법적인 세자인 크세르크세스 2세가 그의 아들 디리우스 2세인 노투스(424-404)에 의해 살해를 당하고, 노투스가 황제로 등극하였다. 그후 서쪽에서 문제가 발생하였다. 아나톨리아와 시리아에서 반란이 일어나 이집트까지 퍼졌고, 엘레판틴의 유대인들 군사 식민지에 있었던 여호와 성전이 파괴되었다.94) 다리우스 2세를 이은 아닥사스 2세(404-359)는 페르샤가 더 이상 서방 세계를 통치하는 일은 무너졌다. 이집트 사람들이 아닥사스사가 자기 동생 고레스와 왕위 투쟁을 할 때 독립을 얻었다. 그 다음 60년간 이집트는 독립을 누렸다.

Some fraternal strife erupted at the death of Artaxerxes(424). Artaxerxes was succeeded, after the legitimate successor, Xerxes II, had been assassinated by his son Darius II Nothus(424-404) took the throne. His reign also witnessed troubles in the west. Revolts

---

94) *ANET*, 492.

broke out in Anatolia and Syria and widespread discontent occurred in Egypt and the Yahwistic temple in the Jewish military colony at Elephantine was destroyed.[94] Under Artaxerxes II(404-359), who succeeded Darius II, Persian control in the west collapsed further. The Egyptians gained their independence when Artaxerxes was forced to fight his brother Cyrus to retain the throne. In the following sixty years, the Egyptians enjoyed their independence.

3-1-2. 사회적 배경 The social context

페르샤 제국의 더 넓은 세계는 성경에서 관심을 끌지 못해서 페르샤 시대 때에 팔레스타인의 유대 공동체의 생활에 대해 궁금해진다. 위에서 살핀 대로, 재건된 유대는 페르샤의 국제 정책의 산물이어서, 유대가 계속 존재할 수 있었던 것은 더 큰 사회적-정치적 존재인 제국과 잘 적응했기 때문이었다.

The larger world of the Persian empire received little consideration in the biblical traditions and we are left to wonder about the course of life in the Palestinian Judean community during the Persian period. As we examined above, the reconstituted Judah was the product of Persian international policy, so that her continued existence depended on her accommodating to this larger social-political reality.

포수기 이후 팔레스타인 내의 유대 공동체 안에, 바벨론 포로로부터 돌아온 귀환민들과 팔레스타인 내에 남아 살았던 유대인들 사이에 긴장이 발전되었다. 또한 북 이스라엘이 멸망한 후 사마리아로부터 유입된 유대인들 공동체도 있었다. 이들 공동체들은 각기 자기들의 상징적 세계들이 있었고 다른 종교적 예배와 생활 방식들이 있었던 것으로 추정한다. 자연스럽게 이 공동체들 내에 긴장이 있었는데 그중에서도 특별히 귀환민 공동체와 팔레스타인에 계속 거주한 공동체 사이가 그러했다. 이 긴장은 종교적인 문제라기보다는 사회적·정치적인 문제였다.[95]

Within the post-exilic Judean community in Palestine, a tension developed between those who had returned from the Babylonian exile and those who had remained in Palestine. And there was another Judean community who came from Samaria's fall. We assume that these communities had their own symbolic universes and followed different religious practices and ways of life. Thus there was naturally tension among these communities, inter alia, between the group that had returned from exile and other groups that had remained in the land of Judah. This tension was not primarily religious but rather essentially socio-political.[95]

페르샤 제국과 유대 공동체도 서로 다른 상징적 세계가 있었다. 호의적 분위기로 보면 유대의 종교적인 지도자들의 관심과 페르샤 제국의 외교 정책이 공동점을 찾았는데, 유대는 페르샤의 주적인 이집트와 완충지대 역할을 수행하는 데 있어서 토라에 기초한 예배를

---

95) C. Schltz, "The political Tensions Reflected in Ezra-Nehemiah", in *Scripture in Context*, eds. by C.D. Evans, W.W. Hallo, J.B. White, Pittsburgh, PA: The Pickwick Press, 1980, 224, 228ff. : "According to the Chronicler, the identity of the opponents to the rebuilding of the temple is (1) adversaries of Judah and Benjamin (2) descendants of those whom Esarhaddon had settled in Palestine (3) the poor people (4) Samarians and (5) neighboring governors."

갱신하도록 허락한다는 것이었다. 그래서 사독계 지도자들이 페르샤 정부와 협력하여 그들의 탁월한 국제적 위치를 보장하는 데 적합했던 것이다.

The Persian empire and the Judean community had also each different symbolic universe. In a propitious manner, however, the interests of the religious leaders of Judah and the established foreign policy of the Persian empire converged: Judah was to be strengthened as a buffer state bordering Persia's chief enemy Egypt by the renewal of the cult on the basis of the Torah. This state of affairs was ideally suited for a Zadokite leadership class willing to collaborate with the Persian authorities as a means of safeguarding its own position of pre-eminence.

에스라와 느헤미야는 페르샤로부터 예루살렘으로 돌아왔을 때 피폐해진 공동체를 개혁하는데 페르샤 왕의 허락으로 회복 사업을 지도했을 때 사독 제사장들 계층과 레위 제사장들 사이에 더 이상 긴장이 없었다. 이들 제사장 그룹들은 종교적인 죄를 함께 지었다. 유대인 공동체는 현상유지를 했고 다른 백성들과 좋은 관계를 유지했다. 사독계와 레위계 제사장들 일부가 다른 백성들과 통혼을 하였다(스 10:18-24).

When Ezra and Nehemiah came to Jerusalem from Persia and conducted their restoration work with Persian royal permission to reform the languishing community, there was no more tension between the Zadokite priestly group and the Levite group. Both priestly groups committed religious sins together. The Judean community maintained the status quo and enjoyed good relation with other peoples. Some priestly families, of both the Zadokites and the Levites, intermarried with other peoples(Ezra 10:18-24).

3-2. 에스라 9-10장 주석 Exegesis of Ezra 9-10

에스라 9-10장은 에스라가 수행한 결혼 개혁을 다루고 있다. 비록 두 장 사이에 인칭의 문법적 변화(1인칭에서 3인칭으로)가 있을지라도, 에스라 9-10장은 문학적·역사적 차원에서 유일한 설화 형식을 가지고 있다.[96] 에스라의 회고록(에스라 7-10장, 느헤미야 8-10장)에서 에스라 7-8장, 느헤미야 8장, 에스라 9장에서는 1인칭의 설명이 나오고, 에스라 10장에서는 3인칭으로 나온다. 이 순서가 그의 페르샤 대군주의 첫 해의 사건들을 기록하고 있다.[97]

Ezra 9-10 deals with the marriage reform under Ezra. Although there is a grammatical change of person between the two chapters(from the first to the third person), Ezra 9-10 forms a single narrative unit at the literary-historical level.[96] Ezra's memoir comprises a first-person account consisting of Ezra 7-8, Nehemiah 8, Ezra 9, and a third-person account found in Ezra 10 - in that order- recording the events of his first year for his Persian overlord.[97]

---

96) H.G.M. Williamson, *Ezra, Nehemiah*, Word Biblical Commentary, vol. 16 (Waco, TX: Word Books, Pub., 1985), 127.; K. Baltzer, *The Covenant Formulary*, ET D.E. Green (Oxford: Blackwell, 1971), 47-48.

97) Ibid.

이 순서에 의하여 에스라는 아닥사스다 1세의 칠년 5월에 도착했고(스 7:7-8), 7월에 율법을 공식적으로 낭독했고(느 7:73하-8:12), 초막절 행사를 가졌다(느 8:13-18). 그리고 백성들의 참회에 이어 대속죄일이 지켜졌고(느 9장), 9월 20일에 결혼 개혁이 시작되어(에 10:9) 3개월 후인 이듬해 초에 마무리되었다(10:16-17).[98]

According to this order, Ezra arrived in the fifth month in the seventh year of Artaxerxes I(Ezra 7:7-8); he read the law publicly in the seventh month(Neh. 7:73b-8:12); the Feast of Tabernacles was celebrated(Neh. 8:13-18); a day of penance, followed by a general confession of sins, was observed(Neh. 9); then began his marriage reform on the twentieth day of the ninth month(Ezra 10:9) and concluded over three months later, that is, at the beginning of the following year(10:16-17).[98]

성경학자들 가운데 에스라가 예루살렘에 도착한 연도를 세 가지로 추정한다. BC 458년, 428년, 398년이다.[99] 이 이론들에 대한 충분한 논의를 여기서 다룰 수 없지만 프랭크 크로스(Frank M. Cross, Jr.)[100]

---

[98] 에스라와 느헤미야의 본문은 전승과정에서 연대별로 정리되지 못했다. The texts of Ezra and Nehemiah have been dislocated in transmission. 이 문제에 대해 다음 자료들을 참고하라. Concerning composition of the books of Ezra and Nehemiah, see Williamson, *Ibid.*, xxix-xxxii.: "As far as Ezra and Nehemiah are concerned, the author proposes three stages of composition: (1) The writing of various primary sources, more of less contemporary with the events they relate; (2) The combination of the Ezra Memoir, the Nehemiah Memoir, and other sources into a document consisting of Ezra 7:1 - Neh. 11:20; 12:27-13:31(11:21-12:26 were added later); (3) The addition of an introduction, Ezra 1-6. The second stage took place about 400 BC and the third about 300 BC."

[99] See J. Bright, A History of Israel, 4th. ed., Excursus II on "The Date of Ezra's Mission to Jerusalem," pp. 391-402. We reject the theory of C. Torrey who regards both exile and restoration as fiction(Ezra Studies, Chicago: University Press, 1910).

[100] Frank M. Cross, Jr.(1921-2012) 교수는 하버드대 고대근동학과 Hancock Professor of He-

의 이론이 적합한 듯하다. 왜냐하면 그의 이론이 1962년에 사마리아에서 발견한 4세기 법적 파피루스를 사용하고 요세푸스의 〈전쟁사〉의 자료[101]를 함께 분석하고 있기 때문이다. 이 분석에 의하면 에스라의 사역이 BC 458년에 시작되었고(에 7:7, 아닥사스다 1세의 7년), 느헤미야의 사역은 BC 445년에 시작되었다(느 2:1, 같은 왕 20년)는 결론으로 인도한다.[102]

Among biblical scholars, there have been three different dates favored for Ezra's arrival in Jerusalem: 458, 428, and 398 BC.[99] Full discussion of these theories cannot be attempted here, but it seems to be inclined to accept the theory of Frank. M. Cross, Jr.,[100] for his theory is more persuasive and scientific, using fourth-century legal papyri found in Samaria in 1962 along with data from Josephus, Antiquities of the Jews.[101] This analysis leads us to conclude that Ezra's mission took place in 458 BC(Ezra 7:7, the seventh year of Artaxerxes I), and Nehemiah's mission in 445 BC(Neh. 2:1, in the twentieth year of the same king).[102]

그러나 점성학(별자리)과 유대교의 안식년 및 컴퓨터로 성경의 연대를 과학적으로 분석하면서 유진 폴스틱(Eugene W. Faulstich)은 에스

---

brew and Other Oriental Languages Emeritus 은퇴교수로, 필자의 논문 지도교수였다.

101) Frank M. Cross, Jr., "A Reconstruction of the Judean Restoration," *JBL* 94 (1975), 4-18. 이 고고학 증거는 여리고 북쪽으로 9마일 떨어진 절벽에 있는 달리예 동굴에서 나옴. This archaeological evidence was from a cave in the Wadi Daliyeh, located in cliffs overlooking the Jordan Valley about nine miles north of Jericho. 이곳에서 발견된 행정 문서들을 통해 역사가들이 느헤미야 시대의 호른사람 산발랏으로부터 사마리아 총독들의 계보를 세울 수 있었음 Administrative documents found there enable historians to establish the sequence of governors in Samaria, beginning with Nehemiah's contemporary, Sanballat the Horonite.

102) Cf. L.J. Hoppe, "The Restoration of Judah," *BT* 24 (1986), 282.

라, 느헤미야 연도를 각각 BC 515년과 502년으로 정한다.[103] 본 연구에서는 올브라이트의 성경 연대기를 참고하면서, 더욱 설득력 있고 합리적이고 과학적인 증거를 제시하는 최근의 연대기를 사용한다.

However, E. W. Faulstich suggested the date of Ezra's mission as BC 515 and Nehemiah's starting mission as BC 502, based on the scientistic method, using the astronomy, the Jewish sabbatical cycles and the computer.[103] We support this recent chronology which provides more acceptable and reasonable analysis in this study, with reference of the Albright's Biblical chronology.

이집트의 왕의 칭호는 바로(Pharaoh)이다. 그런 메데인들과 페르샤인들은 세 가지 호칭을 사용했다. 다리오(Darius), 아닥사스다(Artaxerxes)와 아하수에로(Ahasuerus)이고, 모두 '왕'이나 '위대한 왕'의 의미를 지니고 있다. 학자들이 가끔 칭호를 고유 명사처럼 오해했던 것을 이해하는 것이 중요하다. 절대적인 연대기가 없으면, 우리가 고유한 이름과 왕의 칭호의 차이를 확실하게 결정하는 데 어려움이 있을지 모른다. 고유한 이름 대신에 왕의 칭호를 사용하는 예는 에스라서에서 찾을 수 있다.

An Egyptian king's title is "pharaoh." But there are three titles used by the Medes and Persians: Darius, Artaxerxes, and Ahasuerus, all which have in their meaning, "the king" or "the great king." It is important to understand that scholars have occasionally mistaken a title for a proper name. Without an

---

103) E.W. Faulstich, *Bible Chronology and The Scientific Method*, Spencer, IA: Chronology Books, 1990; 양승원 외 번역, 《성경 연대기와 과학적 검증방법》, 서울: 성경과학원 (IBS) 출판사, 2019. pp. 76f.

absolute chronology, we may have trouble determining with certainty the difference between a proper name and a throne title. An example of the usage of throne titles in place of proper names can be found in the Book of Ezra. 첫째로, 에스라는 건축을 고레스(Cyrus) 아래서 시작한다고 열거하고(스 1:1), 둘째로, 아하스에로와 아닥사스다 아래서 중지되었고(4:6-7), 셋째로 다리오의 2년에 다시 시작되었고(4:25), 넷째로 다리오의 제6년에 완성되었다(6:15). First, Ezra lists the construction beginning under Cyrus(Ezra 1:1). Second, it is halted under Ahasuerus and Artaxerxes(4:6-7). Third, it started again in the second year of Darius(4:25), and Fourth, it was completed in the sixth year of Darius(6:15).

 고레스와 다리오(아하수에로와 아닥사스다) 사이에 열거된 두 왕들은 고레스의 아들 캄비세스(Cambyses)와 그 뒤를 이었던 다리우스 1세이다. 아닥사스다(다리오)의 제 7년에 성전의 완성과 뒤이은 유월절에 바로 이어서 에스라는 율법에 착수했다(스 7:1). 이 예들은 에스라가 고유한 이름들과 왕의 칭호들을 번갈아 사용했다는 것을 입증한다. 아닥사스다의 생애 동안 활동을 수행했던 모든 제사장들은 페르샤의 다리우스 통치 기간 동안에 살았던 것으로 말하고 있다(느 12:1-22).

 The two kings listed between Cyrus and Darius(Ahasuerus ad Artaxerxes) were Cyrus' son Cambyses, followed by Darius I. Immediately following the completion of the Temple and the subsequent Passover, in the seventh year of Artaxerxes[Darius], Ezra went to initiate the Law(Ezra 7:1). These examples demonstrate that Ezra alternately used proper names and throne titles. Nehemiah also alternates between throne titles and names. All the priests which carried on activities during the life of Artaxerxes are said to have lived during the reign of "Darius the Persian"(Neh. 12;1-22).

다리우스에게 보낸 엘레파틴 서신들 하나는 "아닥사스다의 제 37년 마르체쉬안(Marcheshwan)월의 제19일에"라고 진술한다. 우리가 알기로 이것은 다리우스 1세에게 발송되었는데 서신에 언급되어 있는 아르사메스와 다른 자들이 다리우스 1세의 다른 서신들에도 나타나기 때문이다.

On of the Elephantine letters directed to Darius states, "on the 19th of Mancheshwan in the 37th year of Artaxerxes…" We know that this is addressed to Darius I, since Arsames and others who are mentioned in the letter also appear in other letters of Darius I.

에스라는 예루살렘에 도착했을 때 그의 손에는 두 가지 중요한 문서를 가지고 왔다: 하나는 여호와의 율법이고 또 하나는 그에게 권한을 부여한 아닥삭스다 1세[다리우스]의 편지였다. 왕의 임명은 에스라가 "너희들 손에 있는 너희 하나님의 율법"을 가르치고 강화하는 데 힘을 주었다. 에스라의 약력에 대해 아는 바는 거의 없다. 구약성경에 의하면 그는 제사장이며 율법사였고, 바벨론 포로 생활을 한 유대 공동체의 일원인 스라야의 아들이었다(에 7:1-6).

Ezra arrived at Jerusalem with two important documents in his hands: the law of Yahweh and a letter from the Persian king, Artaxerxes I[Darius], giving him authority in Judah. The king's authorization empowered Ezra to teach and to enforce "the law of your God which is in your hand." Comparatively little is known about Ezra's biography. As far as the Hebrew Bible shows, he was a priest and a scribe, the son of Seraiah, a member of the Judean community in Babylonia(Ezra 7:1-6).

그는 모세의 율법에 전문가였다(스 7:6, 11, 21). 그의 공식 직함은 팔레스타인에 조상들의 토라에 근거하여 유대 공동체를 재건하도록 허락 받은 종교적 서기관이었다.[104] 에스라는 예루살렘으로 돌아오는 긴 여정 가운데 약 1760명의 바벨론 포로 생활을 한 유대인들이 동행했다. 이 가운데에는 너무 열정적이지 않는 레위인들(8:15이하)와 다른 성전 종들이 있었다(8:20).

He was skilled in the law of Moses(Ezra 7:6, 11, 21). His official position was that of a religious scribe who was given official Persian permission to reconstitute the Judean community in Palestine on the basis of its ancestral Torah.[104] Ezra was accompanied on the long road to Jerusalem by some 1,760 Babylonian Judeans, including not-too-enthusiastic Levites(8:15ff.) and other temple servants(8:20).

에스라는 아닥사스다 1세[다리우스]에 의해 다음의 네 가지 사명을 성취하기 위해 예루살렘으로 파송받아 왔다: (1) 예루살렘으로 귀환을 원한 유대인들을 인솔함 (2) 성전 예배에 필요한 헌물들을 가지고 옴 (3) 유대와 예루살렘에 질문에 대한 답을 함 (4) 하나님의 율법을 가르칠 판사들과 행정관들을 임명함.

Ezra was sent to Jerusalem by Artaxerxes I[Darius] in order

---

104) Fishbane, *Biblical Interpretation in Ancient Israel*, 107.

to fulfill the following four tasks : (1) to lead any Judeans who wished to return to Jerusalem, (2) to convey some gifts for the temple cult, (3) to conduct an inquiry in Judah and Jerusalem, and (4) to appoint judges and magistrates to teach the divine law.

그의 주된 관심은 여호와의 법을 유대 백성들의 생활을 위한 근거로 세우는 것이었다. 에스라는 새로운 율법을 제시하지 아니했으나 그의 율법에 대한 새로운 해석은 율법에 새로운 의미를 부여했다. 수문[105] 앞에서 에스라는 율법을 낭독(느 8:1-12)한 것이 회개를 촉구했을 뿐만 아니라(백성들의 첫 반응처럼, 느 8:9), 또한 그들이 율법 전체의 긍정적인 메시지를 이해하는 데 도움이 되었다(느 8:10-12).

His principal concern was to establish the law of the Lord as the basis for the life of the Judean people. Ezra did not present a new law, but his new interpretation of the text gave the law new significance. Ezra's reading of the law(Neh. 8:1-12) before the Water Gate[105] was not only to evoke a sense of repentance(like the first reaction of the people, Neh. 8:9), but also to help them understand the positive message of the law in its totality(Neh. 8:10-12).

이제 에스라 9-10장을 살펴보자. 이 본문을 항목별로 해석하면서

---

105) 수문(Water Gate, 느 3:26, 8:1, 3, 16, 12:37): 골짜기 문 맞은편에 있었으며, 기드론 골짜기에 있던 기혼 샘으로 이어진 듯하다. 느헤미야가 귀환하여 예루살렘의 성벽을 재건하기 14년 전에, 에스라가 귀환하여 백성들을 재건하였다. 에스라가 수문 앞 광장에서 백성들에게 율법을 가르쳤다. 백성들이 거기에서 율법을 낭독해 달라고 요청한 것은 놀라운 일이 아니었다. Fourteen years before Nehemiah returned to rebuild the walls of Jerusalem, Ezra returned to rebuild the people. One of the recorded instances in which Ezra taught the people occurred at Jerusalem's Water Gate. So, it's no surprise why the people requested Ezra read them the Bible there.

본문, 문학적 형태, 사회적-주석적 해석과 함께 분석할 것이다. 히브리 성경으로는 마소라 본문을 사용할 것이며 영어 번역으로는 킹제임스와 유대인 성경 타낙(Tanak)을 참고할 것이다.

Let us to examine Ezra 9-10 at this point. We will interpret this text section by section with discussion of text, literary form, and social-exegetical interpretation. We will use the Masoretic Text as the basic text of the Hebrew Bible, with the English version, such as KJB and TNK.

3-2-1. 비극적인 보고 The tragic report (Ezra 9:1-4)

스 9:1 이 일 후에 관리들이 내게 나아와 말하기를 "이스라엘 백성과 제사장들과 레위 사람들이 이 땅 백성과 분리하지 아니하고 가나안 사람과 헷 사람과 브리스 사람과 여부스 사람과 암몬 사람과 모압 사람과 이집트 사람과 아모리 사람의 신성모독적 일을 행하여[a] Now when these things were done, the princes came to me, saying, The people of Israel, and the priests, and the Levites, have not separated themselves from the people of the lands, doing according to their abominations, even of the Canaanites, the Hittites, the Perizzites, the Jebusites, the Ammonites, the Moabites, the Egyptians, and the Amorites.[a] 2 그들의 딸을 취하여 아내와 며느리를 삼아 거룩한 자손으로 이방 족속과 서로 섞이게 하는데 관리들과 지도자들이 이 죄에 더욱 으뜸이 되었다 하는지라 For they have taken of their daughters for themselves, and for their sons: so that the holy seed have mingled themselves with the people of those lands: yea, the hand of the princes and rulers hath been chief in this trespass. 3 내가 이 일을 듣고 속옷과 겉옷을 찢고 머리털과 수염을 뜯으며 기가 막혀 앉으니 And when I heard this thing, I rent my garment and my mantle, and plucked off the hair of my head and of my beard, and sat down astonied. 4 이에 이스라엘 하나님의 말씀을 인하여 떠는 자가 이 사로잡혔던 자의 죄를 인하여 다 내게로 모여 오더라. 내가 저녁 제사 드릴 때까지 기가 막혀 앉았더니 Then were assembled unto me every one that trembled at the words of the God of Israel, because of the transgression of those that had been carried away; and I sat astonied until the evening sacrifice.

3-2-1-1. 본문 노트 (*textual note):

1절 a(v. 1 a). 비록 70인 역과 외경 에스드라 상권(8:69)에서는 아모리인 대신에 '에돔 사람'으로 읽고 있으나, 우리는 마소라 본문이 정확하다고 확신한다. 왜냐하면 에돔 사람들은 그들의 역사적인 죄로 인해 신랄하게 비난을 받아왔기 때문이다(왕하 25:8-12). 그들은 이스라엘이 고난과 파괴를 당할 때 자기 형제를 도와주지 않았다(참고. 시 137:7; 오 1:10-14; 말 1:2-5; 애 4:21; 사 63:1-6; 겔 25:12-14). 어떤 이스라엘 백성들은 에돔 사람과 결혼한 것 같지 않았다. 에스드라서에서는 암몬 자손을 아무런 이유 없이 삭제하고 있다.[106]

---

106) Cf. L. W. Batten, *Ezra and Nehemiah*, ICC, 331.

Although LXX and 1 Esdras(8:69) read the Edomite(ימדאה) for the Amorite, we are sure that MT is correct. For the Edomites had been bitterly blamed for their historical sin(2 Kings 25:8-12), by failing to help Israel their brother in her affliction and destruction(cf. Ps. 137:7, Ob. 1:10-14, Mal. 1:2-5, Lam. 4:21, Isa. 63:1-6, Ezk. 25:12-14). No Israelite was likely to marry any Edomite. Esdras omits Ammonite, for an unknown reason.106)

3-2-1-2. 형식 form

본문은 에스라의 참회기도(스 9:6-15)의 배경을 묘사하는 유대인들의 통혼에 대한 보고이다. 이 보고는 오경의 율법에 대한 성경 내의 주석을 반영한다. 카우프만(Yehezkel Kaufmann)107)은 그의 저서인 《이스라엘 종교사》에서 이 보고를 초기 미드라쉬의 작품으로 발견했다.108) 그는 이 미드라쉬의 두 가지 목적을 지적했다: (1) 오경의 율법에 의해 규정된 관계를 금지한 이방 백성들의 명단을 나열하며 (2) 고대 백성들과 현재 타 백성들을 같이 취급하고 있다.

Our text is a report of Judean intermarriages which describes the background of Ezra's prayer of confession(Ezra 9:6-15). This report shows an inner-biblical exegesis of the Pentateuchal law. Yehezkel Kaufmann107) found an early Midrash at work in this report in his book, History of the Religion of Israel.108) He pointed out two purposes of this Midrash: (1) it enumerates the foreign peoples, relationship with whom has been restricted by the laws

---

107) Yehezkel Kaufmann(1889-1963)은 히브리대학(Hebrew University) 철학과 성경학자임.
108) *Midrash*, vol. IV, ET by M. Greenberg, New York: Schocken Books, 1977, 337-339.

of the Pentateuch, and (2) it shows the equation of the ancient peoples with those of the present other peoples.

피쉬베인은 1-2절은 신명기 7:1-4과 23:3-8을 주석적으로 혼합한 것으로 여긴다.[109] 브렌킨숖은 피쉬베인의 이론인 1절의 열국 목록이, 비록 신 7:1에서는 기르가스 족속과 히위 족속이 이 명단에서 누락되고 이집트인이 첨가되었지만, 신 7:1-4과 23:3-8의 주석적인 재미있는 혼합을 보인다는 데 동의했다.[110]

Fishbane considered vs. 1-2 an exegetical blend of Deuteronomy 7:1-4 and 23:3-8.[109] Blenkinsopp agreed with Fishbane that the list of nations in verse 1 exhibits an interesting exegetical blend of Deut. 7:1-4 and 23:3-8,[110] even though the Girgashites and the Hivites in Deut. 7:1 are omitted from the list and the Egyptians are added.

3-2-1-3. 해석 interpretation:

에스라가 예루살렘에 도착해서 초막절이 끝난 직후(느 8장), 약 4개월 안에 그는 지방 관리들로부터 불평하는 내용 속에 어떤 동료 유대인들이 통혼을 했다는 것을 알게 되었다. 많은 유대인들이 포로생활에서 귀환 후 유대 땅에서 인종과 종교가 다른 백성들과 통혼하였던 것은 분명하다(참고. 느 6:18, 10:31, 13:1-3, 23-30).

---

109) *Biblical Interpretation in Ancient Israel*, 115; Japhet, *The Ideology of the Book of Chronicles and Its Place in Biblical Thought*(Frankfurt: Verlag Peter Lang, 1989), 116.
110) Blenkinsopp, *Ezra-Nehemiah: A Commentary*, The Old Testament Library(Philadelphia: The Westminster Press, 1988), 175.

Within about four months of his arrival in Jerusalem, shortly after the events of the festival of Tabernacles(Neh. 8), Ezra became aware that some fellow Judeans have been intermarriaged through the complaint of local officials. It is clear that many Judeans intermarried with other ethnic and religious groups in the land of Judah after the exiles' return(cf. Neh. 6:18, 10:31, 13:1-3, 23-30).

3-2-1-3-1. 에스라 9:1 주석 Exegesis of Ezra 9:1

> "이 일 후에 관리들이 내게 나아와 말하기를 "이스라엘 백성과 제사장들과 레위 사람들이 이 땅 백성과 분리하지 아니하고 가나안 사람과 헷 사람과 브리스 사람과 여부스 사람과 암몬 사람과 모압 사람과 이집트 사람과 아모리 사람의 신성모독적 일을 행하여"

'이 일 후에': 이 일이 무엇이었는가? 위에서 제시한 대로 이 결혼 개혁이 일어나기 전 7월에 있었던 여호와의 율법을 읽고 해석하는 일(느 8:1-12)과 초막절을 축하한 일이었다(느 8:13-18). 느헤미야 8장의 본래 위치는 연대기적 일치를 위해 여기 있는데, 왜냐하면 에스드라 3서가 우리의 본문(느 8:68-9:36)[111]과 같은 연대기 순서를 따르고 있어 5월(느 7:9)과 9월(느 10:9) 사이의 공백을 메꾸면서 9:36-37에서 전

---

111) Concerning the chronological discussion, see P. R. Ackroyd, *I & II Chronicles, Ezra, Nehemiah*, London: SCM Press Ltd., 1973, 250-251; Howard F. Vos, *Ezra, Nehemiah, and Esther*, Bible Study Commentary, Grand Rapids, MI: Zondervan Pub., 1987, 70.

환하고 있다.[112]

"Now when these things were done, the princes came to me, saying, The people of Israel, and the priests, and the Levites, have not separated themselves from the people of the lands, doing according to their abominations, even of the Canaanites, the Hittites, the Perizzites, the Jebusites, the Ammonites, the Moabites, the Egyptians, and the Amorites."

"Now when these things were done": What are "these things"? As we suggested above, the reading and explanation of the law of the Lord(Neh. 8:1-12) in the seventh month preceded this marriage reform. Thus "these things" include celebration of the Feast of Tabernacles(Neh. 8:13-18) as well. The original location of Neh. 8 here makes for a chronological sequence, for III Esdras follows the same chronological order as our passage(Neh. 8:68-9:36), marking the transition at 9:36-37,[111] filling the gap between the fifth(Neh. 7:9) and the ninth(Neh. 10:9) months.[112]

"관리들이 내게 나아와": 여기서 관리들이란 누구였는가? 알려지지 않은 관리들은 확실히 여호와의 율법을 지키는 데 보수적이었던 백성들의 지도자들이었다. 포수기 이후 시대에 "관리"(śarîm) 개념에는 주가 나눠진 여섯 구역의 행정관들이 포함되었다.[113] 그들이 여호와의 법을 무시하거나 어겼던 다른 유대인들의 지도자들에 반대하여 말했다(스 9:2 하반절). 그들은 에스라의 그룹보다 더 일찍이 포

---

112) Blenkinsopp, *ibid.*, 174.
113) Avi-Yonah, *The Holy Land from the Persian to the Arab Conquest*, Grand Rapids, MI: Zondervan, 1966, 11-31.

로 생활로부터 귀환하였다(느 3:9, 12:31-32). 그들은 최선을 다해 율법을 지켰고 어떤 이방적 요소들로부터 분리하기를 원했다. 에스라가 포로생활로부터 가지고 왔던 여호와의 율법책이 선포되었을 때 그들은 전적으로 그 율법을 순종하려고 했다(느 8:1-12, 10:28). 그들의 관심은 일부 동료 유대인들이 토착민들과 통혼을 함으로 유대 공동체의 전체를 위험에 빠뜨리는 것이었다.

"the officers (מירשה) came near to me" : Who were "the officers"? These unknown officers were surely leaders of the people who were conservative in keeping the law of the Lord. In the post-exilic period, the term(śarîm) included the chief administrators of the six districts into which the province was divided.[113] They spoke against other leading Judeans who violated or disregarded the law of Yahweh in verse 2b. They returned from exile earlier than the group of Ezra(Neh. 3:9, 12:31-32). They did their best to keep the law and wanted to be separated from any foreign elements. When the law of the Lord which Ezra brought from exile was promulgated, they were fully willing to obey the law(Neh. 8:1-12, 10:28). Their concern was that some fellow Judeans' intermarriage with the peoples of the lands might endanger the whole Judean community.

비난을 받은 사람들 가운데는 백성들의 지도자들도 포함되었는데, 심지어 제사장 집안들(즉 사독계 제사장들과 레위계 제사장들)조차 통혼을 하였다. 이들은 스스로를 그 지방 백성들로부터 분리하지 않았다. 연대적인 관점에서 에스라와 함께 귀환한 이들은 이 기소를 당한 자들로부터 제외되었다. 야벳 교수에 의하면, 포로에서 귀환한 그룹들은 스스로 유일한 합법적인 이스라엘 백성들로 여겼다. 다른 이스라엘 그룹들은 존재하지 않았다: "그러나 합법적인 유대 공동체 안에서조차 적어도 세 그룹들이 존재했는데, 여호와의 율법, 즉 통혼, 안식일, 예배, 음식법 등을 지키는 데 보수적, 중립, 그리고 진보적 그룹들이 있었다."114) 그러나 팔레스타인에 남아 있어도 토착민들과 오염되지 않고 분리한 유대인들도 있었다(스 6:21).115)

The accused ones included some leaders of people, even priestly families(i.e. Zadokites and Levites). They had not separated themselves from the peoples of the lands. In chronological perspective, those who returned with Ezra were excluded from these accused ones. According to Japhet, the group that returned from exile saw themselves the only legitimate Israelites, and there were no other Israelite groups at all: "Even within the legitimate Judean community, however, there existed at least three groups: conservative, moderate, and liberal in keeping the law of the Lord, for example, intermarriage, Sabbath, worship and food, etc." 114) But we find some Israelites who remained in Palestine and separated themselves from the pollutions of the peoples of the land in 6:21.115)

"분리하지 아니하고"의 뜻은 다른 백성들과 통혼하는 것이었다(2

---

114) Japhet, *ibid.*, 112.
115) "사로잡혔다가 돌아온 이스라엘 자손과 무릇 스스로 구별하여 자기 땅 이방 사람의 더러운 것을 버리고 이스라엘 무리에게 속하여 이스라엘 하나님 여호와를 구하는 자가 다 먹었다 And the children of Israel, which were come again out of captivity, and all such as had separated themselves unto them from the filthiness of the heathen of the land, to seek the LORD God of Israel, did eat."

절도 보라). 이 구절에 대해 "그들의 딸을 취하여 아내와 며느리를 삼아," "거룩한 자손으로 이방 족속과 서로 섞이게 하는데"(스 9:2)에서 설명하고 있기 때문이다. "삼아"와 "통혼하다"의 두 동사에 대해 2절에서 상세히 설명하겠다.

The meaning of ולדבנ אל "have not separated themselves" surely indicates intermarriage with other people(see v. 2), since it is explained by "they have taken their daughters as wives for themselves and their sons," and "the holy seed have mingled with the people of those lands" in verse 2. We will discuss these two verbs, 'to take' and 'to become intermingled' in the following verse.

"그 땅의 백성들": 이 백성들은 유대 공동체의 밖에 있었던 주변의 여덟 백성들이었다. 본문에 열거된 목록은 본문에 첨가된 것으로 비역사적이다. 왜냐하면 가나안 족, 헷 족, 브리스 족, 여부스 족, 그리고 아모리 족은 에스라 당시에 더 이상 인종적 그룹으로 존재하지 않았기 때문이다. 이 다섯 백성들은 성경에서 이방 족속들의 전형적인 명단에 속했기 때문이다(창 15:19이하; 출 3:8, 17, 33:2, 34:11; 느 9:8 등). 하지만 암몬 족, 모압 족, 이집트 족들은 BC 6세기에 여전히 존재했다(참고. 사 25:10-11; 시 83:6; 느 4:3, 7, 13:1, 7-8). 이 세 백성들은 신 23:3-7에서 이스라엘의 옛 원수들로 간주되어졌다. 본문에 나오는 이방 백성들 목록은 신 7:1-5의 주석적 짜깁기로, 가나안 칠족(헷, 기르가스, 아모리, 가나안, 브리스, 히위, 여부스 족)과 통혼을 금지하고 있다.[116] 신 20:17에서 주변의 열국들(헷, 아모리, 가나안, 브리스, 히위, 여부스)을 완

---

116) Fishbane, *ibid*., 114-117.

전히 멸망시킬 것을 요구한다. 이 열국들의 혐오스러운 제의들(혹 그들의 신성모족에 의하면)이 신명기 사가의 용어로 이단 신들과 제의들(신 20:18, 18:9-14, 참고. 왕상 14:21-24)이었다. 한편 역대기 사가는 자주 마알(ma'al, "불성실," "불신") 단어를 "신성모독, 혐오스러움"이라는 뜻으로 사용했다.117)(대상 2:7, 10:13; 대하 12:2, 26:18, 28:19, 22, 29:6, 19, 30:7, 33:19, 36:14).

"the peoples of the lands"(תוצראה ימעמ): These peoples were from the eight surrounding regions who were outside the Judean community. Our list was an unhistorical addition to the text, for the Canaanites, Hittites, Perizzites, Jebusites, and Amorites no longer existed as racial groups by the time of Ezra. These five peoples belonged to a stereotyped list of heathen peoples(Gen. 15:19ff; Exo. 3:8, 17, 33:2, 34:11; Neh. 9:8, etc.). However, Ammonites, Moabites and Egyptians still existed in the 6th century BC(cf. Isa. 25:10-11; Ps. 83:6; Neh. 4:3, 7, 13:1, 7-8). These three peoples were considered to be old enemies of Israel in Deut. 23:3-7. We may conclude that our list is an exegetical blend of Deut. 7:1-5, prohibiting intermarriage with the seven Canaanite nations(the Hittites, the Girgashites, the Amorites, the Canaanites, the Perizzites, the Hivites, and the Jebusites).116) Deut. 20:17 required to destroy utterly the surrounding nations(the Hittites, the Amorites, the Canaanites, the Perizzites, the Hivites, and the Jebusites), whose abhorrent practices(or according to their abominations) is a Deuteronomic term for false gods and their cults(Deut. 20:18, 18:9-14; cf. 1 K. 14:21-24), while the Chronicler

---

117) See P. Humbert, "Abomination" *ZAW* 72(1960), 217-237.

frequently used ma'al "infidelity, unfaithfulness, undutifulness" as the equivalent of תבעות "something abominable or abhorrent"117) (1Chron. 2:7, 10:13; 2 Chron. 12:2, 26:18, 28:19, 22, 29:6, 19, 30:7, 33:19, 36:14).

이스라엘의 종교 전통에 의하면 통혼은 금지된다. 신 23:4-8(MT)에서 암몬 족과 모압 족들은 예배 공동체 회원이 될 수 없었다(참고. 느 13:1-2). 그러나 신 23:8-9(MT)에 따르면 에돔 족과 이집트 백성 가운데 태어날 3세대의 자녀들은 여호와의 총회에 가입될 수 있다. 그래서 암몬 족, 모압 족 등과 통혼이 금지된 제도는 신 7:1-5에 나오는 율법의 주석적 확대로 신 23:4-8로부터 나온 법을 수용한 것과 겹치는 부분이다(참고. 출 34:15-16; 신 7:3-4). 그들의 공동체를 어떤 외국의 요소들로부터 지키기 위해, 보수 그룹은 모든 통혼들을 신성모독으로 여겼다. 학 2:14에 의하면, 불결한 백성들이 바친 제물조차 불결하다고 했다: "이에 학개가 대답하여 말하기를 '여호와의 말씀에 내 앞에서 이 백성이 그러하고 이 나라가 그러하고 그 손의 모든 일도 그러하고 그들이 거기서 드리는 것도 부정하니라.'"

According to the Israelite religious tradition, intermarriage is to be prohibited. Deut. 23:4-8(MT) excluded Ammonites and Moabites from membership in the worshipping community(cf. Neh. 13:1f). According to Deut. 23:8-9(MT), however, the children of the third generation that would be born to the Edomites and the Egyptians could be admitted to the assembly of the Lord. Thus, the mechanism for prohibiting intermarriage with the Ammonites, Moabites, etc. was an exegetical extension of the law in Deut. 7:1-5 effected by means of an adaptation and interpolation of features from Deut. 23:4-8(cf. Ex. 34:15-16; Deut. 7:3-4). In order to keep their community from any foreign elements, the conservative group considered all intermarriages abominable. According to Haggai 2:14, even the offering made by a defiled people is unclean: "Then answered Haggai, and said, So is this people, and so is this nation before me, saith the LORD; and so is every work of their hands; and that which they offer there is unclean."

3-2-1-3-2. 에스라 9:2 주석 Exegesis of Ezra 9:2

"그들의 딸을 취하여 아내와 며느리를 삼아 거룩한 자손으로 이방 족속과 서로 섞이게 하는데 관리들과 지도자들이 이 죄에 더욱 으뜸이 되었다 하는지라 For they have taken of their daughters for themselves, and for their sons: so that the holy seed have mingled themselves with the people of those lands: yea, the hand of the princes and rulers hath been chief in this trespass."

"그들의 딸을 취하여 아내와 며느리를 삼아": 거룩한 자손(= 포로귀환민)이 그 땅의 백성들과 섞여 살게 되었다. 오경에서 가나안 족들과 통혼하는 위험에 대해 경고한 것이 여기서 당시 토착민에게 적용될 수 있다. 에스라 공동체 내의 통혼 문제는 인종적이며 사회학적이었다(참고. 스 6:21-22, 10:11; 느 13:3, 25). 반면에 포수기 이전의 성경 구절들은 통혼을 종교적인 이유로 금지했다(출 34:15-16; 신 7:3-4, 참고. 신 20:17f. 등). 이스라엘은 자율적인 정치적 세력이 없었고 예루살렘에는 사마리아인들을 비롯한 다른 백성들이 살고 있기에, 통혼은 분명히 포수기 이후 유대 공동체 내에 심각한 인종적, 종교적 정체성의 위기를 가져왔다. 이런 통혼들이 유대 공동체의 사회적 구조의 취약성이 되고 말 것이다. 이방인 부인의 가족들의 일원이 된 유대 남편은 자기의 처가 식구들(장인, 처남, 처제들)로부터 영향을 받게 된다(참고. 신 7:4). 아마도 그의 가족들이 이방인 친척들로부터 영향을 받게 된다.[118]

"they have taken their daughters as wives for themselves and their sons" : The holy seed(=exiles) has become intermingled with the peoples of the land. The warning about the danger of intermarriage with Canaanites in the Pentateuch was here applicable to the contemporary peoples of the lands. The intermarriage issue within Ezra's community was ethnic and sociological(cf. Ezra 6:21-22, 10:11; Neh. 13:3, 25), whereas the pre-exilic biblical passages mainly prohibited intermarriage for a religious reason(Ex. 34:15-16; Deut. 7:3-4, cf. Deut. 20:17f. etc.). Because Israel had no autonomous political power and Jerusalem was inhabited by other peoples including Samaritans, intermarriage clearly led to a serious ethnic and religious identity crisis in the post-exilic Judean community. These intermarriages would result in weakness of the social structure of the Judean community. The Judean husband who became a part of his foreign wife's family was certainly influenced by his foreign father-in-laws and brothers- and sisters-in-laws(cf. Deut. 7:4). Maybe his family members seemed to be also influenced by their foreign relatives.[118]

---

118) F.C.Holmgren, *The Books of Ezra and Nehemiah*, International Theological Commentary, Grand Rapids, MI: Wm. B. Edrdmans Co., 1987, 72.

이 구절은 일부 유대인들이 이방인들의 딸을 아내와 며느리로 삼았다는 것이다. 그러나 어떤 유대인의 부인들이 이방 백성들의 아들들을 자기의 남편이나 사위로 삼았다고는 하지 않는다. 새로운 유대 공동체 내에 부인들이 부족했다는 암시를 준다.[119] 그러나 신명기적인 금지에는 양성(남성, 여성)을 포함하며(신 7:3), 성결 법전에서는 이스라엘 여인이 이집트의 남자와 혼인하는 경우를 제시하고 있다(레 24:10-23, 참고. 결혼에 관련하여 이집트의 관습을 거부, 레 18:3).[120] 엄마가 아빠보다 자녀들의 신앙 교육에서 더 큰 영향을 끼친다는 추측 아래, 결혼 배우자들로 이방 여성들을 제거하는 것을 강조하는 것이 이해될 수 있다."[121] 에스라에게 온 관리들은 자신들은 "거룩한 자손"으로 간주했다. 그러나 일부 거룩한 자손("거룩한 족속 그룹." 참고. 느 9:2; 말 2:15; 사 6:13; 신 7:6; 대하 20:7)이 현재 다른 토착 백성들과 섞여 살고 있었다. "섞여 산다"는 단어는 "통혼하다"(스 9:14)는 동사와 "(이방 여인과) 산다"는(스 10:2, 참고. 시 106:35) 동사와 상징적 대칭을 이룬다. 이 결혼들은 거룩한 자손의 타락의 결과로 보여진다.

Our passage indicates that some Judeans took the daughters of the peoples as their wives and daughters-in-law. But there is no hint that some Judean women took the sons of the peoples as their husbands and sons-in-law. This is attributable to the lack of women in the new Judean community.[119] However, the

---

119) Cf. L.W. Batten, *The Books of Ezra and Nehemiah*, The International Critical Commentary, Edinburgh: T. & T. Clark Ltd., 1913, 331.
120) "너희는 그 거하던 이집트 땅의 풍속을 좇지 말며, 내가 너희를 인도할 가나안 땅의 풍속과 규례도 행하지 말고 After the doings of the land of Egypt, wherein ye dwelt, shall ye not do: and after the doings of the land of Canaan, whither I bring you, shall ye not do: neither shall ye walk in their ordinances."
121) J. Blenkinsopp, *Ezra-Nehemiah: A Commentary*, The Old Testament Library, Philadelphia: The Westminster Press, 1988, 177.

Deuteronomic prohibition includes both sexes(Deut. 7:3), and the Holiness Code presents the case of an Israelite woman married to an Egyptian man(Lev. 24:10-23, cf. the rejection of Egyptian customs in relation to marriage, Lev. 18:3).[120] On the assumption that the mother has the greater influence on her children's religion than the father, "emphasis on excluding foreign women as marriage partners is readily understandable."[121] The officers who came to Ezra seemed to consider themselves as a "holy seed." But some holy seeds(זרע הקדש "the holy kin group," cf. Neh. 9:2; Mal. 2:15; Isa. 6:13; Deut. 7:6; 2 Chron. 20:7) were now intermingled with the peoples of the land. The word "to intermingle" has symbolic symmetry of the verbs והתחתן "to intermarry" in 9:14 and וישב "to make(a foreign woman) a resident" in 10:2(cf. Ps. 106:35). These marriages were seen as resulting in the corruption of the holy seed.

"관리들과 지도자들이 이 죄에 더욱 으뜸이 되었다 하는지라"(문자적으로, "관리들과 지도자들의 손이 이런 불성실한 죄에 으뜸이 되었더라."): 실망스럽게 평신도 지도자와 귀족 계층이 이런 통혼들에 더욱 앞장서게 되었다(느 13:4, 28). 엘레판틴에서, 평신도 지도자들과 성전 관리들이 또한 비-유대인들과 결혼했다고 알려졌다.[122] 느헤미야 2장에 보니 적어도 여덟 지방관리들 가운데 네 명이 이방인의 아내를 두고 있었다(참고. 10:25, 41-42). 지도자라는 단어는 본래 바벨론 어로 마을의 장로들 같은 낮은 직급의 지도자를 말하며, 페르샤 시대에는 지방 감사 혹은 동네 서기와 같은 임명된 관리였다(참고. 겔 23:6, 12, 23;

---

122) B. Porten, *Archives from Elephantine. The Life of an Ancient Jewish Military Colony* Berkeley, CA., 1968, 250.

렘 51:23, 57; 사 41:25).[123]

"it is the officers and rulers who have taken the lead in this trespass"(Literally, "the hand of the officials and rulers has been first in this unfaithfulness"): Discouragingly, the lay and the clerical aristocracy took the lead in these intermarriages(Neh. 13:4, 28). At Elephantine, lay leaders and temple officials were also known to have married non-Judeans.[122] At least four among eight district officials(הסרשים) mentioned in Neh. 2 could be identified as husbands of foreign wives(cf. 10:25, 41f). The rulers(הסגנים), a term originally Babylonian, were minor(or lesser) appointed officials, such as village elders, and in the Persian period even superintendents or foremen(cf. Ezek. 23:6, 12, 23; Jer. 51:23, 57; Isa. 41:25).[123]

3-2-1-3-3. 에스라 9:3 주석 Exegesis of Ezra 9:3

"내가 이 일을 듣고 속옷과 겉옷을 찢고 머리털과 수염을 뜯으며 기가 막혀 앉으니 And when I heard this thing, I rent my garment and my mantle, and plucked off the hair of my head and of my beard, and sat down astonied."

에스라가 이런 보고를 들었을 때에 그의 반응은 예민하고 즉시

---

[123] "관료"와 "통치자"는 가끔 동일시되기도 하며, "귀족들" 혹 "지도자들"로 간주된다. The two terms "official" and "ruler(or prefect)" are sometimes regarded as identical and could be identified with the "nobles" or "leaders." D. J. Clines, *Ezra, Nehemiah, Esther*, The New Century Bible Commentary, Grand Rapids, MI: Wm. B. Eerdmans Pub. Co., 1984, 120; R. A. Bowman, "The Book of Ezra and the Book of Nehemiah," in *The Interpreter's Bible*, Nashville, Tenn.: Abingdon Press, 1954, 645.

행동에 옮겼다. 그의 세 가지 전통적인 애곡의 행동(속옷과 겉옷을 찢고, 머리털과 수염을 뜯고, 기가 막혀 앉음)은 큰 슬픔, 치욕 및 탄원을 표시하는 것이었다. 에스라와는 달리 느헤미야는 이방 여인들과 결혼한 유대인들의 머리털을 뽑았다(느 13:23-25). 에스라는 자기 백성들의 죄가 자기가 지은 죄로 여기고 그들을 대신하여 중보 하였다(참고. 출 32:33이하, 사 6:5-9).

After Ezra heard this report, his reaction was sharp and immediate. His three classic gestures of mourning (to tear up garment and robe, to pluck off the hair of head and beard, and to sit down astonied) were to express great grief, humiliation and lamentation. Unlike Ezra, Nehemiah pulled out the hair of Judean men who married foreign women(Neh. 13:23-25). Ezra identified himself with the sin of his people and became an intercessor for them (cf. Exod. 32:33ff, Isa. 6:5-9).

"내가 속옷과 겉옷을 찢고": 이 구절은 매우 과격한 행동을 표현한다. 본래 모든 옷을 찢으면 나체가 드러나게 된다.[124] 그는 큰 슬픔과 신적인 분노(참고. 미가 1:8)를 나타내는 표로 겉옷뿐만 아니라 속옷과 찢어 버렸다(칠십인 역, 옷들)(참고. 창 37:29, 34; 삼하 1:11; 에 4:1; 욥 1:20, 2:12). 신적인 분노를 나타내기도 한다(참고. 미 1:8).[125]

"I tore up my garment and my robe": This phrase expressed

---

[124] Morris Jastrow, "The Tearing of Garments as a Symbol of Mourning with Especial Reference to the Customs of the Ancient Hebrews," *Journal of the American Oriental Society* 21 (1900), 23-39.
[125] "이러므로 내가 애통하며 애곡하고 벌거벗은 몸으로 행하며 들개 같이 애곡하고 타조 같이 애통하리니 Therefore I will wail and howl, I will go stripped and naked: I will make a wailing like the dragons, and mourning as the owls."

very violent action, originally the tearing off of all clothing to the point of nakedness.[124] He tore up not only his outer robe but also his inner garment(LXX, garments), as a token of great grief(cf. Gen. 37:29, 34; 2 Sam. 1:11; Est. 4:1; Job. 1:20, 2:12) and dread of divine wrath(cf. Micah 1:8).[125]

"머리털과 수염을 뜯으며": 애통은 보통 머리털과 수염을 밀어버리는 것이 수반된다(참고. 욥 1:20; 사 22:12; 렘 16:6, 41:5; 겔 5:1-4, 7:18; 암 8:10 등). 이런 행동은 이방인의 풍습과 연관이 되기에 율법에서는 금지하기 때문에(참고. 레 19:27-28, 21:5; 신 14:1), 에스라는 밀어버리는 대신 머리털과 수염을 뜯는다.

"plucked off the hair from my head and beard": Mourning is usually accompanied by the shaving of the hair and beard(cf. Job 1:20; Isa. 22:12; Jer. 16:6, 41:5; Ezek. 5:1-4, 7:18; Amos 8:10, etc.). Because this act is condemned by the law because of its pagan associations(cf. Lev. 19:27-28, 21:5; Deut. 14:1), Ezra pulled out hair from his head and beard instead.

"기가 막혀 앉으니": 감정을 억제하고, 에스라는 기가 막혀 침묵하면서 앉아 있었다.[126] (참고. 겔 26:16; 욥 2:12-13). 저녁 소제를 드릴 때까지 아무런 말도 없이 침묵했다. 그의 상징적 행동은 예배적 의미를 가졌는데, 그 이유는 아홉시(오후 3시) 즉 저녁 예배 시간까지 기도로 예배를 준비하며 조용히 앉아 있었던 것이다(참고. 출 29:39, 41; 왕상

---

126) 외경 에스드라 8:71에는 "그가 염려와 슬픔 가운데 앉아 있었다"로 번역하고 있다. 루시언 본문(헬라)에서는 "침묵하며 궁금하며"로 번역함. 1 Esdras 8:71 renders "and sat down in anxiety and grief" and the Lucian text (GL) renders 'silent and wondering.'

18:36; 왕하 16:15; 단 9:21; 마 27:46; 행 3:1, 10:3, 30)

"I sat down astonied": Overcome by emotion, Ezra sat down in silence, appalled(NEB, "dumbfounded")126)(cf. Ezek. 26:16; Job 2:12f). Ezra was silent, uttering no cry until the evening sacrifice. His symbolic actions had a cultic significance, for Ezra sat in silence until the appropriate time to offer a prayer, the time of the evening sacrifice, the ninth hour(3 pm, cf. Exod. 29:39, 41; 1 Kgs 18:36; 2 Kgs. 16:15; Dan. 9:21; Mt. 27:46; Acts 3:1, 10:3, 30).

3-2-1-3-4. 에스라 9:4 주석 Exegesis of Ezra 9:4

"이에 이스라엘 하나님의 말씀을 인하여 떠는 자가 이 사로잡혔던 자의 죄를 인하여 다 내게로 모여 오더라. 내가 저녁 제사 드릴 때까지 기가 막혀 앉았더니 Then were assembled unto me every one that trembled at the words of the God of Israel, because of the transgression of those that had been carried away; and I sat astonied until the evening sacrifice."

에스라의 행동은 이스라엘의 하나님의 말씀을 두려워하고 그분의 말씀을 기다리던 군중들을 매혹시켰다. 에스라가 슬픔에 잠겨 거기서 조용히 앉아 있을 동안 그들은 서서히 그 주변에 모여들었다. 그들 중 대부분은 그의 지지 그룹이 되었다(참고. 10:1-7). 이 그룹에는 이 문제를 그에게 상기시킨 관리들(스 9:1), 귀환한 포로민들의 불성실로 인해 이스라엘 하나님의 말씀을 두려워하면서 말씀에 충성한 이들도 포함되었다.

Ezra's action attracted a crowd who feared the words of the God of Israel and waited for His words. While Ezra was sitting there in silent grief, they slowly gathered around him. Most of them became his support group(cf. Ez. 10:1-7). Now his support group included the officers who brought the matter to his attention(Ez. 9:1) and all who remained loyal, fearing the words of the God of Israel because of the unfaithfulness of their fellow returned exiles.

3-2-2. 에스라의 참회 기도 (스 9:5-15) Ezra's prayer of confession (Ezra 9:5-15)

에스라 9:5 저녁 제사를 드릴 때에 내가 근심 중에 일어나서 속옷과 겉옷을 찢은 대로 무릎을 꿇고 나의 하나님 여호와를 향하여 손을 들고 And at the evening sacrifice I arose up from my heaviness; and having rent my garment and my mantle, I fell upon my knees, and spread out my hands unto the LORD my God, 6 말하기를 "나의 하나님이여, 제가 부끄러워 낯이 뜨뜻하여 감히 저의 하나님을 향하여 얼굴을 들지 못하오니 이는 저희 죄악이 많아 정수리에 넘치고 우리 허물이 커서 하늘에 미침이니이다. And said, O my God, I am ashamed and blush to lift up my face to thee, my God: for our iniquities are increased over our head, and our trespass is grown up unto the heavens. 7 저희 조상 때로부터 오늘까지 저희 죄가 심하기에 저희의 죄악으로 인하여 저희와 저희 왕들과 저희 제사장들을 만국의 왕들의 손에 붙

이사 칼에 죽으며 사로잡히며 노략을 당하며 얼굴을 부끄럽게 하심이 오늘날 같으니이다. Since the days of our fathers have we been in a great trespass unto this day; and for our iniquities have we, our kings, and our priests, been delivered into the hand of the kings of the lands, to the sword, to captivity, and to a spoil, and to confusion of face, as it is this day. 8 이제 저희 하나님 여호와께서 저희에게 잠깐 은혜를 베푸사 얼마를 남겨두어 피하게 하신 저희를 그 거룩한 처소에 박힌 못과 같게 하시고 저희 눈을 밝히사 저희로 종 노릇 하는 중에서 조금 살아남게 하셨나이다 And now for a little space grace hath been shewed from the LORD our God, to leave us a remnant to escape, and to give us a nail in his holy place, that our God may lighten our eyes, and give us a little reviving in our bondage. 9 저희가 비록 노예가 되었사오나 저희 하나님이 저희를 그 복역하는 중에 버리지 아니하시고 페르샤 열왕 앞에서 저희로 긍휼히 여김을 입고 소성하여 저희 하나님의 전을 세우게 하시며 그 허물어진 것을 수리하게 하시며 유다와 예루살렘에서 저희에게 울타리를 주셨나이다. For we were bondmen; yet our God hath not forsaken us in our bondage, but hath extended mercy unto us in the sight of the kings of Persia, to give us a reviving, to set up the house of our God, and to repair the desolations thereof, and to give us a wall in Judah and in Jerusalem. 10 저희들의 하나님이여, 이렇게 하신 후에도 저희가 주님의 계명을 배반하였사오니 이제 무슨 말씀을 하오리이까? And now, O our God, what shall we say after this?

for we have forsaken thy commandments, **11** 전에 주님께서 주님의 종, 대언자들로 명하여 말씀하시기를 '너희가 가서 얻으려 하는 땅은 더러운 땅이니 이는 이방 백성들이 더럽고 가증한 일을 행하여 이 가에서 저 가까지 그 더러움으로 채웠음이라 Which thou hast commanded by thy servants the prophets, saying, The land, unto which ye go to possess it, is an unclean land with the filthiness of the people of the lands, with their abominations, which have filled it from one end to another with their uncleanness. **12** 그런즉 너희 여자들을 저희 아들들에게 주지 말고, 저희 딸을 너희 아들을 위하여 데려오지 말며, 그들을 위하여 평강과 형통을 영영히 구하지 말라. 그리하면 너희가 창성하여 그 땅의 아름다운 것을 먹으며 그 땅을 자손에게 유전하여 영원한 기업을 삼게 되리라' 하셨나이다. Now therefore give not your daughters unto their sons, neither take their daughters unto your sons, nor seek their peace or their wealth for ever: that ye may be strong, and eat the good of the land, and leave it for an inheritance to your children for ever. **13** 저희의 악한 행실과 큰 죄로 인하여 이 모든 일을 당하였사오나 저희들의 하나님이 저희 죄악보다 형벌을 경하게 하시고 이만큼 백성을 남겨 주셨사오니 And after all that is come upon us for our evil deeds, and for our great trespass, seeing that thou our God hast punished us less than our iniquities deserve, and hast given us such deliverance as this; **14** 저희가 어찌 다시 주님의 계명을 거역하고 이 가증한 일을 행하는 족속들과 통혼하오리이까? 그리하오면 주님께서 어찌 진노하사 저희를 멸하시

고 남아 피할 자가 없도록 하시지 아니하시리이까? Should we again break thy commandments, and join in affinity with the people of these abominations? wouldest not thou be angry with us till thou hadst consumed us, so that there should be no remnant nor escaping? 15 이스라엘 하나님 여호와여, 주님께서 의롭도소이다. 저희가 남아 피한 것이 오늘날과 같사옵거늘 도리어 주님께 범죄하였사오니 이로 인하여 주님 앞에 한 사람도 감히 서지 못하겠나이다" O LORD God of Israel, thou art righteous: for we remain yet escaped, as it is this day: behold, we are before thee in our trespasses: for we cannot stand before thee because of this.

3-2-2-1. 본문 노트 textual note

5절 상반절. 외경 에스드라 상 8:73에서는 "그런 후 내가 내 옷과 내 거룩한 예복을 찢으며 금식으로부터 일어섰다"라고 번역한다(NRSV). 칠십인 역에서는 "내가 수치에서 일어났다; 내가 옷을 찢었을 때 나는 떨렸다"라고 번역하고 있다.

5a 1 Esd. 8:73 renders "Then I rose from my fast, with my garments and my holy mantle torn"(NRSV). And LXX renders "I rose up from my humiliation; and when I had rent my garments, then I trembled." καὶ ἐν θυσίᾳ τῇ ἑσπερινῇ ἀνέστην ἀπὸ ταπεινώσεώς μου· καὶ ἐν τῷ διαρρῆξαί με τὰ ἱμάτιά μου καὶ ἐπαλλόμην ערקבי can be read as(קמשי "shears").

6절 상반절. 문자적으로 "머리 위로 많아졌다." 마소라 본문도

BHS 비평장치에 제안한 해로, 아마 "중자 탈락"(중자-비슷한 단어, 행의 탈락)으로 추정될 정도로 읽혀져야 한다(참고. 대하 34:4). 사라 자펫교수는 주장하기를 본문은 본래 "머리 위로"로 읽혀야 하나 그 단어들이 전승 과정에서 잘못 나뉘어졌다고 한다.[127]

6a Lit. "have become many above/upwards head." MT should probably read שארה לעם הלעמל, assuming haplography(cf. 2 Chr. 34:4), as suggested in the critical apparatus of BHS. S. Japhet insisted that the text may have originally read שארה לעם, but that the words were wrongly divided in the course of transmission.[127]

7절 상반절에서 칠십인역을 따른다. 마소라 본문에는 접속사가 없다. 이 접속사는 중자 탈락에 의해 상실된 것으로 보인다.[128]

7a We follow LXX. MT omits ו. The conjunction in MT may have been lost by haplography.[128]

7절 하반절에서 Ms Vrs에서 접속사를 이 단어 앞에 첨가하고 있다.
7b Ms Vrs put "and (ו)" in front of this word.

8절 상반절의 "못"의 문자적 뜻은 "텐트의 말뚝"이다. 한 사본에서는 이 단어를 "남은 자"로 수정하는데 그럴 필요는 없다. 왜냐하면 이 단어는 성경의 다른 구절에서 자기 나름의 은유적 의미가 있기 때문이다(사 33:20, 54:2).[129]

---

127) S. Japhet, "The Supposed Common Authority of Chronicles and Ezra-Nehemiah Investigated Anew," *VT* 18 (1968), 357-358.
128) Cf. H. G. M. Williamson, *Ezra, Nehemiah*, Word Biblical Commentary, Waco, TX: Word Books, Pub., 1985, 126.
129) *BDB*, # 3489.

8a Lit. "a tent peg." There is no need to emend(with one manuscript) to רתי, "remnant." For this word has its own metaphorical meaning in other biblical passages(Isa. 33:20, 54:2).129)

13절 상반절. 시리아역과 칠십인역에 따르면 "주님께서 가볍게 방문하셨다"임.

13절 하반절. "오 우리 하나님, 당신께서 우리의 죄악들을 인해 매를 드시지 않고"임.130)

13a According to Syriac and LXX, "you have lightly visited"(תבשח).

13b If the word is הטמל, lit. "You, O our God, have kept from the rod some of our iniquities."130)

3-2-2-2. 문학적 형태 form

여기서 1인칭 단수("내가", "나의")가 사용되었지만 이 본문의 문학적 형식은 공동체 참회 기도이다(참고. 느 9:6-37; 단 9:4-19). 문학 장르는 아마도 사회적 문맥에 순응하여 수사학적으로 죄를 지은 자들이 그들의 외국 아내들을 버리도록 설득하는 데 목적이 있는데,131) 왜냐하면 기도는 현재 군중들에게도 전달되었기 때문이다. 다른 말로 표현하자면 에스라의 기도는 유대 공동체 전체를 향한 기도적 설교였다(참고. 슥 1:7-8, 7:12-14).132)

Although the first person singular ("I," "my") was here used, the

---

130) J. M. Myers, *Ezra, Nehemiah*, Anchor Bible, Garden City, NY: Doubleday & Company, Inc., 1965, 75; cf. M. Dahood, *Proverbs and Northwest Semitic Philology*, 1963, 51, n.2.
131) Blenkinsopp, *Ezra-Nehemiah*, 181.
132) Vos, *Ezra, Nehemiah, and Esther*, 71.

form of this unit is a communal prayer of confession of sin(cf. Neh. 9:6-37; Dan. 9:4-19). The genre was probably adapted to the social context, being aimed rhetorically at persuading the guilty ones to get rid of their foreign wives,[131] for the prayer was delivered for its present audience. This prayer of Ezra was, in other words, a prayer sermon, directed to the whole Judean community (cf. Zech. 1:7-8, 7:12-14).[132]

이 기도는 다음과 같이 분석될 수 있다: 불성실에 대한 일반적 고백(6-7절); 하나님이 현재 은총들을 묵상, 페르샤인들에 의해 가능했던 새로운 시작(8-9절); 통혼 금지와 위반(10-12절); 미래의 결심과 일반적 고백의 결론(13-15절).

This prayer may be analyzed as follows: general confession of infidelity(vv. 6-7); reflection on God's present mercies, the new beginning made possible by the Persians(vv. 8-9); prohibition against intermarriage and violation(vv. 10-12); statement of future intent and concluding general confession(vv. 13-15).

3-2-2-3. 해석 interpretation

위에서 언급한 대로 에스라가 알았던 내용에 대한 반응은 슬픔과 참회적 침묵(혹 금식)이었다. 오후 예배드릴 시간에 에스라는 공중 참회기도시간에 참석했다. 온 공동체를 대표해서 에스라는 현재 상황을 사회적 현상으로 본 것이 아니라 이스라엘의 하나님께 큰 죄를 지은 것으로 보았다. 일반적 관점에서 그는 이스라엘의 역사를 이스라엘이 당한 재앙들을 죄의 심판으로 해석한 신명기 사가 신학의 관점에서 보았다. 역대기 사가의 글에서 신명기 사가의 요소들을 발견하는 일은 놀라운 일이 아니다.133)

As mentioned above, Ezra's response to what he learned was mourning and penitential silence (or fasting). At the evening sacrifice Ezra engaged in a public prayer of confession. Ezra, representing the whole community, considered the present situation, not as a social phenomenon, but as a great sin against Israel's God. In general terms, he reviewed Israel's history in the light of the Deuteronomistic(Dtr) theology which accounted for the disasters of Israel as punishment for sin. It is not surprising to find the Dtr elements in the Chronicler's work.133)

3-2-2-3-1. 에스라 9:10-12 주석적 해석 (통혼의 금지와 위반) Exegesis of Ezra 9:10-12 (prohibition against intermarriage and violation)

이 기도는 오경의 율법과 대언서의 견해에 대한 성경 내적 법적 주석의 또 다른 실례이다. 아마 그는 모세를 대언의 기초자로 여겼던 신명기 사가의 영향을 받은 것 같다(신 18:15-18, 34:10; 참고 왕하 17:13, 23, 21:10; 렘 7:25-26 등). 피쉬베인은 이 성경 내적 주석을 사회적-종교적 권위에 의지한 "함축된 어휘 의미 통사부 전이 주석"이라고 정의를 내렸다.134) 주석적 논쟁의 힘은 권위적 전승(즉 오경의 어휘, 의미, 통사부 전이)에 매여 있음을 뜻한다. 에스라 9:11하-12에 나오는 본문의 혼합은 신 7:1-3, 23:3-8과 레 18:24-30(근친상간에 대해)과 다른 구절들로 구

---

133) Cf. S. L. McKenzie, *The Chronicler's Use of the Deuteronomistic History*, Harvard Semitic Monographs 33, Atlanta: Scholars Press, 1984.
134) *Biblical Interpretation in Ancient Israel*, 266-267, 535.

성되어 있다. 이 주석에 사용된 주요 자료는 다음과 같다:[135]

This prayer is another example of inner-biblical legal exegesis of the Pentateuchal laws and prophetic ideas, probably under the influence of the Deuteronomist, who regarded Moses as the fountainhead of prophecy(Deut. 18:15-18, 34:10, cf. 2 Kgs. 17:13, 23, 21:10; Jer. 7:25-26 etc.). Fishbane designated this inner-biblical exegesis as "implied lemmatic exegesis" resting on social-religious authority.[134] By this is meant that the force of the exegetical polemic is bound to an authoritative traditum(i.e. a Pentateuchal lemma). The textual blend in Ezra 9:11b-12 consists of quotations from Deut. 7:1-3 and 23:3-8 and allusions to Lev. 18:24-30(regarding incest) and other passages. The principal material used in this exegesis is as followings:[135]

"너희들이 차지하려는 땅"(신 4:5이하, 7:1)
"The land that you are about to possess"(Deut. 4:5ff., 7:1)

"토착민들과 오염된 불결한 땅"(레 18:24-30, 20:21이하; 겔 7:19-20)
"a land unclean with the pollutions of the peoples of the lands(Lev. 18:24-30, 20:21ff; Ezk. 7:19-20)

"그들의 신성모독 죄와 함께"(신 18:9; 왕하 16:3, 21:2 참고. 대하 28:3, 33:2)

---

135) Myers, Ezra, *Nehemiah*, 79; Blenkinsopp, *Ezra-Nehemiah*, 185.

"with their abominations"(Deut. 18:9; 2 Kgs. 16:3, 21:2; cf. 2 Chron. 28:3, 33:2)

"그들이 이 끝에서 저 끝까지 채워졌다"(왕하 21:16)
"They have filled it from one end to the other"(2 Kgs. 21:16)

"너의 딸들을 그들의 아들과 결혼시키거나 그들의 딸들로 너희들의 아들들과 결혼 시키지 말라"(신 7:3)
"do not give your daughters in marriage to their sons or let their daughters marry your sons"(Deut. 7:3)

"그들의 평안이나 번영을 위해 아무것도 하지 말라"(신 23:6; 히브리 성경 본문은 7절)
"do nothing for their well-being or prosperity"(Deut. 23:6 [Heb. 7])

"그러면 너희들이 강하여 지고 땅의 좋은 것을 즐기리라"(신 6:11, 11:8; 참고. 사 1:19; 창 45:18)
"then you will be strong and enjoy the good of the land" (Deut. 6:11, 11:8; cf. Isa. 1:19; Gen. 45:18)

"너희 자녀들에게 유업으로 영원히 남겨라"(신 1:38-39; 참고. 겔 37:25하)
"and leave it for an inheritance to your children forever" (Deut. 1:38-39; cf. Ezk. 37:25b)

이것은 예언적 명령으로 기술된 것에 의하면, 비록 어떤 정확한 인용이 아니더라도 더 이른 구약성경의 회고담으로 가득찬 인용에 기초하여, 예언적 명령으로 표현된 실패의 고백이다.136) 이 기도의 주요 관심은 하나님의 법을 유대 공동체의 생활을 위한 기반으로 세우는 것이었다.

This is a confession of failure expressed in terms of what was described as prophetic command, based on a quotation full of reminiscences of earlier Old Testament passages, though not itself a precise quotation of any one.136) The principal concern of this prayer was to establish the law of God as the basis for the life of the Judean community.

토착민들과 통혼들이 투쟁하는 유대 공동체의 무서운 결과들로 충만했다. 특히 유대인들의 지배 가족들이 포함되었기 때문이다. 아마도 통혼이 불법의 종교적 제의들로 인도한다는 관찰 때문에(참고. 삿 3:5-6; 왕상 11:1, 16:31), 일찍이 율법에서는 가나안이 어떤 부족들과 결혼하는 것을 금지하였다(출 34:16).

Intermarriages with "the peoples of the lands" were fraught with dire consequences for the struggling Judean community, especially since it involved the ruling families of the Judeans. Earlier, legal prohibitions were placed on marriages with certain groups in Canaan (Exod. 34:16), probably because of the observation that they might lead to illicit religious practices (cf. Judg. 3:5-6, 1 Kgs. 11:1, 16:31).

"주님의 종, 대언자들"(스 9:11; 참고. 렘 7:25, 25:4, 26:5, 29:19, 35:15, 44:4;

---

136) Ackroyd, *I & II Chronicles, Ezra, Nehemiah*, Torch Bible, London: SCM Press LTD, 1973, 255.

슥 1:6; 단 9:6, 10; 왕하 17:23, 21:10): 하나님께서 모세에게 여호와의 이름으로 대언하며 그분을 성실하게 섬기는 대언자라고 하셨다(참고. 신 18:15-22). 왜 이 단어를 복수로 사용했을까? 이 개념은 율법적 가르침들이 모세와 같은 대언자들을 통해 명령되었고 의사 전달이 되었음을 반영하고 있다.137)

"Your servants, the prophets"(Ezra 9:11; cf. Jer. 7:25, 25:4, 26:5, 29:19, 35:15, 44:4; Zech. 1:6; Dan. 9:6, 10; 2 Kgs. 17:23, 21:10): God told that Moses would be the prophet who would speak in the Lord's name and serve him faithfully(cf. Dt. 18:15-22). Why was the word plural? This reflected a notion that the legal teachings were commanded and communicated through "a succession of prophets like Moses."137)

3-2-2-3-2. 에스라 9:13-15 (일반적 참회로 결론맺음) Exegesis of Ezra 9:13-15 (concluding general confession)

위에서 지적한 대로 이 기도는 기도 설교이다. 13-14절에서 권면조의 말씀을 발견할 수 있다. 이스라엘은 이미 포로생활에서 그들의 종교적 불성실로 인한 하나님의 심판 척도를 경험했다. 이제 이스라엘이 존재하는 것은 하나님의 은총 때문이다. 여호와께서 그들의 죄로 인한 대가만큼 처벌 받을 필요를 하감하셨다. 그래서 하나님의 명령들(여기서 특히 "통혼")을 더 이상 어기면 공동체 전체가 없어질 위기에 처할 것이다(14절 "그리하오면 주님께서 어찌 진노하사 저희를 멸하시고 남아 피할 자가 없도록 하시지 아니하시리이까?). 합법적으로 살아 남은

---

137) Cf. Fishbane, *Biblical Interpretation in Ancient Israel*, 116n.; See G. von Rad, *Deuteronomy*, 17:15ff.

자로 믿는 유대 백성들은 그들 자신의 운명에 책임을 졌다.[138]

As we pointed out above, this prayer was a prayer sermon. We find the hortatory tone in verses 13-14. Israel already experienced a measure of God's judgment in the exile because of her religious infidelity. Now Israel existed only due to divine mercy. The Lord did not requite them to the extent their sins deserved. Thus further violations of the divine commandments(here especially "intermarriage") would put the community at risk of total annihilation(v. 14). The Judean people, who were believed to be a surviving legitimate remnant, were responsible for their own destiny.[138]

14절에 나오는 수사학적 질문인 "저희가 어찌 다시 주님의 계명을 거역하고 이 가증한 일을 행하는 족속들과 통혼하오리이까?"는 간접적으로 죄를 지은 자들이 스스로 신성모독에서 벗어나려는 희망 속에 대중들에게 전달되었다. 기도는 우리가 나라의 참회 시편들에서 보는 대로 하나님의 정의를 인정하면서 국가의 죄와 공동체의 잘못에 대해 크게 참회함으로 끝을 맺고 있다(시 44, 60, 74, 79, 80, 83, 85, 90, 108, 126, 129, 137).

The rhetorical question in v. 14 "Shall we once again break your commandments by intermarrying with these peoples who follow such abhorrent practices?" was indirectly addressed to the congregation, in the hope that the guilty ones might resolve to rid themselves of abomination. The prayer ends with

---

138) Blenkinsopp, *Ezra-Nehemiah*, 185; Williamson, *Ezra, Nehemiah*, 137.

a great confession of national sin and corporate guilt in an acknowledgment of the justice of God, which we find in most national laments(Pss. 44, 60, 74, 79, 80, 83, 85, 90, 108, 126, 129, 137).

"저희 죄악보다 형벌을 경하게 하시고": 이 구절은 사 40:2에 나오는 대로 제2이사야가 "이스라엘이 모든 죄를 인하여 여호와의 손에서 배나 받았느니라"의 말씀과 짝을 이루고 있다.

"punished us less than our iniquities deserved": This phrase can be contrasted with Isa. 40:2 in which Second Isaiah said "Israel had received for Yahweh's hand double for all her sins".

"우리에게 화를 내사": 하나님께서 이스라엘이 하나님과의 언약을 어겼기 때문에 이스라엘 백성들에게 진노하셨다(신 7:4, 11:16-17, 29:26-28; 수 23:16; 삿 2:20). 포수기 이전의 이스라엘 백성들의 죄 행실로 인해 포로 생활을 했다(참고. 13절 첫 절인 "이 모든 일이 일어난 후).

"angry with us": God's anger came upon the Israelites because they had violated God's covenant with them (Dt. 7:4, 11:16-17, 29:26-28; Jos. 23:16; Judg. 2:20). The reference was to the exile which resulted from the sinful deeds of the pre-exilic Israelites(cf. the first phrase in v. 13 "After all that has happened").

"주님은 의로우사": 이 구절은 이 참회기도의 정점을 이룬다. 이 인정은 다른 참회 기도문과 비교될 수 있다(출 9:27; 대하 12:6; 느 9:33; 단 9:14; 참고. 시 4:1, 119:137, 129:4).

"thou art righteous": This phrase showed the climax of this prayer of confession. This acknowledgment came at an equivalent point in other comparable prayers (Ex. 9:27; 2 Chron. 12:6; Neh. 9:33; Dan. 9:14; cf. Ps. 4:1, 119:137, 129:4).

이 기도문은 에스라 개혁의 중심 주제인 인종의 순결을 요구하는 데 매우 중요했다. 포수기 이후 유대 공동체가 하나님께 전적으로 의지하는지를 보여주는 원인을 제공했다. 살아남은 유대인들은 결코 포로생활과 같은 경험을 원하지 않았지만 하나님의 법을 순종하기를 원했다.

This prayer passage was of great importance in shedding light upon the demand for racial purity which was made a central theme of the reform of Ezra. It provided an occasion for showing how the post-exilic Judean community could see itself as totally dependent upon God. The survived Judean people never wanted to experience the disaster like the exile, but to obey the law of God.

3-2-3. 에스라 (10:1-8) 주석—백성들의 회개 Exegesis on Ezra 10:1-8—Repentance of the people

에스라 10:1 에스라가 하나님의 성전 앞에 엎드려 울며 기도하여 죄를 고백할 때에 많은 백성이 심히 통곡하니 이스라엘 중에서 백성의 남녀와 어린아이의 큰 무리가 그 앞에 모인지라. Now when Ezra had prayed, and when he had confessed, weeping and casting himself down[a] before the house of God, there assembled unto him out of Israel a very great congregation of men and women and children[b]: for the people wept very sore. 2 엘람 자손 중 여히엘의 아들 스가냐가 에스라에게 말하기를 "우리가 우리 하나님께 범죄하여 이 땅 이방 여자를 취하여 아내를 삼았으나 이스라엘에게 오히려 소망이 있나니 And Shechaniah the son of Jehiel, one of the sons of Elam[a], answered and said unto Ezra, "We have trespassed against our God, and have taken[b] strange wives of the people of the land: yet now there is hope in Israel concerning this thing. 3 곧 내 주님의 교훈을 좇으며 우리 하나님의 명령을 떨며 준행하는 자의 의논을 좇아 이 모든 아내와 그 아이들을 다 내어 보내기로 우리 하나님과 언약을 세우고 율법대로 행할 것이라. Now therefore let us make a covenant with our God to put away[a] all the wives, and such as are born of them, according to the counsel of my lord[b], and of those that tremble at the commandment of our God; and let it be done according to the law. 4 이는 당신의 주장할 일이니 일어나소서. 우리가 도우리니 힘써 행하소서." Arise; for this matter belongeth unto thee: we also will be with thee: be of good courage, and do it." 5 이에 에스라가 일어나 제사장들과 레위 사람들과 온 이스라엘에게 이 말대로 행하기를 맹세하게 하니 회중이 맹세하니라. Then arose Ezra, and made the chief priests, the Levites, and all Israel, to swear that they should do according to this word. And they sware. 6 이에 에스라가 하나님의 성전 앞에서 일어나 엘리아십의 아들 여호하난의 방으로 들어가니라. 그가 들어가서 사로잡혔던 자의 죄를 근심하여 떡도 먹지 아니하며 물도 마시지 아니하더니 Then Ezra rose up from before the house of God, and went into the chamber of Johanan the son of Eliashib: and when he came thither[a], he did eat no bread, nor drink water: for he mourned because of the transgression of them that had been carried away. 7 유다와 예루살렘의 사로잡혔던 자의 자손들에게 공포하기를 너희는 예루살렘으로 모이라 And they made proclamation throughout Judah and Jerusalem unto all the children of the captivity, that they should gather themselves together unto Jerusalem; 8 누구든지 방백들과 장로들의 훈계를 좇아 삼일 내에 오지 아니하면 그 재산을 몰수하고 사로잡혔던 자의 회중에서 쫓아내리라 하매 And that whosoever would not come within three days, according to the counsel of the princes and the elders, all his substance should be forfeited, and himself separated from the congregation of those that had been carried away.

3-2-3-1. 본문 노트들(textual notes)

1a 칠십인역이 이것을 "기도하면서"로 번역함
1a LXX reads this as καὶ προσευχόμενος "praying".

1b 에스드라 8:91에 따르면, 회중들은 예루살렘에서 몰려들었는데 왜냐하면 군중은 짧은 시간에 모든 유대로부터 올 수 없었다. 그러나 대부분 귀환한 유대인들은 예루살렘 내에 혹은 근처에 살았던 것 같다. 그래서 그들이 한 두 시간 내에 성전으로 올 수 있었다고 추정할 수 있다. 외국 아내들도 분명히 거기에 있었다. 어떤 헬라 본

문들은 자녀들 다음에 "그리고 노예들"을 추가하고 있다.¹³⁹⁾

1b According to Esd. 8:91, "the congregation were from Jerusalem, for the crowd could hardly come from all Judah in a short time. But it is assumed that most returned Judeans lived in or near Jerusalem, so that they might come to the temple within a few hours. The foreign wives were surely there. Some Greek texts added "and slaves" after children.¹³⁹⁾

2a 대부분 본문들(Q mlt Mss LXX, Syr., Vul.)에서 마소라 본문의 'ôlām 대신 'Ēlām으로 읽는데, 우리도 엘림으로 읽는다.

2a Most texts (Q mlt Mss LXX, Syr., Vul.) read as סלים rather than MT סלוע We follow the former.

2b 문자적으로 "우리가 (외국 여인들을) 데리고 살았다" "우리가 (각자의 집에) 살게 했다"의 뜻이다. 이 표현은 비록 "결혼하다"의 단어와 같지 않지만, 스 10장에서 네 번 나오고(9, 14, 17, 18절). 또한 느 13:23에도 나온다. 이 동사와 비교되는 동사가 3절에 나오는 "내 보내다" "이혼하다"이다.

2b Literally, "we made (a foreign women) reside," "we caused to dwell (in one's house)." This expression occurred four times in this chapter (vv. 9, 14, 17, 18) and Neh. 13:23, though it is not the usual word for "to marry." We can compare this verb with חלש "to send away" or "divorce" in v. 3.

---

139) L. W. Batten, *The Books of Ezra and Nehemiah*, The International Critical Commentary, Edinburgh: T. & T. Clark Ltd., 1913, 340.

3a 헬라어 루시안 본문과 시리아 본문에서는 '여인들' 다음에 '이 방 여인들'이 추가 되었다. 외경 에스드라서 8:90에서 이 번역을 반영 하고 있다. "외국의 뿌리를 둔 우리 모든 아내들"

3a The Lucianic Text and Syr. added תויכנה after nashim. 1 Esd. 8:90 follows this reading: "all our wives who are of alien race."

3b 에스드라 상 8:94에 따르면 "내 주"는 에스라를 지칭한다. 참고. 칠십인역과 아퀼라 헬라 본문에서는 "당신에게"라고 번역함.

3b Ms emended MT "my lord," with reference to Ezra, following 1 Esd. 8:94. Cf. LXX and Aquila σοι "to you".

6a 마소라 본문에서 "그는 거기에 갔다"가 아마도 서기관의 실수 인 것 같다(에스다라 상 9:2, 칠십인역, 헬라 루시안 본문에서 "밤새도록 남아 있음" "철야하다"로 번역함)

6a MT "he went there" is probably a scribal error (1 Esd. 9:2, LXX, the Lucianic Text read και αυλισqeij, that is, l n" to remain overnight " or "stay through the night").

3-2-3-2. 문학적 형식 form

본문의 문학 형식은 에스라 비망록의 한 부분인 설화이다. 이 설화는 스 7:1-26처럼 3인칭으로 계속 되었다(위에서 주석한 에스라 9:6을 보라).140)

---

140) 인칭변화에 대하여 다음 자료를 참고하라. Concerning the change in person, see Williamson, *Ezra, Nehemiah*, 145: 모빙켈은 본 설화에서 일인칭에서 삼인칭으로 변화된 이유를 네 가지로 든다. Mowinckel lists four possible reasons for the change from

The form of this text is a narrative which belonged a part of the Ezra memoirs. This narrative continued in the third person as in Ezra 7:1-26 (see above 9:6).[140]

3-2-3-3. 주석적 해석 interpretation

본문은 스 10:1-5절(계약을 체결함)과 6-8절(회의의 순서)로 나눠질 수 있다. 에스라의 공중 기도는 즉각적인 효과가 나타났다. 기도하기 전에 에스라 주변에 모였던 군중들 외에(9:4), 이제 유대인들의 큰 무리들이 에스라가 기도하고 있었던 성전 주변으로 모여 들었다. 그들은 귀환한 포로민들의 불성실(참고. 스 9:4) 때문에 이스라엘의 하나님의 심판을 두려워했다. 그래서 그들은 슬픔의 표현으로 에스라와 함께 애통하며 회개하기 시작했다. 그때 엘람 자손 중 여히엘의 아들 스가냐가 유대인들이 잘못했고 통혼한 자들이 외국인 부인들과 이들 사이에 태어난 자녀들을 내보내는 일에 맹세하자고 제안했다. 공동

---

the first person to the third person in the narrative: i) 두 가지 다른 자료들이 합쳐졌다 two separate sources, one first-person and the other third-person, may have been combined; ii) 본래 일인칭 설화가 나중에 삼인칭 설화로 바뀌어졌다 an original first-person narrative has been later changed in a number of passages into the third person; iii) 본래 삼인칭 설화가 후대 확장되면서 일인칭으로 바뀌어졌다 an original third-person narrative has been later changed into the first person for much of its extent; iv) 본래부터 인칭변화가 있는 설화로 저자에 의해 인칭변화가 있었음 the difference is original, having been intended from the first by the author(Requoted from S. Mowinckel, "Ich und Er in der Ezrageschichte," in *Verbannung und Heimkehr*, ed. A.Kuschke, T bingen: Mohr, 1961, 211-33). 모빙켈은 네 번째 가능성을 좋아한다. 즉 인칭변화는 수사학적 변화라는 것이다. Mowickel himself favors the fourth possibility, namely that the change was present for a stylistic variation; v) 포러는 에스라 10장이 에스라가 전수받은 비망록의 형태를 따라 역대기사가에 의해 개작되었다고 주장함 favored by G. Fohrer, is that "Ezra 10 was composed de novo by the Chronicler after the pattern of the Memoir which he inherited" (*Introduction to the Old Testament*, ET D. Green, London: S.P.C.K., 1970, 243.

체로부터의 추방은 이혼 혹은 결혼 무효를 포함했다. 에스라와 그의 주변에 모여든 대부분 유대인들은 이 제안을 수락했고 하나님과 언약을 체결했다. 에스라가 대제사장 방에서 공개 금식한 후 그는 모든 유대인들이 이 문제를 해결하기 위해 삼 일 안에 다 모이라고 선포를 했다. 만약 모이지 않을 경우 재산 몰수와 파문의 처벌을 내리기로 했다.

This text can be divided into vv. 1-5(the making of a covenant) and vv. 6-8(an order for assembly). Ezra's public prayer had an immediate effect. Besides the crowd who gathered around Ezra before his prayer(9:4), a big crowd of Judeans now gathered in the temple area where Ezra was praying. They feared the punishment of the God of Israel, because of the unfaithfulness of the returned exiles(cf. Ezr 9:4). So they began to repent and join with him in weeping as an expression of distress. At that time, Shecaniah admitted that Judeans had done wrong and proposed that the offenders be put under oath to expel their foreign wives and the children born by them. Exclusion from the community involved divorce or annulment. Ezra and most Judeans who gathered around him accepted this proposal and made a covenant with God. After Ezra's public fast in the room of the high priest, he issued a proclamation directing all Judeans to convene within three days to deal firmly with the matter under penalty of confiscation and excommunication.

3-2-3-3-1. 에스라 10:1-5 주석(계약을 체결한 이야기): Exegesis of Ezra 10:1-5(the story of making a covenant):

에스라의 기도와 크게 애통함이 큰 군중들을 모았다. 왜냐하면 그의 기도는 하나님께 드린 순수한 참회였고 백성들에게 선포한 설교였기 때문이다. 크게 우는 소리가 백성들을 모았다(스 3:13를 보라. 느 1:4, 8:9; 욜 2:12; 참고. 단 9:4, 20; 대하 20:9). 에스라는 회중들이 행해야 할 일에 대하여 그들 자신들이 결론을 이끌어 내도록 기다렸다(참고. 에스라 9:2; 느 13:27)

Ezra's praying and loud weeping attracted a very large crowd, for his prayer was both a genuine confession of sin to God and a sermon directed to the crowd. The sound of high-pitched weeping attracted people (see 3:13; Neh. 1:4, 8:9; Joel 2:12; cf. Dan. 9:4, 20; 2 Chron. 20:9). Ezra waited for his congregation to draw their own conclusions about what should be done(cf. Ezra 9:2; Neh. 13:27).

"엎드려"(1절): 이 자세는 자신의 몸을 땅에 엎드려 이마와 배와 다리가 땅에 닿는 자세로 기도와 예배의 자세이다(느 8:6). 그러나 문맥을 보면 이 단어는 단순히 무릎을 꿇는 자세였다(스 9:5).

"prostrate" in v.1: ("throwing himself down") To cast oneself down on the ground was a posture of prayer and worship(Neh. 8:6). But according to the context, this word may simply refer to his kneeling posture(Ezra 9:5).

"많은 백성들이 크게 통곡하니"(1절): 아마도 에스라를 지지하는 그룹들이 함께 울며 회개하였다. 많은 여인들과 자녀들도 그들의 임

박한 운명에 때문에 비참하게 애통했을 것이다.[141] 스가냐는 포로의 첫 귀환 동안 엘람으로부터 유대로 돌아온 가족에 속했다(참고. 스 2:7, 31, 8:7). 스 10:26에 의하면, 스가냐의 아버지, 여히엘을 포함한 여섯 명의 엘람 사람들이 외국인 부인과 결혼했다. 만약 그렇다면, 스가냐는 확실히 자기 아버지가 비 유대인 여인(자기 어머니가 아님!)과 결혼한 것에 대해 비통했을 것이다.[142] 비록 스가냐의 가족이 주로 통혼에 포함되었을지라도, 그는 18-43절에 나오는 범죄자들의 명단에 포함되어 있지 않았다. 만약 스가냐의 아버지가 다른 이방 여인과 결혼을 했다면 그는 슬픔에 잠겼을 것이다.[143] 에스라처럼 자신이 공동체의 불성실함과 동일시하면서, 그는 모든 외국 여인들을 유대 공동체로부터 추방할 것을 건의했다. 그가 제안한 과격한 해결은 많은 호응을 얻었다는 것은 주목할 만하다. 어떤 희망을 지탱하면서 그는 에스라보다 더 나아갔다.

"the people were weeping bitterly" in v.1: Presumably Ezra's support group joined in weeping and repenting. Possibly some of the women and children wept bitterly because of their imminent fate.[141] Shecaniah belonged to a family that returned to Judah from Elam during the first return(cf. Ezra 2:7, 31, 8:7). According to Ezra 10:26, six Elamites, including Shecaniah's father, Jehiel, married foreign wives. If so, Shecaniah was doubtless grieved that his father married a non-Judean woman(not his mother!).[142] Although Shecaniah's family was pimarily involved in the

---

141) J.G. McConville, *Ezra, Nehemiah and Esther*, The Daily Study Bible Series, Philadelphia: The Westminster Press, 1985, 68.
142) *Ibid*.
143) Contra D. J. Clines, *Ezra, Nehemiah, Esther*, 126.

intermarriages, he was not included in the list of offenders in vv. 18-43.[143] Identifying himself, like Ezra, with the faithlessness of the community, he proposed to put away all the foreign women from the Judean community. It is noteworthy that the radical solution that he proposed found general agreement. In holding out some hope, he went further than Ezra.

"언약을 체결하고"(3절): 구약성경에서 어떤 이스라엘 왕들이 이미 존재한 언약에 순종할 것을 맹세하며 언약을 체결하였다고 나온다 (왕하 23:1-3; 대하 29:10; 참고. 대하 15:12, 23:16, 34:31-32). 포수기 이후 "언약"이란 용어는 맹세에 의해 확인된 어떤 법의 규정들에 대한 집단적 헌신을 말했다.[144] 이 언약은 외국 여인들과 결혼한 모든 자들이 즉시 이들과 이혼해야 한다는 에스라 지지 그룹의 편에서 체결한 약속이었다(5절. 참고 느 10:1 "맹세", 느 10:30 "서약").[145] 이 약속 합의는 요시아 왕 아래에 생존을 위한 언약이었다(왕하 23:1-3).

"make a covenant" in v.3: In the Hebrew Bible, some Israelite kings were said to make a covenant, pledging their obedience to the covenant that already existed(2 Kgs. 23:1-3, 2 Chron. 29:10, cf. 2 Chr. 15:12, 23:16, 34:31-32). The term "covenant"(תירב) in the post-exilic period was used for a collective commitment to certain stipulations of law confirmed by an oath.[144] This covenant was a sworn agreement on the part of Ezra's support group that all

---

144) Blenkinsopp, *Ezra-Nehemiah*, 188.
145) See further D. R. Hillers, *Covenant: The History of a Biblical Idea*, Baltimore: Johns Hopkins Press, 1969, 148. ; G. J. Botterweck & H. Ringgren (eds), ET by J.T. Willis, *Theological Dictionary of the Old Testament II*, "covenant," Grand Papids, 1974, 253-279; D.J. McCarthy, *Treaty and Covenant*, Rome: Biblical Institute Press, 1981.

those who have married foreign women should divorce them immediately(v. 5, cf. Neh.10:1 הנמא "a pledge", Neh. 10:30 העובש "an oath,").145) This sworn agreement was a covenant for the sake of revival, as under Josiah(2 Kgs. 23:1-3).

"모든 여인들(에스드라 상 8:90에서는 보다 강한 용어로 "우리의 아내들")과 이들 사이에서 태어난 자녀들을 다 내어보내기로"(3절): "추방하다" 혹 "내쫓다"의 동사146)는 이혼의 가혹한 조치를 말한다. 학문적인 신명기 사가의 법적 용어로 "내보내다"의 동사를 사용하는 것 같다 (신 21:14, 24:3-4; 렘 3:1). 고대 근동 시대에는 결혼이 깨어질 때 아이들의 양육권이 엄마에게 주어졌다. 예를 들면, 함무라비 법전 137번에 의하면,147) 바벨론에서 이혼을 당한 여인들이 자기의 자녀들을 데리고 갔으며, 이들이 장성할 때까지 기다렸다가 재혼을 하였다고 한다. 하갈이 쫓겨나갈 때 이스마엘이 엄마와 함께 내보내졌다(창 21:14).

"expel all the women(1 Esd. 8:90 "our wives", a stronger term) and those who were born to them." in v.3: The verb הוציאל("to expel" or "to cast out")146) refers to the harsh measure of divorce. The technical deuteronomistic legal term appeared to be חלש (Deut. 21:14, 24:3-4 and Jer. 3:1). Mothers were given custody of their children when marriages were dissolved in the ancient Near East. For example, in Babylonia divorced women were granted their children and had to wait for them to grow up before remarrying,

---

146) 이 아카디언 파생어가 이혼의 절차에 사용됨 The Akkadian cognate was used in divorce proceedings; cf. the texts in C. H. Gordon, "Hos. 2:4-5 in the Light of New Semitic Inscription," *ZAW* 54 (1936), 278-280.
147) *ANET*, 172.

according to the law code of Hammurabi(#137).[147] When Hagar was dismissed, Ishmael was sent away with her(Gen. 21:14).

"율법대로 행할 것이라"(3절): 여기서 말하는 율법은 신 7:1-4에 나오는 신명기 법이나 혹은 에스라가 공표한 법규(참고. 느 8; 스 9:11-12)를 말한다. 그런 경우에 이혼을 요구하는 법이 없다. 이혼은 남편이 아내에게 불결 혹은 불성실을 발견할 때만 허락되었다(신 24:1-4; 대하 34:31-33; 참고. 마 19:8-9).[148] 스가냐와 회중은 율법을 해석하여 그로 하여금 통혼을 파기하도록 격려하는 데 에스라의 지도력을 인정했다. 왜냐하면 그들은 에스라가 율법에 정통하다고 믿었기 때문이다(참고. 7:6, 11, 14, 25-26; 느 8:1-8).

"let the law be done" in v.3: The law here doubtless refers to a radical interpretation of the Deuteronomic law in Deut. 7:1-4 or the regulation issued by Ezra(cf. Neh. 8, Ezra 9:11-12), since no extant law requires divorce in such cases. Divorce was otherwise permitted only in the event of a husband's finding some "indecency" or "uncleanness" in his wife(Deut. 24:1-4, 2 Chron. 34:31-33, cf. Mt. 19:8-9).[147] Shecaniah and the congregation recognized Ezra's leadership in interpreting the law and encouraged him to outlaw intermarriage, for they believed that Ezra was the expert in the law(cf. 7:6, 11, 14, 25-26, Neh. 8:1-8).

"무리가 맹세를 하는지라"(5절): 참고. 느 5:12. 회중들의 지지로 에스라는 모여든 제사장들과 회중의 평신도 지도자들과 더불어 3절에

---

148) Clines, *Ezra, Nehemiah, Esther*, 126-127.

서 스가랴가 제안한 언약을 약속하도록 하였다. 그 맹세는 상호 신뢰성을 가지는 종교적 행동이었다. 왜냐하면 하나님 앞에서 가진 신실하고 신성한 약속이었기 때문이었다.

"they took the oath" in v. 5: cf. Neh. 5:12. With public support, Ezra made the priests and the leaders of the lay Judeans who were present in the congregation swear an oath which affirmed the covenant proposed by Shecaniah in v. 3. The oath was a religious action creating mutual confidence because it was a sincere and solemn promise before God.

3-2-3-3-2. 에스라 10:6-8 주석 (회중 모임의 순서) Exegesis of Ezra 10:6-8 (an order for assembly)

에스라가 여호하난의 방에서 참회하는 강한 행동은 신성한 종교 행위를 위한 준비를 암시하였다. 에스라가 계속 금식하고 기도를 계속하는 동안 회중의 지도자들이 모든 유대인들을 예루살렘으로 집합을 시켰다.

Ezra's strong penitential action in the room of Jehohanan suggests preparation for a solemn religious action. While Ezra continued to fast and pray, the leaders of the congregation ordered all Judeans to assemble in Jerusalem.

"엘리아십의 아들 여호하난의 방으로 들어가니라"(6절): 에스라는 대제사장 엘리아십의 손자인 여호하난의 방에서 철야를 하였다.[149]

---

[149] It is clear that Joshua was the high priest, contemporary with Ezra in 458 BC [or 515 BC] (Clines, 127-8; Blenkinsopp, 1988:190; Bowman, 654; Williamson, 151-154; contra

여기에 언급된 엘리아십는 다리우스 2세(BC 424-405) 때의 대제사장이 된 인물과 다르다. 프랭크 크로스 교수는 느 12:10-11의 대제사장 족보에서 두 사람의 이름이 빠졌다고 주장한다: 여호야김의 동생 엘리아십과 그의 아들 요하난이다.150)

"went into the room of Jehohanan son of Eliashib" in v.6: Ezra spent the night in the room of Jehohanan, the grandson of Eliashib the high priest.148) The Eliashib here mentioned was not identical with the person who became high priest under Darius II (424-405). We agree with F. M. Cross who suggested that the high priestly genealogy of Neh. 12:10-11 omitted two names: Eliashib, brother of Joiakim, and Johanan his son.149)

"음식도 먹지 않고 물도 마시지 않더라"(6절): 음식과 물을 금하는 철저한 금식을 의미한다. 비록 모세가 이런 금식을 두 번씩(출 34:28; 신 9:18) 했고, 니느웨 백성들이 했는데(욘 3:7), 보통 금식은 먹는 것만 금지했다(삼상 1:7; 삼하 3:35).

"ate no food and drank no water" in v.6: This means complete fasting from both food and water. Although Moses did this complete fast twice (Ex. 34:28; Dt. 9:18), and so did the Ninevites(Jon. 3:7), fasting usually involved abstaining only from eating(1 Sam. 1:7; 2 Sam. 3:35).

"근심하여"(6절): 히브리 단어는 마땅히 받아야 할 심판의 위협을 아는 사람들의 행동을 말한다(참고. 출 33:4; 민 14:39).

Myers, 85-86).
150) F. M. Cross, "A Reconstruction of the Judean Restoration," 10, 17.

"in mourning" in v.6: The Hebrew often meant the reaction of those aware of the threat of deserved judgment (cf. Ex. 33:4; Num. 14:39).

"공포하기를"(7절): 이 구절은 제사장 문서에서 처음 나오는 표현으로 후기에 속한다(출 36:6). 히스기야가 유월절 선언과 관련하여 역대기 사가가 사용했다(대하 30:5). 고레스가 유대인들을 해방할 때도 사용했다(대하 36:22; 스 1:1). 그리고 느헤미야가 장막절을 축하할 때도 사용했다(느 8:15).151)

"a proclamation was issued" in v.7: This phrase was a late expression found first in P(Ex. 36:6). It was used by the Chronicler in connection with Hezekiah's Passover announcement(2 Chron. 30:5), with Cyrus' decree granting release of the Judeans(2 Chron. 36:22; Ezra 1:1), and with the celebration of the Feast of Tabernacles under Nehemiah(Neh. 8:15).150)

"삼 일 내에"(8절): 유대 나라의 경계가 페르샤 시대에 다소 축소되었기에 대부분 유대 백성은 예루살렘의 50마일(약 80킬로미터) 반경에서 살았다. 북쪽 경계는 벧엘, 남쪽은 브엘세바, 동쪽은 여리고, 서쪽은 오노였다(참고. 느 7:26-38, 11:25-35). 쿰란사본 IQ Sam. 1:25-27에서 "삼 일간"의 거룩하게 구별하는 일은 어떤 절기를 준비하면서 회집 전에 필수였다.152)

"within three days" in v.8: Since the territory of Judah was a little reduced in the Persian period, most Judean people lived

---

151) Myers, *Ezra, Nehemiah*, 83.
152) *Ibid*.

within 50 miles of Jerusalem. The borders were Bethel in the north, Beersheba in the south, Jericho in the east, and Ono in the west(cf. Neh. 7:26-38, 11:25-35). In 1Q Sam. 1:25-27, three days' sanctification was required before assembly on certain occasions.[152]

"몰수하고"(8절): 히브리 동사 BDL의 뜻은 "세속적 사용을 금지하고 여호와께 헌신함"인데, 파괴(보라. 출 22:20; 신 13:12-18) 혹은 여호와의 창고에 줌(참고. 레 27:28; 수 6:19, 7:1-15)으로 그 재산을 처분하는 것이었다.

"forfeited" in v.8: The Hebrew for this word means "to ban from profane use and to devote to the Lord", either by destruction (see Ex. 22:20; Dt. 13:12-18) or by giving it to the Lord's treasury (cf. Lev. 27:28; Jos. 6:19, 7:1-15).

3-2-4. 스 10:9-17 주석 (조사와 항의) Exegesis of Ezra 10:9-17 (Survey and protest)

에스라 Ezra 10:9 유다와 베냐민 모든 사람이 삼 일 내에 예루살렘에 모이니 때는 구월 이십일이라. 회중이 하나님의 성전 앞 광장에 앉아서 이 일과 큰 비를 인하여 떨더니 Then all the men of Judah and Benjamin gathered themselves together unto Jerusalem within three days. It was the ninth month, on the twentieth day of the month; and all the people sat in the street of the house of God, trembling because of this matter, and for the great rain. 10 제사장 에

스라가 일어서서 그들에게 말하기를 "여러분들이 범죄하여 이방 여자로 아내를 삼아 이스라엘의 죄를 더하게 하였으니 And Ezra the priest stood up, and said unto them, "Ye have transgressed, and have taken strange wives, to increase the trespass of Israel. 11 이제 여러분 조상의 하나님 앞에서 죄를 자백하고 그 뜻대로 행하여 이 땅 백성들과 이방 여인을 끊어 버리라." Now therefore make confession unto the LORD God of your fathers, and do his pleasure: and separate yourselves from the people of the land, and from the strange wives." 12 회중들이 큰 소리로 대답하여 말하기를 "당신의 말씀대로 우리가 마땅히 행할 것이니이다. Then all the congregation answered and said with a loud voice, "As thou hast said, so must we do. 13 그러나 백성이 많고 또 큰 비가 내리는 때니 능히 밖에 서지 못할 것이요 우리가 이 일로 크게 범죄하였으니 하루 이틀에 할 일이 아니오니 But the people are many, and it is a time of much rain, and we are not able to stand without, neither is this a work of one day or two: for we are many that have transgressed in this thing. 14 이제 온 회중을 위하여 우리들의 관리들을 세우고 우리 모든 성읍에 이방 여자에게 장가든 자는 다 정한 때에 본성 장로들과 재판장과 함께 오게 하여 우리 하나님의 이 일로 인하신 진노가 우리에게서 떠나게 하소서" 하나 Let now our rulers of all the congregation stand, and let all them which have taken strange wives in our cities come at appointed times, and with them the elders of every city, and the judges thereof, until the fierce wrath of our God for this matter be turned from us." 15 오직 아사헬의 아들 요나단과 디과의 아들 야스야가 일어나 그 일을 반대하고 므술람과 레위 사람 삽브대가 저희를 돕더라. Only Jonathan the son of Asahel and Jahaziah the son of Tikvah were employed[a] about this matter: and Meshullam and Shabbethai the Levite helped them[b]. 16 사로잡혔던 자의 자손이 그대로 한지라. 제사장 에스라가 그 백성을 따라 각기 지명된 족장 몇 사람을 위임하고 시월 초하루에 앉아 그 일을 조사하여 And the children of the captivity did so. And Ezra the priest, with certain chief of the fathers, after the house of their fathers, and all of them by their names, were separated[a], and sat down in the first day of the tenth month to examine[b] the matter. 17 정월 초하루에 이르러 이방 여인을 취한 자의 일 조사하기를 마치니라. And they made an end with all the men[a] that had taken strange wives by the first day of the first month.

3-2-4-1. 본문 노트 textual notes

15a 칠십인 역에서는 "나와 함께" 즉 "에스라와 함께"로 되어 있다.
15a LXX "with me," i.e., "with Ezra."

15b 복수로 읽는 루시안 헬라어 본문을 따라 마소라 본문의 단수 보다는 므술람과 사베타이로 읽는다. 칠십인 역에서는 "오직 아사헬의 아들 요나단과 디과의 아들 야스야가 일어나 이 일에 나와 함께하고, 므술람과 레위 사람 삽브대가 그들을 돕더라"로 읽는다.

이렇게 읽어 번역하는 것153)은 이 문학적 상황에서 받아들여질 수 없다. 왜냐하면 본 절의 시작에서 특별한 언급이 우리를 앞으로 일어난 사건의 일의 정반대로 인도하기 때문이다.

15b We follow the Lucianic Text, reading a plural, which designates Meshullam and Shabbethai, rather than a singular as in MT(םיולה). LXX reads this whole verse as follows: "Only Jonathan son of Asahel and Jahzeiah son of Tikvah were with me concerning this. Meshullam and Shabbethai, the Levites, helped them." This alternative translation153) was not acceptable in this literary context, for the particle mention at the start of the verse led us to expect a contrast with the foregoing event.154)

16a 비록 마소라 본문에서 동사가 히필형 복수로 되어 있을지라도, 우리는 에스드라 상 9:16과 몇몇 사본에 있는 대로 히필형 단수("그가 자신을 위하여 지명하다")를 택한다. 왜냐하면 확실히 에스라가 이 지명을 주도했기 때문이다.

16a Although MT has a plural, hiph'l verb, we prefer a singular, hiph'l as in 1 Esd. 9:16 ("chose for himself") and some MSS, because Ezra evidently made the selection himself.

16b וישרדל를 많은 대사본, 칠십인역, Vrs와 더불어 וישורדל로 읽는다. 마소라 본문(문자적으로 "다리우스의")에서 요드 י가 첨가되었는데 성경을 필사한 서기관의 시대착오의 실수로 보여진다.155)

---

153) Cf. 1 Esd. 9:14-15. 참고. 에스드라 상 9:14-15.
154) Williamson, *Ezra, Nehemiah*, 156.
155) *Ibid.*, 144.

16b וירדל שוירדל must be read with some MSS, LXX and Vrs ורדל ש. MT(lit. "of Darius") was only slightly different(the addition of י), and is probably to be explained as the work of a careless scribe who expected such a reference after the date.154)

17a 마소라 본문 대신에(헤이 ה가 없음) 칠십인역, 시리아역, 라틴역을 따른다.

17a We follow LXX, Syriac, and Vulgata instead of MT (without ה).

3-2-4-2. 해석 Interpretation

스가냐의 제안에 따라 예루살렘에서 대규모 집회가 열렸다. 출석이 강하게 요구되었는데, 불참할 경우 심한 처벌이 주어진다는 위협이 있었다(참고. 8절). 회중들은 주장하기를 대회의 참가 숫자가 많고 일기가 불순한 관계로 짧은 시간에 이 문제를 해결하기가 불가능하다고 했다. 이들의 제안을 따라 이 문제를 조사하기 위해 위원회를 지명하기로 결정했다. 비록 에스라의 개혁 제안에 대한 반대도 있었지만(15절), 대부분의 회중들은 동의를 했다.

In accord with Shecaniah's proposal there was held in Jerusalem a mass assembly, attendance at which was required under threat of severe penalties(cf. v. 8). The congregation argued that the great number of the assembly and the inclement weather prevented them from solving the matter in a short time. Following their proposal, it was decided to appoint a committee to investigate the matter. Although there was some opposition to Ezra's proposed reform(v. 15), the main body of the congregation were in agreement.

그러한 해결이 채택되어졌을 때 회중들은 확실하게 해산되었다. 16절과 17절에서 선택된 위원들이 그들의 작업을 어떻게 수행했는지에 대해 상술하고 있다. 조사는 열 번째 달(테벳, 양력으로 하면 12월과 1월 경) 초하루에 시작하여, 이듬해 첫 달(니산, 양력으로 3월과 4월 경) 초하루에 마쳤다.[156] 사마리아인, 가나아인을 포함한 다른 민족들로부터의 반응은 유대인들과 위원들에게 보고된 내용은 없었다.

When such a solution was accepted, apparently the assembly was dismissed. Verses 16 and 17 detail the manner in which the selected officials went about their work. The investigation commenced on the first of the tenth month (Tebet, December-January), and was completed on the first of the first month of the next year (Nisan, March-April).[155] We had no report of a response from the other peoples, such as Samaritans and Canaanites, to this Judean assembly and its proposed investigation.

3-2-4-2-1. 에스라 Ezra 10:9

"광장에": 성전의 바깥 광장이거나 수문 앞 광장이거나 율법이 읽혀진 장소를 말함(느 8:1, 3, 16; 참고. 대하 32:6; 욥 29:7; 잠 1:20)

"open square": Either the outer court of the temple or the open space before the Water Gate, where the law was read (Neh. 8:1, 3, 16; cf. 2 Chron. 32:6; Job 29:7; Prov. 1:20).

---

156) Fishbane insisted that the period referred to was from 20 December, 458 BC to 27 March, 457 (*Biblical Interpretation*, 115n).

"큰 비를": (키슬레브 월에 흔히 있던) 큰 비의 언급은 13절에 언급한 불순한 일기와 더불어 이곳에서는 심판의 일에 대한 상징적 뜻을 가리킨다. 이 단어의 히브리어(הגשמים)는 복수로 되어 있어 장대비와 같은 폭우를 가리킨다. 아홉 번째 달인 키슬레브(양력, 11월과 12월)는 우기의 중간에 해당되어 장마비가 내리는 시기였다(13절). 보통 우기는 10월에 보슬비로 시작되었고 4월 중순까지 비가 내린다. 12월과 1월은 또한 춥고 비가 내리는 때요 예루살렘은 화씨로 50-40도(섭씨 10-4도)이다. 이 회중의 많은 이들이 비로 인해 젖어서 떨기도 했지만 이 폭우 가운데 하나님의 진노하심 때문에 떨기도 했다(겔 13:11, 13을 보라). 폭우 때문에 그들은 어떤 조치도 취하지 못했다.

"the heavy rain": The casual mention of "the heavy rain" (which was usual in the month of Kislev) pointed to the symbolic meaning of the matter(judgment) here as well as the inclement weather in v. 13. The Hebrew for this word(הגשמים) is a plural of intensity, indicating heavy torrential rains. The ninth month, Kislev(November- December), was in the middle of the "rainy season" (v. 13), which began with light showers in October and lasted to mid-April. December and January were also cool rainy months, with temperatures in the 50's(F) and even 40's(F) in Jerusalem. The members of this congregation shivered not only because they were drenched, but also because they sensed divine displeasure in the heavy rains(see Ezek. 13:11, 13). The heavy rain prevented them from taking any effective steps.

3-2-4-2-2. 에스라 Ezra 10:14

"본성 장로들과 재판장": (보라. 스 7:25; 신 16:18, 19:12, 21:3, 19; 대하 29:10, 30:8; 룻 4:2). 지방 장로들과 재판장들은 가족과 마을의 역사를 알고 있기에 증거를 제시할 수 있었다.157)

"the elders and judges of each town": (see Ezra 7:25; Dt. 16:18, 19:12, 21:3, 19; 2 Chron. 29:10, 30:8; Ruth 4:2). The local elders and judges would be able to offer evidence from their personal knowledge of family and village history.156)

3-2-4-2-3. 에스라 Ezra 10:15

아마 이들 네 사람(아사헬의 아들 요나단, 디과의 아들 야스야, 므술람, 레위 사람 삽브대)[에스드라 상 9:14에 의하면 할레비가 추가되어 있고 마소라 본문에도 "레위인들"이 추가됨]이 이러한 조치에 반대했다(히브리어 문자적으로 "이 일에 반대하여 일어섰다"). 이것은 유대 공동체 회원들 가운데에는 에스라의 극적인 개혁을 실제로 지원하는 것이 상대적으로 약했다는 것을 의미했다. 두 가지 이유로 반대를 한 것 같다.

Perhaps these four men(five in 1 Esd. 9:14 which has Hallevi, even though MT has "the Levites" in this verse) opposed this measure (זאת עמדו על literally, "stood against this"). This meant that there was relatively little real support for Ezra's drastic reform among the Judean community members. There were two reasons for this opposition.

---

157) Clines, *Ezra, Nehemiah, Esther*, 130.

첫째는 그들 자신과 친척들을 보호하고 싶었다. 만약 므술람이 29절에 나오는 므술람[158]이라면, 그는 이방 여인과 결혼을 했다. 그는 이 조치가 너무 가혹하다고 생각했을 것이다. 두 번째 이유는 이 문제를 여기서 당장 해결한다는 것 보다 행동을 연기하자고 권면했다.[159] 삽브대는 율법이 공개적으로 낭독될 때에 회중들이 이해하도록 도운 자였다(느 8:7). 그의 이름은 나중에 예루살렘에서 살았던 레위 집안 가운데 지도자들 명단에도 있었다. 그는 신속하게 문제를 해결하는 데 반대를 했다.

The first reason was that they wanted to protect themselves and their relatives. If Meshullam was the Meshullam[158] of v. 29, he himself married a foreign woman. He would view the measure as being too harsh. The second reason was that they recommended to postpone action rather than settling the matter here and now.[159] Shabbethai(or Shabbethai) helped the congregation to understand the law at the public reading of the law(Neh. 8:7). His name was listed among those of leading Levites resident later on in Jerusalem. He would oppose the hurry decision.

3-2-4-2-4. 에스라 Ezra 10:16-17

에스라 자신은 조상들의 계보에 따라 선택된 가장 중심으로 평신도 지도자들로 구성된 위원회를 선발하였다. 본문은 위원들의 명단을 제공하지 않는다. 위원들은 삼 개월 내에 그들의 작업을 완수하

---

158) This name was popular among Jews of the Persian period. See K. L. Tallqvist, *Neubabylonisches Namenbuch*, Helsingfors, 1905, 113-114.
159) Blenkinsopp, *Ezra-Nehemiah*, 194.

여 약 111(칠십인역에서는 110)명의 유대인 남자들이 외국 부인들과 결혼하는 데 동참했음을 밝혀내었다.

Ezra himself selected the committee which was composed of the lay leaders(the heads of families) chosen by ancestral line. The text did not provide the list of the committee members. The committee completed their task in three months, discovering that about 111(LXX, 110) Judean men were guilty of marrying foreign women.

3-2-5. 이방 여인들과 결별한 남자들의 명단 (스 10:18-44) List of men who separated from foreign wives (10:18-44)

스 10:18 제사장의 무리 중에 이방 여인을 취한 자는 예수아 자손 중 요사닥의 아들과 그 형제 마아세야와 엘리에셀과 야립과 그달랴라. Among the priestly families who had married foreign women were the descendants of Jeshua son of Jozadak and his brothers :Maaseiah, Eliezer, Jarib, and Gedaliah. 19 그들은 다 손을 잡아 맹세하여 그 아내를 보내기로 하고 또 그 죄를 인하여 수양 하나를 속건제로 드렸으며 They gave their hand to expel their wives [a] and their guilt offering was a ram from the flock for their guilt. 20 또 임멜 자손 중에는 하나니와 스바댜요 Of the sons of Immer:Hanani and Zebadiah; 21 하림 자손 중에는 마아세야와 엘리야와 스마야와 여히엘과 웃시야요 of the sons of Harim: Maaseiah, Elijah, Shemaiah, Jehiel, and Uzziah; 22 바스훌 자손 중에는 엘료에내와 마아세야와 이스마엘과 느다넬

과 요사밧과 엘라사였더라 of the sons of Pashhur: Elioenai, Maaseiah, Ishmael, Nethanel, Jozabad, and Elasah; 23 레위 사람 중에는 요사밧과 시므이와 글라야라 하는 글리다와 브다히야와 유다와 엘리에셀이었더라 of the Levites: Jozabad, Shimei, Kelaiah who is Kelita, Pethahiah, Judah, and Eliezer. 24 노래하는 자 중에는 엘리아십이요 문지기 중에는 살룸과 델렘과 우리였더라 Of the singers: Eliashib. Of the gatekeepers: Shallum, Telem, and Uri. 25 이스라엘 중에는 바로스 자손 중 라먀와 잇시야와 말기야와 미야민과 엘르아살과 말기야와 브나야요 Of the Israelites: of the sons of Parosh: Ramiah, Izziah, Malchijah, Mijamin, Eleazar, Malchijah [a], and Benaiah; 26 엘람 자손 중 맛다냐와 스가랴와 여히엘과 압디와 여레못과 엘리야요 of the sons of Elam: Mattaniah, Zechariah, Jehiel, Abdi, Jeremoth, and Elijah; 27 삿두 자손 중 엘료에내와 엘리아십과 맛다냐와 여레못과 사밧과 아시사요 of the sons of Zattu: Elioenai, Eliashib, Mattaniah, Jeremoth, Zabad, and Aziza; 28 베배 자손 중 여호하난과 하나냐와 삽배와 아들래요 of the sons of Bebai: Jehohanan, Hananiah, Zabbai, and Athlai; 29 바니 자손 중 므술람과 말룩과 아다야와 야숩과 스알과 여레못이요 of the sons of Bani: Meshullam, Malluch, Adaiah, Jashub, Sheal, and Jeremoth; 30 바핫모압 자손 중 앗나와 글랄과 브나야와 마아세야와 맛다냐와 브살렐과 빈누이와 므낫세요 of the sons of Pahath-moab: Adna, Chelal, Benaiah, Maaseiah, Mattaniah, Bezalel, Binnui, and Manasseh; 31 하림 자손 중 엘리에셀과 잇시야와 말기야와 스마야와 시므온과 of the sons of Harim: Eliezer, Isshijah, Malchijah, Shemaiah, and Shimeon; 32 베냐민과 말룩과 스마랴요 Benjamin, Malluch, and Shemariah; 33 하숨 자손 중 맛드내와 맛닷다와 사밧과 엘리벨렛과 여레매와 므낫세와 시므이요 of the sons of Hashum: Mattenai, Mattattah, Zabad, Eliphelet, Jeremai, Manasseh, and Shimei; 34 바니 자손 중 마아대와 아므람과 우엘과 of the sons of Bani [a]: Maadai, Amram, and Uel; 35 브나야와 베드야와 글루히와 Benaiah, Bedeiah, Cheluhi, 36 와냐와 므레못과 에랴십과 Vaniah, Meremoth, Eliashib, 37 맛다냐와 맛드내와 야아수와 Mattaniah, Mattenai, Jaasai[a], 38 바니와 빈누이와 시므이와 Bani, Binnui [a], Shimei, 39 셀레먀와 나단과 아다야와 Shelemiah, Nathan, Adaiah, 40 막나드배와 사새와 사래와 Machnadebai, Shashai, Sharai, 41 아사렐과 셀레먀와 스마랴와 Azarel, Shelemiah, Shemariah, 42 살룸과 아마랴와 요셉이요 Shallum, Amariah, and Joseph; 43 느보 자손 중 여이엘과 맛디디야와 사밧과 스비내와 잇도와 요엘과 브나야더라 of the sons of Nebo: Jeiel, Mattithiah, Zabad, Zebina, Jaddai, Joel, and Benaiah. 44 이상은 모두 이방 여인을 취한 자라 그중에 자녀를 낳은 여인도 있었더라 All these had married foreign women, among whom were some women who had borne children [a].

3-2-5-1. 본문 노트 Texual Notes

19절 상. 레 5:15를 보라.
19a See Lev. 5:15.

25절상. 에스드라 상 9:26에서 "하사비야"로 읽고 칠십인역에서는 "아사비야"로 읽음.
25a 1 Esd. 9:26 reads "Hashabiah" (LXX, "Asabia").

34절상. 칠십인역에서 "바누이"로 읽으나 38절에서는 "비누이"로 읽음. 루돌프는 여기서는 "비그바이"로 읽어야 한다고 생각한다. 34절에서 "바니"로 나온다.
34a LXX "Banoui," but "Binnui" appears in v. 38. Rudolph thinks "Bigvai"ought to be read here since Bani occurs in v. 34.

38절상. 칠십인역에서 "비누이"의 아들들 가운데로 읽음.
38a LXX reads "of the sons of Binnui."

44절상. 마소라 본문의 뜻은 불확실함. 문자적으로 "그들로부터 아내들이 있었고 그들인 아들들을 두었다." 이것은 단순히 남자들이 아내들과 자녀들이 있음을 뜻하는 것 같다. 에스드라 상 9:36하 반절은 스 10:3의 관점에서 문제가 있는 본문을 교정하여 "그들이 여인들과 그들의 자녀들을 내어 보냈다"(NRSV)로 읽음.[160]
44a Meaning of MT is uncertain, lit. "and there were wives

---

[160] Fishbane, *Biblical Interpretation*, 115.

from them and they placed sons" This seems simply to note that the men had wives and children. 1 Esd. 9:36b corrects this troubling text in the light of Ezra 10:3, and reads "they sent them away with their children"(NRSV).160)

3-2-5-2. 본문 형식 Form

본문의 문학적 형식은 사람들의 명단이다. 에스라와 느헤미야서에는 많은 명단들이 있다. 아마 에스라와 느헤미야의 4분의 1이 명단, 대부분 사람들의 명단으로 이뤄지고 있다.161)

The literary form of the text is a list of persons. There are many lists in the books of Ezra and Nehemiah. Approximately one quarter of the books of Ezra and Nehemiah is made up of lists, mostly lists of people.161)

이 명단에 대해 윌리엄슨은 결론내리기를 이 명단은 처음부터 에스라 비망록(EM)에 포함되어 있었다. 현재의 형태는 후기 편집활동의 결과임을 알 수 있다.162)

Concerning the setting of this list, Williamson concluded that the list was included in the Ezra Memoir (EM) from the start, and its present form may owe something to later editorial activity.162)

이 명단 이외에 에스라-느헤미야서에는 여러 관료 명단들과 지명 명단이 있다. 1차 귀환자들(스 2장과 느 7장), 에스라와 함께 귀환한 자들(스 8:1-19), 건축자들(느 3:1-32), 통역자들(느 8:4-7, 9:4-5), 개혁 문서에

---

161) T. C. Eskenazi, *In An Age of Prose: A Literary Approach to Ezra-Nehemiah*, Atlanta: Scholars Press, 1988, 180.
162) Williamson, *Ezra, Nehemiah*, 148-149.

서명한 자들(느 10:1-28), 서기관 족보(느 12:1-26), 성벽 봉헌 참석자들(느 12:31-43), 유다와 베냐민 지역에 정착한 마을들(느 11:25-36), 그리고 인구 조사(느 11:3-24) 명단이 있다.163)

Besides this list, there are several personnel lists and one topographical list in Ezra-Nehemiah: of those in the first return (Ezra 2 and Neh.7), of returnees with Ezra(Ezra 8:1-19), of builders (Neh. 3:1-32), of interpreters(Neh. 8:4-7, 9:4-5), of signatories on the reform document(Neh. 10:1-28), of clerical genealogies(Neh. 12:1-26), of participants in wall-dedication(Neh. 12:31-43), of occupied towns in Judah and Benjamin(Neh. 11:25-36) and a census(Neh. 11:3-24).163)

이 명단의 순서는 2장(세스바살과 함께 귀환한 이들의 명단, 느 7:6-73상, 지도자들, 평신도들, 성전 관리들, 애매한 족보의 사람들, 종들, 동물들)보다는 순서를 거꾸로 하는 8장(에스라와 함께 귀환한 제사장들과 평신도들 명단)의 순서를 따르고 있다. 제사장들 먼저, 평신도들 그 다음이다. 발표되지 않는 본문에 근거하여, 귀환자들 3만 명 중, 성직자들 중 27명의 이름과 평신도들 가운데 84명 이름을 합쳐 111명(칠십인역 110명)이 거명되고 있다.164)

The order of the list follows that of chapter 8(a list of priestly and lay clans who returned with Ezra) - clergy first, then laity - rather than that of chapter 2(a list of those who first returned with Sheshbassar = Neh. 7:6-73a, leaders, laymen, temple officials, those of dubious genealogy, servants, and animals), which reverses the sequence. On the basis of the unemended text, 27 names of clergy occur and 84 names

---

163) Myers, *Ezra, Nehemiah*, 223-245.
164) *Ibid.*, 87; Williamson, *op. cit.*, 157-158.

of laymen, or a total of 111(LXX 110) persons in a group of around 30,000.[164]

총합은 명단에 따라 다소 차이가 있다: 칠십인역에는 27명 성직자들 및 82명(+2 혹은 3, 37절 끝과 38절 시작에서 본문의 불확실 때문) 평신도들이 포함되어 있다; 에스드라 상 9장에서는 26명의 성직자와 75(혹 76)명의 평신도로 101명(만약 32절의 시몬 코사메우스가 두 사람으로 읽히면 1명 추가).[165] 통혼한 자의 수가 2장의 인구 조사된 4,236명에 비해 상대적으로 매우 적은 숫자였다. 세 가지 설명이 가능하다: (a) 통혼 문제가 수면에 오를 만큼 심각하지 않았다. (b) 개혁이 역대기 사가가 주장한 대로 성공적이지 못했다. (c) 이 명단은 부분적인 명단일 뿐인데 마지막 편집자가 본래 명단을 축소한 것이다.

The totals vary somewhat in the lists: LXX has 27 clergy and 82(+2 or 3) laymen, which comes to 110(+2 or 3, due to the uncertainty in the text at the end of v. 37 and the beginning of v. 38); 1 Esd. 9 has 26 clergy and 75(or 76) laymen, which comes to 101(+1, if Simon Chosamaeus in v. 32 is to be read as two names).[165] The number of offenders was extraordinarily small considering the census figures(4,236) in chapter 2. Three explanations suggest themselves: (a) the problem was not as serious as appears on the surface, (b) the reform was not as successful as the Chronicler would have us believe, (c) this was only a partial list, for the final editor has abbreviated the original list.

---

165) Williamson, *ibid.*, 157f; Clines, *Ezra, Nehemiah, Esther*, 131; W. Rudolph, *Esra und Nehemia samt 3. Esra*, Tübingen, 1949, 97-98.

3-2-5-3. 해석 Interpretation

개혁 설화는 그들의 결혼을 파혼시키면서 이방 부인들을 쫓아 내보낸다는 데 동의한 포로 귀환민들의 명단으로 끝이 난다. 명단에는 17명의 제사장들(18-22절, 에스라 2:36-39에 제사장들 네 가족이 제사장들의 4분의 1에 해당된다), 이중 네 가정은 여호수아 대제사장 가족이며, 6명은 레위인들(23절), 한 명은 노래하는 자(24절 상), 3명은 문지기들(24절 하), 그리고 84명의 평신도들(25-43절)로 모두 111명이다.

The reform narrative closes with a detailed roster of the exiles who agreed to dissolve their marriages and send their foreign wives away. The list included 17 priests(vv. 18-22; in Ezra 2:36-39, four clans of priests were about a fourth of the total), 4 of whom are from the high priestly family of Joshua; 6 Levites(v. 23), 1 singer(v. 24a), 3 gatekeepers(v. 24b), and 84 laymen(vv. 25-43), a total of 111 persons.

3-2-5-3-1 에스라 10:18-22 (제사장들의 명단과 속건제): Ezra 10:18-22 (list of priests and a guilt offering):

17명의 제사장들이 죄를 지었다. 명단의 시작은 대제사장 예수아의 자손들(마아세야, 엘리에셀)과 그의 형제들(야립, 그달랴)이다. 대제사장 집안 출신인 이들 네 명의 남자들은 그들의 범죄를 인정해서(참. 레 21:14-15 "과부나 이혼된 여인이나 더러운 여인이나 기생을 취하지 말고 자기 백성 중 처녀를 취하여 아내를 삼아 그 자손으로 백성 중에서 더럽히지 말지니 나는 그를 거룩하게 하는 여호와임이니라"), 숫양 한 마리로 속건제를 드렸다. 그 서원과 속건제가 대제사장 가족과 연관할 때만 언급되었다. 나중에 살피겠지만 느헤미야 때에 한 대제사장 가문이 이방 여인과의 통혼 문제에 포함(느 13:28-29)되었다. 대제사장 가문 이외에 네 명의 제사장 가정들이 유죄로 판명 났다(참고. 느 23:36-39).

A total of seventeen priests were found guilty. Heading the list were sons of the high priest Jeshua(Maaseiah, Eliezer) and his brothers(Jarib, Gedaliah). These four men from the high priestly family acknowledged their transgression(cf. Lev. 21:14-15, "the priest shall marry a virgin of his own kin, so that he may not profane his offspring among his kin"), and then offered a ram as a guilt offering. The pledge and guilt offering were mentioned only in connection with the high priestly family members. As we shall see later, one high priestly family at the time of Nehemiah was involved in foreign marriage alliances(Neh. 13:28-29). Besides the family members of the high priest, four priestly families (cf. Neh. 23: 36-39) were found guilty.

19절 "손을 내밀어"(NRSV "스스로 서원하여"): 이런 태도는 어떤 결정을 내릴 때 거룩한 맹세를 표시할 때 취하는 것이었다. 왕상 10:15와 겔 17:18에서는 악수를 한다.

"gave their hand" in v.19:(NRSV "pledged themselves"): This gesture signifies a solemn covenant to make a decision about something. We find the symbolic use of the handshake in 2 Kgs. 10:15 and Ezek. 17:18.

19절 "숫양 한 마리를 속건제로 드렸으며": 대제사장 집안의 통혼의 죄로 인하여(ma'al, 스 9:2, 4, 10:2, 6, 10; 느 13:27), 실수로 거룩성을 범했을 때 드리는 속건제를 드려야 했다. 속건제는 고의적으로 죄를 범했을 때(레 6:1-7)나 혹 성물에 대해 부지중에 범죄하였을 때(레 5:14-19; 참고. 민 5:8) 드렸고, 흔히 이런 경우 숫양을 번제로 드려졌다(레 5:15, 6:6).

"their guilt offering was a ram" in 19: For the sin of intermarriage (which is referred to as ma'al Ezra 9:2, 4, 10:2, 6, 10; Neh. 13:27) in a high priest family, the correct offering was a guilt offering (אשם) which signified that the wrong had been righted. A guilt offering was to be made for sins committed unintentionally(Lev. 5:14-19; cf. Num. 5:8) as well as intentionally(Lev. 6:1-7), and ordinarily the offering was a ram in either case(Lev. 5:15, 6:6).

3-2-5-3-2. 에스라 10:23-24 (레위인들의 명단) Ezra 10:23-24 (List of the Levites)

레위인들 중 적은 숫자(10명만) 통혼 죄를 지었다. 레위인들(참고 출 6:25)은 항상 명단에서 제사장들과 연관이 되었다(참고. 에스라 2:40). 노래하는 자 1명과 문지기들 3명이 이 일에 연루되었다. 성전에서 일하는 자들(느디님 같은 집안의 자손, 2:43-54) 혹은 솔로몬의 종들의 후손들(2:55-57)은 이 명단에서 발견되지 않는다. 그들은 이미 외국인들 혹은 율법 밖의 사람들로 취급받았기 때문이었다.[166]

A small number (only ten) of the Levites were singled out as being guilty of intermarriage. The Levites(cf. Ex. 6:25) were always associated with the priests(cf. Ezra 2:40) in the list. It is striking that only one singer and three gatekeepers were involved. No

---

166) Bowman, *ibid.*, 659.

temple servants(such as Nethinim)(2:43-54) or descendants of Solomon's servants(2:55-57) were found in the list, for they were already treated largely as foreigners and outside the law.[166]

"그리다가 그라이야": 에스드라 상 9:23보다 더 오래된 각주에 보면 그라이야가 그리다였다(참고. 느 8:7, 10:10).[167]

Kelaiah who was Kelita: Kelaiah was identified as Kelita(cf. Neh. 8:7, 10:10) in a gloss older than 1 Esd. 9:23.[167]

3-2-5-3-3. 에스라 10:25-43 (평신도 명단, 스 2:3-20을 보라) Ezra 10:25-43 (List of the laity, see Ezra 2:3-20)

이 명단은 에스라 2:3-35에서 보는 평신도 이름들과 같은 이름을 많이 찾아 볼 수 있는 죄를 지은 평신도 명단이다. 43절의 "느보"는 바벨론의 신 나부(사 46:1을 보라)의 히브리어 식 이름으로 여기서만 개인 이르므로 나온다.

This list is a long list of the guilty laymen in which we may observe a number of the same family names as in Ezra 2:3-35. "Nebo" in v. 43: The Hebrew equivalent of the name of the Babylonian god Nabu(see Isa. 46:1), found only here as a personal name.

---

167) Ibid.

3-2-5-3-3. 에스라 10:44 Ezra 10:44

마지막 구절(문자적으로 "그들 가운데 어떤 이들은 여성들이며, 그들(남성)이 자녀들을 낳았다")로 된 문장이 전승 과정 속에서 일부가 파괴된 것 같다. 이 절은 에스드라 상 9:36에 의하면 관련된 남자들이 맹세를 충실히 지켜(참고. 10:3-5) 그들의 이방 아내들과 낳은 자식들을 모두 내어 쫓았다고 회복될 수 있다(NRSV, REB). 통혼의 결과 자식들이 태어났으나 이혼 절차를 중지시키는 이유로 채택되지 못했다. 이방 부인들과 자식들은 자기들의 민족으로 돌아갔을 것이다. 관련된 여인들과 자식들에게 닥친 고통과는 별도로 이런 이혼들이 유대 공동체 가운데 살았던 이웃들에게는 큰 미움의 대상이 되었을 것이 분명하다.

The last verse(lit. "and some of them were women, and they (masc.) had given sons") seemed to have been partly destroyed in transmission. This verse can be restored on the basis of 1 Esd. 9:36 which suggested that the men concerned put away both their wives and their children(NRSV, REB), as the faithful had sworn to do(cf. 10:3-5). Some of the marriages had produced children, but this was not accepted as a reason for halting the divorce proceeding. It may be presumed that the foreign women and their children returned to their homes. It was not difficult to see that, apart from the hardships to the women and children concerned, these divorces might have created a great deal of resentment among the Judean neighbors.

3-3. 느헤미야 13:23-30 주석 Exegesis of Nehemiah 13:23-30

다리우스 1세(일명 다리우스 대제, 550-486, 재임 522-486, BC)[168]가 그의 통치 20년째인 해(502 BC, Neh. 2:1-10, 5:4)에 자기의 술 맡은 관원(당시 왕으로부터 가장 신임 받던 장관)인 느헤미야를 페르샤의 유대국의 총리로 임명하였다. 그는 예루살렘에 돌아오자마자 산발랏, 도비야, 게셈으로부터 반대에 직면한 가운데 엄청나게 신속하게 무너진 성벽을 재건하였다(느 4:1-7:5).

DariusI(550-486 BC, rule during 522-486 BC)[168] appointed Nehemiah, his cupbearer(the royal sincerest official), as the governor over Judah in the twentieth year of his rule(502 BC, Neh. 2:1-10, 5:4). Once Nehemiah returned to Jerusalem, he rebuilt the wall of Jerusalem with deliberate haste in spite of opposition from Sanballat, Tobiah and Geshem(Neh. 4:1-7:5).

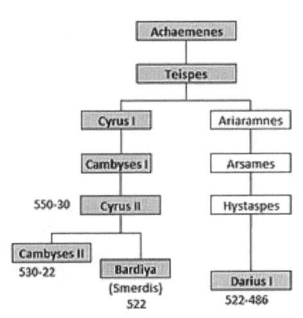

느헤미야서에 기록된 성벽 건축과 다른 사건들이 그의 총리직 첫 해에 일어났다. 하나님의 도우심으로(느 6:15-16) 52일 만에 성벽을 재건한 후 느헤미야는 유대 공동체의 사회적-종교적 개혁과 영적 부흥운동을 일으켰다. 개혁은 통혼 금지

---

168) 종전의 견해로는 느헤미야가 아닥사스다 1세(465-424 BC) 치하의 장관으로 알려졌는데, 본 연구에서는 베히스툰 석비에 의해 소개된 계보대로 다리우스 대제 20년에 임명받음으로 본다. Wikipedia: "Darius" Lineage of Darius the Great according to the Behistun Inscription.

(느 10:30. 히브리 원문에는 10:31), 안식일에 상업 행위 금지(10:31상; 출 23:12, 34:21, 35:3; 민 15:32-36; 암 8:5), 토지에 대한 안식년 준수(10:31하; 출 23:10), 빚으로 인해 노예된 자들의 불평에 관한 법(느 5; 신 15:1-3), 성전 봉사 제공과 다른 헌금들(느 10:32-39)이 포함되어 있었다. 왜냐하면 페르샤 정부의 관용이 그리 길지 못했기 때문이었다.[169] 그가 12년 연속 예루살렘에 머물렀는지는 확실하지 않다(느 5:14).[170] 그의 총독 첫 임기를 큰 성공으로 수행했다.

The building of the wall and other major events recorded in the book of Nehemiah had occurred within about the first year of his governorship. After the rebuilding of the wall had been accomplished in fifty-two days with the help of God(Neh. 6:15-16), Nehemiah moved on to the spiritual revival and socio-religious reform of the Judean community. The reform included prohibition against intermarriage(Neh. 10:30, Heb. 10:31), interdiction of Sabbath commercial activity(Neh. 10:31a, Ex. 23:12, 34:21, 35:3, Num. 15:32-36, Amos 8:5), observance of the seventh year of rest for the land(Neh. 10:31b, Ex. 23:10) laws related to the complaint of debt slavery(Neh. 5, Deut. 15:1-3), and provision for the temple service and other contributions(Neh. 10:32-39), because the generosity of the Persian government would not last long.[169] It is questionable whether he had remained in Jerusalem the whole twelve years(Neh. 5:14).[170] He served his first term of administration with great success.

---

[169] See Vos, 123; Blenkinsopp, *Ezra-Nehemiah*, 315.
[170] Darius I (502-490 BC). 개역, 개역개정에서 아닥사스다로 나오는 것은 페르샤 언어로 '위대한 왕'이란 호칭으로 다리우스 대왕(Darius I)을 가리킨다.

다리우스 1세 황제의 32년(BC 490년)에, 그는 페르샤 제국의 수도인 수사성으로 돌아왔다. 어느 정도 시간이 흐른 후(아마 1년 내에) 그는 페르샤 왕에게 허락을 받고 예루살렘으로 돌아가서(느 13:6-7) 다리우스 1세 33년(489 BC)에 총독 2기를 봉사했다. 그는 돌아와서 바로 성전을 청결하게 하고, 안식일을 회복하고 통혼을 금지시켰다(느 13:4-31).

In the thirty-second year of Darius I(490 BC), he went back to Susa the capital of the Persian empire. After some time(probably within one year) he was permitted to return by the Persian king and was back to Jerusalem(Neh. 13:6-7) for his second term of governorship in the thirty-third year of Artaxerxes I(489 BC). Soon after his return, Nehemiah set about reforming the Judean community by cleansing the temple, restoring the Sabbath, and inveighing against intermarriage(Neh. 13:4-31).

느헤미야서의 개요는 에스라 개요보다 더 시민적이고 세속적이다. 그러나 제사장의 관점에서 씌여졌다. 느헤미야서는 크게 두 부분으로 나뉘어져 있다. 1-7장은 성벽 재건에 대한 사건에 대해 말하며, 8-13장에서는 에스라와 느헤미야의 사회적이며 종교적인 개혁을 서술되고 있다. 우리의 본문(느 13:23-30)은 느헤미야가 총독 2기를 수행하기 위해 예루살렘으로 돌아온 후에 일어난 일을 적고 있다. 23-27절에서 다룬 통혼문제에 관한 결론으로 29절 하반절에서 마무리되고 있다.

The orientation of the book of Nehemiah is more civil and secular than that of the book of Ezra, but it was still written from the priestly point of view. The book is divided into two main parts, with chs. 1-7 telling the event of the rebuilding of the wall and chs. 8-13 describing the social and religious reforms of Ezra and Nehemiah. Our text(13:23-30) was written after Nehemiah's return to Jerusalem for his second term of governorship. The pericope closed in v.29b with a notation that referred to the problem of intermarriage dealt with in vv. 23-27.

에스라 10:18-44에 나오는 죄 지은 유대 남자들의 명단 이후 유대 가정들의 생활에 대한 더 이상의 보고를 듣지 못한다. 그러나 에스라의 개혁은 예루살렘에 제한됨이 분명하고, 그의 통혼에 대한 공격은 지속적인 영향을 마치지 않았다. 왜냐하면 느헤미야도 유대인들 가운데 통혼을 발견했기 때문이다. 심지어 대제사장의 손자도 사마리아의 총독의 딸과 결혼을 했다(느 13:28).[171]

We have no further report of the Judean families' life after list of the guilty Judean men in Ezra 10:18-44. But it is clear that Ezra's reform was limited to Jerusalem, and his attack on intermarriage had little lasting effect, for Nehemiah also found intermarriage common among the Judeans. Even a grandson of the high priest was married to a daughter of the governor of Samaria(Neh. 13:28).[171]

---

[171] 요세푸스의 보고에 의하면 "많은 제사장들과 이스라엘 백성들이 이 시기에 이런 통혼에 연루되었다…예루살렘의 한 대제사장 집안의 사람이 암몬 자손들 중 유력한 집안의 여인과 결혼했다(신 23:3에 의하면 암몬 자손이나 모압 자손은 여호와의 총회에 들어가지 못한다고 되어 있다). According to the report of Josephus, "many priests and Israelites were involved in such intermarriage in this period…one high priestly family of Jerusalem intermarried with a prominent family of Ammonites(cf. Deut. 23:3 "Ammonites or Moabites shall not be admitted into the congregation of Yahweh; none of their descendants")" (Ant. XI, 312; XII, 160).3

3-3-1. 통혼의 결과와 느헤미야의 반응 (느 13:23-27) Result of intermarriage and response of Nehemiah (Neh. 10:23-27)

느헤미야 Nehemiah 13:23 그때에 내가 또 본즉 유다 사람이 아스돗과 암몬과 모압 여인을 취하여 아내를 삼았는데 In those days also, I found that [a] some Judeans had married [b] women of Ashdod, Ammon, and Moab; 24 그 자녀가 아스돗 방언을 절반쯤은 하여도 유다 방언은 못하니 그 하는 말이 각 족속의 방언이므로 Half of their children spoke the language of Ashdod but could not speak the language of Judah, and [a] spoke according to the language of each people [a]. 25 내가 책망하고 저주하며 두어 사람을 때리고 그 머리털을 뽑고 말하기를 "너희는 너희 딸들로 저희 아들들에게 주지 말고 너희 아들들이나 너희를 위하여 저희 딸을 데려오지 않겠다"라고 하나님을 가리켜 맹세하라 하고 And I contended with them, cursed them, flogged them, pulled out their hair; and I had made them take an oath by God, saying, "You shall not give your daughters to their sons in marriage[a], nor shall you take any of their daughters for your sons or yourselves. 26 또 말하기를 "옛적에 이스라엘 왕 솔로몬이 이 일로 범죄하지 아니하였느냐? 그는 열국 중에 비길 왕이 없이 하나님의 사랑을 입은 자라. 하나님이 그로 왕을 삼아 온 이스라엘을 다스리게 하셨으나 이방 여인이 그로 범죄케 하였나니 Was it not on account of these that King Solomon of Israel sinned? There was not a king like him among many nations, and he was beloved by God, who made him king over all Israel. Yet even he was led by foreign wives into sin. 27 너희가 이방 여인을 취하여 크게 악을 행하여 우리 하나님께 범죄하는 것을 우리가 어찌 용납하겠느냐? How, then, can we listen to[a] you and do this great wrong, breaking faith with our God by marrying foreign women?

3-3-1-1. 본문 노트 Textual Notes

23a절. 관계대명사인 'ăšer("누구, 어느")가 없다.
v.23a This is a relative clause without 'ăšer "who, which."

23b절. 에스라 10:2b의 본문 노트를 보라.
23b See textual note on Ezra 10:2b.

24a-a절. 마소라 본문에 문자적으로 "백성의 언어와 백성에 따라서." 칠십인역에는 없다. 암몬 사람들과 모압 사람들을 포함시키기 위해 첨가된 어구 주해로 보임.[172)]

24a-a MT: literally "according to the language of people and people," absent from LXX. This may be a gloss added to include Ammonites and Moabites.[172)]

25a절. 저자에 의해 "혼인관계로"가 첨가됨.
25a "in marriage" supplied by the writer.

---

172) Blenkinsopp, *Ezra-Nehemiah*, 362; Williamson, 393.

27a절. נשמע를 일인칭 복수 미완료 칼 동사로 번역함. 그러나 3인칭 남성 단수 완료형 니팔로 뜻은 "너희들에 대해 …한 것을 들으며…"인데 훨씬 덜 자연스럽다. 본절의 시작하는 단어 순서를 좋아해서, 솔로몬과 느헤미야의 시대 사람들 사이를 대조하며 가장 강조점을 두고 있다.[173)]

27a We translate נשמע as first-person plural imperfect Qal. But it could also be third-person masc. sing. perfect Niphal, meaning something like, "and as for you, is it heard to do…" which, however, was much less natural. In its favor was the word order at the start of the verse, which put most emphasis on the contrast between Solomon and Nehemiah's contemporaries.[173)]

3-3-1-2. 문학 형식 Literary Form

본문은 느헤미야의 총독 2기 동안 행한 개혁을 보고하고 있는 비망록(1인칭 단수 설화)에 속한다(느 13:4-31). 우리 본문은 구조적으로 바로 전의 본문 느 13:15-22과 병행을 이루는데, 이 두 구절은 "그때에 내가 본즉"으로 시작한다. 이들은 느헤미야의 반응을 일으킨 문제 상황을 기술하고 있다. 그의 반응은 역사에 호소하는 충고의 형태를 취하고 있다.[174)]

This text belongs to the memoir(the first person singular narrative) which reported Nehemiah's reform during his second term as governor(13:4-31). The text is structurally parallel with the previous passage(13:15-22), for these two passages open in the

---

173) Blenkinsopp, *ibid*.; Williamson, *ibid*.
174) Blenkinsopp, *ibid*., 358.

same formulaic manner "in those days I found." They describe a problematic situation which evoked a response from Nehemiah, and the response took the form of remonstrance with appeal to history.[174]

3-3-1-3. 해석 Interpretation

느헤미야는 BC 490년에 다시 돌아온 직후, 어떤 유대인들이 아스돗, 암몬, 모압 여인들과 결혼했다는 것을 알고 매우 화를 냈다. 일찍이 에스라와 느헤미야의 회중들, 지도자들, 레위인들, 제사장들은 하나님의 성전을 도와 그들 스스로를 지역 백성들로부터 헤어지기로 언약을 맺었다(느 9:38-10:39).

Soon after his return to Jerusalem in 490 BC, Nehemiah was very angry to find that some Judeans married women of Ashdod, Ammon, and Moab. Earlier the congregation of Ezra and Nehemiah, including the leaders, Levites, and priests, made a covenant to support God's house and to separate themselves from the peoples of the lands(Neh. 9:38-10:39).

그 당시, 회중들은 다음과 같이 서약을 했다: "우리 딸은 이 땅 백성에게 주지 아니하고 우리 아들을 위하여 저희 딸을 데려오지 아니하며"(느 10:30, 히브리어 원문 10:31). 이제 그는 제사장들과 레위인들을 모든 이방적 요소들로부터 정결케 하는 데 최선을 다했다. 왜냐하면 이방 영향들로부터 격리시켜야 예배의 순수성을 보전하면서 동시에 율법을 더욱 성실히 준수할 수 있게 하기 때문이었다. 성전예배와 유대인 가족들의 순수성을 지키지 않으면, 유대 공동체는 외국 정부 아래서 살아남기 어려웠다. 특히 주변의 이방 여인들과 통혼하는 일은 유대 공동체를 통째로 삼킬 수 있었다. 왜냐하면 그 결과 하나님의 백성이라는 정체성을 잃을 수 있었기 때문이다.

At that time, the congregation took a pledge as follows: "And that we would not give our daughters unto the people of the land, nor take their daughters for our sons:"(Neh. 10:30; MT 10:31). Now he did his best to cleanse the priests and the Levites from everything foreign, for separation from foreign influence derived from an increasingly intense adherence to the law as well as to insistence on purity of worship. Without the maintenance of the purity of temple worship and of Judean families, the Judean community could hardly have survived under foreign government. Especially intermarriage with foreign peoples surrounding them would totally engulfed the Judean community, with the result that they would lose their identity as the people of God.

3-3-1-3-1. 느 10:23-24 (통혼의 결과) Neh. 10:23-24 (result of intermarriage)

어떤 유대인들은 아스돗, 암몬, 모압의 여인들과 통혼했다. 그런 통혼들이 심각한 문제를 야기했는데, 그 자녀들이 유다 언어를 구사할 수 없었다. 느헤미야와 그를 지지하는 이들은 믿기를 그들의 언어는 이스라엘 공동체의 독특한 정체성을 유지하는 데 필수적이라는 것이다.

Some Judeans had intermarried with women from Ashdod, Ammon, and Moab. Such intermarriages led to a serious problem: the children could not speak the language of Judah. Nehemiah and his supporters believed that their language indicated the survival of the distinctive identity of the Israelite community.

"아스돗"(참고 느 4:7; 사 20:1): 아스돗은 예루살렘의 남서쪽에 위치한 블레셋 고대 다섯 성읍 중 하나였다. 이 도시는 가자 북동쪽 18마일에 떨어진 곳으로 지중해 근처에 있다.
"Ashdod"(cf. Neh. 4:7; Isa. 20:1): Ashdod was one of the five ancient Philistine cities south-west of Jerusalem (1 Sam. 6:17). This city was located near the Mediterranean Sea about 18 miles northeast of Gaza.

"암몬과 모압"(참고. 창 19:30-38; 신 2:9, 19): 이 두 족속들은 아브라함의 후손들과 지독한 원수들이 되었다(보라. 삼상 14:47; 대하 20:1). 암몬과 모압은 신 23:3-6의 성경 내의 주석이었던 느 13:1-3에 나오는 요약과 연결고리를 제공한다:
"Ammon and Moab" (cf. Gen. 19:30-38; Dt. 2:9, 19): These two nations had become bitter enemies of Abraham's descendants(see, 1 Sam. 14:47; 2 Chron. 20:1). Ammon and Moab provided a link back to the summary account in Neh. 13:1-3 which was another inner-biblical exegesis of Deut. 23:3-6:

> 느 13:1 그날에 모세의 책을 낭독하여 백성에게 들렸는데 그 책에 기록하기를 암몬 사람과 모압 사람은 영영히 하나님의 회에 들어오지 못하리니 On that day they read in the book of Moses in the audience of the people; and therein was found written, that the Ammonite and the Moabite should

not come into the congregation of God for ever; 2 왜냐하면 그들이 양식과 물로 이스라엘 자손을 영접하지 아니하고 도리어 발람에게 뇌물을 주어 저주하게 하였음이라. 그러나 우리 하나님이 그 저주를 돌이켜 복이 되게 하셨다 하였는지라. Because they met not the children of Israel with bread and with water, but hired Balaam against them, that he should curse them: howbeit our God turned the curse into a blessing. 3 백성이 이 율법을 듣고 곧 섞인 무리를 이스라엘 가운데서 몰수히 분리케 하였느니라. Now it came to pass, when they had heard the law, that they separated from Israel all the mixed multitude.

아스돗 방언: 알트에 의하면,[175] 이 언어는 아람어 혹은 블레셋 언어의 방언 형태이다. 모압과 암몬의 언어는 메사의 석비에서 배울 수 있듯이 히브리어와 매우 밀접하다. 모압어, 암몬어, 히브리어는 상호간에 이해할 수 있음을 추정한다. "the language of Ashdod": This language could be a dialectal form of Aramaic or Philistine, according to Alt.[175] And the language of Moab and Ammon were very close to Hebrew, as we know from the Mesha inscription. We assume that Moabite, Ammonite and Hebrew were mutually comprehensible.

"유다 방언(문자적으로 유대어)": 우리가 히브리어로 아는 유일한 히브리 용어이다[참고. 왕하 18:26, 28(=사 36:11, 13, 대하 32:18)]. 유대인들

---

[175] A. Alt, Pal stinajahrbuch des deutschen evangelischen Institutes f r Altertumwissenschaft des heiligen Landes zu Jerusalem 25 (1925), 86.

과 결혼한 이방 여인들은 그들의 자녀들에게 유대어를 가르치지 아니하여 유대인의 전통의 삶과 사상을 전수하지 못했다. 유대인 엄마들만 이를 할 수 있었다.[176] 통혼의 두려움은 여기에 참여한 개인들만 아니라 유대 공동체의 미래를 위한 걱정을 반영하였다. 왜냐하면 이방 여인들과 결혼함으로 히브리 자녀들이 자기 언어로 말할 수 있고 자신들의 전통을 이해하는 능력에 위협을 주었기 때문이다.

"the language of Judah"(lit. "Judean"): This is the only Hebrew term we know for the "Hebrew language"[cf. 2 Kgs. 18:26, 28 (= Isa. 36:11, 13, 2 Chron. 32:18)]. The foreign women who married Judeans would not teach their children the language of Judah and transmit the life and thought of the Judean tradition. Only a Judean mother could do this.[176] The fear of intermarriage reflected concern not only for the individuals who took part in this union but also for the future of the Judean community, for marriage to a foreign woman threatened the ability of Hebrew children to speak their own language and to understand their own tradition.

3-3-1-3-2. 느 10:25-27 (느헤미야의 반응) Neh. 10:25-7 (response of Nehemiah)

통혼에 관해서 느헤미야는 이혼을 요구한 에스라(9-10장)만큼 단호하지는 않았다. 그는 단순히 더 이상 통혼이 없기를 요구했다. 본문 말씀은 성경 내의 주석이 포함되어 있다. 피쉬베인이 주장하기

---

[176] See further R. de Vaux, *Ancient Israel: Its Life and Institutions*, 48-51.

를 "느헤미야 13:23-27에 나오는 신 23:4-9의 언급은 간접적으로 느 13:1-3에서 이방인들을 추방하라는 말씀과 관련하여 오경의 자료를 명백하게 사용함으로 강화되었다."[177]

In regard to intermarriage, Nehemiah did not go so far as Ezra(chs 9-10), who demanded divorce; he simply demanded an end to further intermarriage. Our passage includes an inner-biblical exegesis; Fishbane insists, "The allusion to Deut. 23:4-9 in Nehemiah 13:23-27 is indirectly strengthened by the explicit use of that Pentateuchal source in Neh. 13:1-3, also in connection with the expulsion of foreigners."[177]

25절에서 통혼에 유대인들을 향한 느헤미야의 강력한 행동(참고 11, 17절)은 감정 폭발이라기보다는 오히려 격변에 대한 제의적 태도로 간주될 수 있었다. 그는 통혼에 가담한 이들과 논쟁을 벌이면서 그들에게 종교적 저주를 내린다(또한 29절을 보라). 그는 그들을 매질하며 머리털을 뜯었다(참고. 신 25:2; 삼하 10:4-5; 에스라 9:3; 사 50:6). 그런 후 그는 그들에게 13년 전에 회중들이 체결한 맹세를 갱신하도록 강요했다(느 10:30): "우리 딸을 이 땅 백성에게 주지 아니하고 우리 아들을 위하여 저희 딸을 데려오지 아니하며."

Nehemiah's violent action against the guilty Judeans in verse 25(cf. vv. 11, 17) could be regarded as largely a ritual gesture of revulsion rather than an outbreak of emotion. He contended with those who have entered into intermarriage, bringing down a religious curse upon them(also see v. 29). He flogged them and pulled out their hair(cf. Deut. 25:2; 2 Sam. 10:4-5; Ezra 9:3; Isa. 50:6). Then

---

177) Fishbane, *Biblical Interpretation*, 126ff.

he forced them to renew the oath that the congregation took about thirteen years earlier(Neh. 10:30): "And that we would not give our daughters unto the people of the land, nor take their daughters for our sons."

솔로몬의 예를 든 것은(26절) 왕상 11:1-8(참고 왕상 3:12-13)를 인용하는 것으로, 왕의 약점이 이스라엘의 남북 분열이 된 원인 제공을 하였다. 이 내용은 역대하에서 솔로몬을 하나님의 성전을 지은 이상적인 왕으로 묘사하는데 관련 내용이 없다. 훗날 그의 이방인 부인들이 솔로몬에게 다른 신들을 섬기게 하여 그는 모압의 신인 그모스를 위한 신당을 세웠다.178) 26-27절(23절; 스 10:2)에서 느헤미야 시대 당시 유대인들의 죄와 솔로몬의 죄악 사이를 비교하고 있다. 이것은 유대 지도자들에 대하여 경고한 것이었다. 만일 위대한 왕이며 하나님의 사랑을 받은(여디디아, 참고 삼하 12:25) 솔로몬이 이방 여인들로 말미암아 타락되었다면, 일반 백성들은 배교를 피하기 위해 무슨 희망이 있느냐 하는 것이 논쟁이다.

The example of Solomon(v.26) was an allusion to 1 Kings 11:1-8(cf. 1K. 3:12-13), where this king's shortcomings were set out as a preliminary to an account of the division of the kingdoms of Israel and Judah. This section had no parallel in 2 Chronicles which described Solomon as an ideal king who built the temple of God. In later years his foreign wives led him to worship other gods, so that he built a high place for Chemosh, the god of the Moabites.178) Verses 26-27(v. 23, Ezra 10:2) drew a parallel

---

178) Cf. Ackroyd, *I & II Chronicles, Ezra, Nehemiah*, 319.

between the culpability of Solomon and the guilt of the Judeans during Nehemiah's time. This was directed against the leaders of Judah. The argument was that if Solomon, the great king and the beloved of God("Jedidiah" cf. 2 Sam. 12:25), could be led astray by foreign women, what hope was there for his ordinary people to avoid apostasy?

3-3-2. 제사장의 통혼과 개혁(느 13:28-31) A priestly intermarriage and reform (Neh. 13:28-31)

느헤미야 Nehemiah 13:28 대제사장 엘리아십의 손자 요야다의 아들 하나가 호론 사람 산발랏의 사위가 되었으므로 내가 쫓아내어 나를 떠나게 하였느니라. One of the sons of Jehoiada, son of the high priest Eliashib, was the son-in-law of Sanballat the Horonite; I drove him away from me. 29 "내 하나님이여 그들이 제사장의 직분을 더럽히고 제사장의 직분과 레위 사람에 대한 언약을 어기었사오니 저희를 기억하옵소서." "Remember them, O my God, because they polluted the priesthood, and the covenant of the priesthood and the Levites [a]. 30 내가 이와 같이 그들로 이방 사람을 떠나게 하여 깨끗하게 하고 또 제사장과 레위 사람의 반열을 세워 각각 그 일을 맡게 하고 Thus I purified them from every foreign element, and I made the priests and the Levites resume the duties of their office. 31 또 정한 기한에 나무와 처음 익은 것을 드리게 하였사오니 "내 하나님이여 나를 기억하사 복을 주옵소서. And for the wood offering, at times appointed, and for the firstfruits. "Remember me, O my God, for good.

3-3-2-1. 본문 노트 Textual Notes

29a절. "레위인들"이 확실히 추가되었다. 신 33:9과 말 2:4, 8에 나오는 "레위와의 언약"를 참고하면서 생긴 것 같다. 루시언 본문, 시리아, 이디오피아, 아랍어 본문에서는 "제사장" 대신에 "제사장들"로 읽는데 후에 추가된 것으로 레위인들을 암시하는 듯하다.[179]

29a "The Levites" was certainly added, perhaps occasioned by the reference to the "covenant of Levi" at Deut. 33:9 and Mal. 2:4, 8. The Lucianic text, Syr., Eth., and Arab. read סינהכה for הנהכה in which case allusion to the Levites may be still a later addition.[179]

3-3-2-2. 문학 형태 form

본문은 위에서 지적한 대로, 23-27절처럼 비망록(1인칭 단수 설화)에 속한다.

This text belongs to the memoir (the first person-singular-narrative) like vv. 23-27, as we pointed out above.

3-3-2-3. 해석 Interpretation

28절에 나오는 요야다(혹 여효야다)의 아들 중 하나가[180] 23절에 나

---

[179] Blenkinsopp, *ibid.*, 362; U. Kellermann, *Nehemia: Quellen, Überlieferung und Geschichte*, BZAW 102 (Berlin: T pelmann, 1967), 54.
[180] 느 12:11과 22에 의하면 요나단과 요하난은 그의 아들들이다. According to Neh. 12:11

오는 민족(아스돗, 암몬, 모압) 중 하나와 통혼을 하지 아니하였더라도 그는 느헤미야의 강력 원수인 호론 사람 산발랏(참고 2:10)의 딸과 통혼을 하여 서약을 파기했다. 대제사장이 이방인과 결혼을 못하게 되어 있는 규정을 확대 적용(참고. 레 21:14)하여, 그는 유대인 공동체로부터 추방을 당해야 했다(참고. 스 7:26, 10:8). 대제사장의 자녀는 차기 대제사장이 될 수 있기에 그는 이런 통혼을 금지당해야 한다.

One of the sons[180] of Jehoiada(or Joiada) in v. 28, though he did not intermarry with any of the peoples mentioned above in v. 23, had violated the pledge by marrying a daughter of Nehemiah's arch-enemy, Sanballat the Horonite(cf. 2:10). He had to be expelled from the Judean community(cf. Ezra 7:26, 10:8), because of a natural extension of the prohibition about the high priest marrying an outsider(Lev. 21:14). Since the son of the high priest may conceivably become the high priest, he should be prevented from such an intermarriage.

이 경우는 느헤미야와 엘리아십 사이의 긴장감을 보여주는 또 하나의 실례였다(느 12:10). 엘리아십은 느헤미야와 동시대의 대제사장이었다(느 3:1, 20-21, 12:10, 22). 그의 대제사장 직을 요야다가 승계했다(느 12:10-11, 22). 느 13:4-9에서 요야다는 느헤미야의 원수들 하나인 도비야와 연합했다. 이제는 산발랏 집안과 결혼으로 친척이 된 것이다(느 2:10, 19).

This may be a further illustration of the tension between Nehemiah and Eliashib(Neh. 12:10). Eliashib was the high priest,

---

and 22, Jonathan and Johanan were also his sons.

contemporary with Nehemiah(Neh. 3:1, 20-21, 12:10, 22), and he was succeeded by Jehoiada(Neh. 12:10-11, 22). In Neh. 13:4-9, he was in league with one of Nehemiah's enemies, Tobiah; now he was shown to be related by marriage to Sanballat(2:10, 19).

이 문제로 느헤미야는 두 가지 문제에 직면하게 되었는데, 공동체의 순수성을 지키는 데 위기가 생겼고 동시에 거룩한 공동체 자체에 인간의 원수가 침투한 일이 발생한 것이다. 요야다의 아들이 이방 여인과 이혼하는 것을 거부했을 가능성이 있다. 어떤 경우에든지, 그는 느헤미야가 산발랏에 대해 가지는 역겨운 기분 때문에 추방되었다. 추정하건데 그는 예루살렘으로부터 추방된 후 사마리아로 가서 거주하였을 것이다.[181]

The point illustrated the double problems faced by Nehemiah, that is, the urgency of maintaining purity and at the same time the need for watchfulness against human enemies, who might find allies even in the holy community itself. It is possible that the son of Jehoiada refused to divorce his wife. In any case, he was expelled because of Nehemiah's bad feeling toward Sanballat. Presumably he retired to Samaria after the banishment from

---

[181] 요세푸스에 의하면(유대전쟁사 11장, 7항 2), 대제사장 야두아의 형제인 마나세가 산발랏의 딸인 니카소와 결혼해서 그 이유 때문에 예루살렘 장로들로부터 추방되어 그린심산에서 산발랏이 지은 사마리아 성전의 대제사장으로 새로운 경력을 시작했다고 한다. 요세푸스는 이 사건이 다리우스 3세(BC 335-330년)와 알렉산더 대제 때 생겼다고 한다. Josephus (Ant. XI. vii. 2) stated that a brother of the high priest Jaddua by the name of Manasseh married Nikaso, the daughter of Sanballat, and was for that reason expelled by the Jerusalem elders and began a new career as high priest of the Samaritan temple built for him by Sanballat on Mount Gerizim. Josephus places this incident at the time of Darius III (BC 335-330) and Alexander the Great. Myers, 217-8; Blenkinsopp, *Ezra-Nehemiah*, 365; Bowman, 818.

Jerusalem.[181]

29-30절은 느헤미야의 예배 개혁의 요약이다. 느헤미야는 29절에서 기도하기를 그를 반대한 자로 유대 공동체 밖으로 쫓겨 나간 자들을(느 6:14; 참고 느 4:3-5) 기억해 달라고 하나님께 기도를 드렸다. 그러나 내부 반항자들(예, 제사장들, 레위인들)은 지속적인 외부인들(예, 사마리아인들, 다른 외국인들)의 반대보다 더 아픈 부담이 되었다. 페르샤 왕이 부여한 권한이 오랫동안 무시당했던 제사장과 레위인들의 반열을 갱신함으로 확실히 나타나게 되었다(느 13:11; 참고 느 10:28-30, 37-39, 12:30, 44-47, 13:3, 10-14; 참고. 스 6:20; 말 2:4-9).

Verses 29-30 are a summary statement of Nehemiah's cultic reform. Nehemiah called upon God to remember those outside of the Judean community who opposed him(Neh. 6:14, cf. Neh. 4:3-5) in v. 29. But the rebellion of the insiders(e.g. priests, Levites) was more painful than the burden of the continual opposition of the outsiders(e.g. Samaritans, other foreigners). The authority given to him by the Persian king was clearly shown by the renewal of the priestly and Levitical orders of service which had long been neglected(Neh. 13:11; cf. Neh. 10:28-30, 37-39, 12:30, 44-47, 13:3, 10-14; cf. Ezra 6:20; Mal. 2:4-9).

3-4. 요약 Summary

본 장에서 우리는 에스라 9-10장과 느헤미야 13:23-31 주석을 통하여 에스라와 느헤미야가 인도한 결혼 개혁을 살펴보았다. 에스라와 그의 지지자 그룹은 에스라 9-10장에서 강하게 이방 부인들과 이혼을 주장했고, 느헤미야는 죄를 지은 평신도들에게 초기 서약을 강제로 상기시켜 그는 대제사장의 죄 지은 손자를 유대 공동체로부터 추방시켰다. 분명하게 에스라와 느헤미야의 결혼 개혁은 유대 공동체의 내부자와 외부자 사이에 있는 강한 "경계선"[182]을 제공했다.

통혼은 결혼한 두 사람들의 일만 아니다. 특히 매우 다른 문화와 종교 전통들이 관여한 경우에 이것은 현재와 미래의 전체 공동체에게 중요하다. 통혼의 두려움은 이 결합에 참여한 개인들뿐만 아니라 유대 공동체의 미래에 대한 염려도 반영했다. 왜냐하면 이방 여인들과 결혼한 것이 유대인들 자녀들이 유대 언어를 말하고 그들 자

---

[182] "경계선"은 공동체의 내부와 외부 사이의 경계선을 말한다. 메리 더글러스가 저서에서 밝히듯이 내부선과 외부선 사이의 경계이다. "Border line" refers to the boundary, the line of demarcation, between inside and outside a community. It includes 'external boundaries and internal lines', as Mary Douglas describes in her book (*Purity and Danger: An analysis of concepts of pollution and taboo*,\ London and Henley: Routledge & Kegan Paul, 1966, 1969). 다른 말로 표현하면, 어떤 특수한 공동체에 가입할 때 규정하는 요구사항의 기준을 말한다. 예를 들면, 순결, 세례, 할례, 통관 제의, 음식, 윤리 규범, 절기와 정경 준수 등을 말한다. 경계선은 공동체를 어떤 외부적 위협으로부터 보호하며, 공동체의 기초 구조를 유지할 수 있게 한다. "내부"란 말은 "포함, 내적 회원, 공동체의 나와 너와의 관계성"을 말하며, "외부"라는 말은 "제외, 외적, 이방인, 공동체의 나와 그것과의 관계성"을 말한다. In other words, it is a criterion or requirement for admission into any specific community; for example, purity, baptism, circumcision, rite of passage, food, ethical norm, observance of days and canon. The border line can protect the community from threat from the outside and maintain the plausibility structure of the community. By "inside", we mean "inclusion, internal, membership, I-Thou relation with the community"; and by "outside," we mean "exclusion, external, stranger, I-It relation with the community." 이 짝은 좋은 상징적 비교를 보인다. 한 공동체 내에도 "외부적 요인"이 존재하며, 한 공동체 외부에도 "내부적 요인"이 있다. 거의 모든 공동체들은 그들의 사회적 삶속에서 배제와 포함의 긴장을 가지고 있다. 그러나 구별 없이 어떤 사람을 포함하는 일은 위험하며 마찬가지로 정당한 이유 없이 사람을 제외시키는 것도 위험하다.This pair shows a good symbolic comparison. It is a common phenomenon that there is "outside-ness" even within a community, and there is "inside-ness" even outside the community. Almost all communities have the tension of exclusion and inclusion in their social lives. But to include people without distinction is precarious, and, likewise, exclusion without justifiable reason is also dangerous.

신의 전통을 아는 능력에 위협을 받기 때문이었다. 유대인들과 결혼한 이방 여인들은 자녀들에게 유대 언어를 가르치지 않았다.

In this chapter we have examined the marriage reform led by Ezra and Nehemiah through exegesis of Ezra 9-10 and Nehemiah 13:23-31. While Ezra and his support group strongly insisted upon the divorce of foreign wives in Ezra 9-10, Nehemiah forcibly reminded the guilty lay persons of the earlier pledge, and he expelled the guilty grandson of the high priest from the Judean community. Evidently this marriage reform of Ezra and Nehemiah offered a distinct "border line"[182] between insiders and outsiders of the Judean community. Intermarriage was not just an affair of the two persons who married. It has importance for the whole community, present and future, especially when very different cultures and religious traditions were involved. The fear of intermarriage reflected concern not only for the individuals who take part in this union but also for the future of the Judean community, for marriage to a foreign woman may threaten the ability of Hebrew children to speak their own language and to know their own tradition. The foreign women who married Judeans would not teach their children the language of Judah.

다음 장에서, 우리는 페르샤 제국 시대에 유대 공동체 정체성의 위기와 에스라와 느헤미야가 주도한 개혁의 합법적 구조들을 살필 것이다. 이것은 당시 유대 공동체의 실제적인 사회적 조건들을 재구성하는 일을 포함할 것이다. 그런 후 우리는 결혼 개혁을 합리화한 "상징적 세계"를 다룰 것이다.

In the following chapter, we will examine the crisis of Judean communal identity in the Persian period and the structures of legitimation of the reform led by Ezra and Nehemiah. This will entail reconstructing the actual social conditions of the contemporary Judean community. Then we will deal with the "symbolic universe" which legitimatized the marriage reform.

IV

결혼개혁과 유대 공동체의 사회적 기반 회복

THE MARRIAGE REFORM AND THE RESTORATION OF THE SOCIAL BASIS OF JUDEAN COMMUNITY

본 장에서, 우리는 에스라와 느헤미야의 결혼 개혁이 페르샤 시대에 유대의 종교적이며 인종적인 공동체를 재구성하는 데 어떻게 공헌했는지를 살필 것이다. 포수기 이후 유대 공동체의 사회적 기반을 회복하는 데 대한 사회학적 질문들에 답하는 것이 본 항의 과제이다.

In this chapter, we will examine how the marriage reform of Ezra and Nehemiah contributed to reconstruct the Judean religious and ethnic community in the Persian period. Our task is to address sociological questions in restoring the social basis of the post-exilic Judean community.

예루살렘이 함락한 후 포로민들은 외국의 땅에서 그들의 정체성을 확립하려고 노력했다. 그들은 자신들의 종교적 전통을 지키고 회당에서 예배를 통해 공동체를 공고히 하였다. 바벨론 포로생활 속에서 유대인들이 통혼했다는 증거는 없다. BC 515년 제2성전이 봉헌되고 어떤 귀환한 유대인들이 이방 여인들과 결혼을 하기 시작했다. 이 통혼들은 경건한 유대인들에게 심각하게 받아들여졌다.

After the fall of Jerusalem, the exiles tried to establish their identity on foreign soil. They kept their own religious traditions and consolidated their community through worship in the synagogue. We have no extant evidence of the Judean intermarriage in the Babylonian exile. Right after the rededication of the temple in 515 BC, some returned Judeans married foreign women. These intermarriages were considered very serious for the pious Judeans.

본 장에서 우리는 페르샤 시대에 유대인 공동체 정체성 위기와 에스라와 느헤미야의 결혼 개혁의 합법성의 과정을 살펴볼 것이다. 그런 후 우리는 에스라와 느헤미야와 그들의 지지 그룹이 합법화의 마지막 단계로 상징적 세계를 분석할 것이다.

In this chapter, we will deal with the crisis of Judean communal identity in the Persian period and the process of legitimation of the marriage reform of Ezra and Nehemiah. Then we will analyze a symbolic universe, which was the common ground of Ezra and Nehemiah and their support group, as the final level of legitimation.

4-1. 유대 공동체 정체성의 위기 The crisis of Judean communal identity

통혼이 확산되니 귀환한 유대 공동체의 예배와 인종의 순수성과 국가의 정체성이 무너지는 위협을 받았다. 어떤 유대인들이 외국인들과 통혼한 이유들이 몇 가지 있었다. 포수기 이후 초창기에 유대인들 가운데 몇 명이 팔레스타인에서 오랫동안 정착한 부유한 혹은 강력한 외국 가정들과 결혼함으로 그들의 운명을 더 나은 것으로 추구하는 데 유혹을 받았을 것이다. 이 외국인들은 BC 588년의 포로생활로 발생된 빈 공간을 메꾼 혼합 민족 인구였을 뿐만 아니라 포수기 이후 정착한 이방 부동산 소유주였을 것이다. 의심할 나위도 없이 그들은 경제적으로 꽤 좋은 환경 속에 살았다. 다른 한편, 포로생활로부터 귀환한 대부분의 유대인들은 가난했고 아마도 가뭄과 농작물 실패(학 1:6-11)로 기근에 시달렸다. 현상유지를 원했던 유대인들 가운데 더 부유하기를 원했던 이들이 이방 이웃들에게 편안하게 대하며, 심지어 그들과 결혼을 하는 데까지 이르렀다.

The spread of intermarriage threatened to disintegrate the national identity and the purity, cultic and ethnic, of the returned Judean community. There were some reasons why some Judeans intermarried with foreign peoples. During the earlier post-exilic period, it must have been tempting for some Judeans to seek to better their fortunes by marrying into more well-to-do or powerful foreign families, long enough established in Palestine. These foreign peoples were not only the mixed population that filled the vacuum created by the exile of 588 BC, but also were outside landholders who took over after the exile. Undoubtedly they were in fairly good circumstances economically. On the other hand, most Judeans who returned from exile were poor and were probably reduced to want because of drought and crop failure (Hag. 1:6-11). Some of the wealthier class among the Judeans who wanted to maintain the *status quo* took an easygoing attitude toward their foreign neighbors, even to the point of mingling and intermarrying with them.

유대인들의 종교적 생활에서도 발견되는 다른 이유가 있었다. 비록 그들이 성전을 가지고 있었지만 그들은 어떤 예배의 규정인 예배와 윤리의 순수성에 대한 어떤 기준이 없었다. 제사장들조차 강제로 뺏은 제물이나 절름발이 혹 병든 제물을 가지고 왔다(말 1:12-13). 앞장에서 살펴본 대로 제사장이나 평신도들이 통혼 문제에 연루되었다.

There was another reason found in the religious life of the Judeans. Even though they had the temple, they did not have any stipulation of worship or any criterion of purity, cultic and ethnic. Even the priests brought what was taken by violence or was lame or sick (Mal. 1:12-13). Both the clergy and the layperson got involved in the problem of intermarriage, as we examined in the previous chapter.

예루살렘의 성벽들이 느헤미야와 그의 추종자들에 의해 재건되어질 동안, 사마리아 총독인 산발랏과 그의 동조자들은 이 건축계획을 저지하기 위해 그들의 권한으로 모든 일을 동원했다(느 4:1-6:18). 왜냐하면 예루살렘의 성벽이 회복되면 예루살렘에 있었던 그 당시 사마리아 공동체가 없어질 위협을 받았기 때문이다. 산발랏이 유대인 지경에 지분을 주장했는데, 그 이유는 예루살렘 멸망 후 바벨론인들에 의해 사마리아의 도로 분할이 되었기 때문이다. 사마리아인들은 처음으로 유대인들을 미워하는 조직된 그룹으로 언급되었다(느 4:2). 그들은 그들의 새로운 나라의 수호자 신을 예배하는 데 맞는 이론이라면 유대인들의 종교를 채택했다. 더구나 요단강 동쪽의 암몬인들과 예루살렘 남방의 에돔인들이 유대인들의 활동들에 대해 시기를 가지고 바라보았다. 이 그룹들은 유대인들이 페르샤 정부에 대해 반기를 드는 혁명을 기획하여 성벽의 취약한 힘을 조롱하여, 마침내 공격을 위협했다고 정죄하였다.

During the days when the walls of Jerusalem were being rebuilt by Nehemiah and his followers, Sanballat, the governor of Samaria, and his allies did everything in their power to frustrate the project(Neh. 4:1-6:18). For the restoration of the walls of Jerusalem threatened to destroy the contemporary Samaritan society within Jerusalem.

Sanballat laid claim to the Judean territory, for it had been assigned to the province of Samaria by the Babylonians after the destruction of Jerusalem. The Samaritans were mentioned in this context for the first time as an organized group hostile to the Judeans(Neh. 4:2). They had adopted the religion of the Judeans, on the theory that it was fitting to worship the tutelary god of their new country. Moreover, the Ammonites of Transjordan and the Edomites to the south of Jerusalem looked with a jealous eye upon the Judeans' activities. These groups accused the Judeans of plotting a revolution against Persia; then they ridiculed the feeble strength of the walls; and finally they threatened to attack.

페르샤 시대의 초기에 통혼은 생존을 위해 필요했을 것이다. 에스라와 느헤미야 시대 때 통혼문제는 공동체 전체의 성격을 위협하기도 했다. 왜냐하면 통혼으로 문화와 인종이 동화되었다. 느헤미야는 이 문제의 현상으로 자녀들의 언어 문제를 관찰하였다. 왜냐하면 어머니들이 자연스럽게 자기 자녀들에게 그들이 아는 언어만 말하도록 가르쳤기 때문이다. 통혼에 대해 느긋한 유대 공동체에 일어난 일은 에스라와 느헤미야의 동시대인 이집트의 엘리판틴 정착지의 예에서 보여진다.[183] 비 유대인 여인들과 결혼한 유대인들이 여호와 이외에 그들의 이방신에게 헌신하는 테도를 보였다. 그러나 엘리판틴 공동체는 점차로 동화되어서 마침내 사라져 버렸다.

In the early Persian period, intermarriage might have been necessary for survival. In the time of Ezra and Nehemiah, however, it was threatening the whole character of the community. For intermarriage resulted in the cultural and ethnic assimilation. Nehemiah observed this phenomenon first in the speech of children, since the mothers naturally taught their children to speak the only language they knew. What happened to a Judean community that was lax concerning intermarriage can be seen in the example of the Elephantine settlement in Egypt, which was contemporary with Ezra and Nehemiah.[183] There the Jews who married non-Jewish women expressed their devotion to pagan gods in addition to Jehovah. But the Elephantine community was gradually assimilated and finally disappeared.

이방 여인들과 결혼함으로 유대인과 이방인 사이, 유대인과 사마리아 사람 사이의 경계선이 흐려졌다. 그래서 유대인 공동체의 개연구조는 해체되거나 무너지기 시작했다. 그들의 공동체의 개연구조를 지키기 위해서, 귀환한 그룹의 지도자들이 정치적(아닥사스다의 편지), 종교적(씌여진 토라와), 경제적(왕의 금고로부터 재정 지원과) 세력을 가졌던 에스라에게 통혼에 관한 사실을 보고했다. 개인의 사회적 역할은 내적인 위협과 외적인 위협에 대항하여 공동체의 순결성과 정체

---

[183] James B. Pritchard, *ANET*, 491-493.

성을 지키는 것이었다.[184]

By marrying foreign women, the border line between Judean and Gentile, and between Judean and Samaritans became vague. Thus the plausibility structure of the Judean community began to be deconstructed or disintegrated. In order to keep the plausibility structure of their community, the leaders of the returned group made report of the facts about intermarriage to Ezra who had the political(with Letters of Artaxerxes), religious(with the written Torah), economic(with the financial support from the king's treasury) power. The social role of individual was to defend purity and identity of community[184] against internal as well as external threats.

긴 포로 시기를 경험한 유대인 성도들에게 통혼 제도가 불건전하다는 확신을 심어주었다. 확실히 종교적인 열정이 여기에 있었는데, 왜냐하면 과거에도 그러했듯이 외국인 여성들이 자기 남편들을 잘못된 신들을 숭배하도록 하는 심각한 위험이 있기 때문이다. 에스라의 관점에서 보면 포로생활은 우상숭배의 죄에 대한 처벌이었고, 통혼이 퍼지면서 비슷한 처벌이 다시 일어났던 것이다. 또한 에스라와 느헤미야가 평신도들과 제사장들의 통혼을 금지한 다른 이유가 있었는데, 귀환한 유대인들은 숫자가 많지 않는 그룹(참고, 스 2:64-67)으

---

184) 공동체는 전통적으로 처녀(왕하 19:12; 사 37:22; 애 1:15, 2:13; 렘 14:17), 신부(렘 2:2-3; 호 2:15하), 음녀(호 1-4; 겔 16)로부터 과부(애 1:1; 사 54:4-8)에 이르기까지 여성 형상으로 표시한다.The community is traditionally represented by female figures ranging from the virgin(2 Kigs 19:12; Isa. 37:22; Lam. 1:15, 2:13; Jer. 14:17) to the bride(Jer. 2:2-3; Hos. 2:15b) to the whore(Hos 1-4; Ezk 16) to the widow(Lam 1:1; Isa. 54:4-8) [Amy-Jill Levine, "Character Construction and Community Formation in the Book of Judith," *SBL Seminar Papers*, Annual Meeting 1989, 561].

로 당시 예루살렘에 살았던 다수 이방인 인구들에게 흡수되고 있었기 때문이다.[185]

The experience of the exile convinced the zealous Judean believers that the custom of intermarriage was unwholesome. Religious fervor was certainly at work here, for there was the serious danger that the foreign women would lead their husbands to the worship of false gods, like something which had happened in the past. The exile was, from Ezra's point of view, the punishment for the sin of idolatry, and, with the spread of intermarriages, the similar punishment might be happened again. There was also a further reason for Ezra and Nehemiah to discourage intermarriages of laypersons and clergy; the returned Judeans were a small group(cf. Ezr. 2:64-67), so that they might be absorbed by the surrounding peoples who formed the majority.[185]

유대 공동체의 존재에 대한 심각한 위협에 대처해 유대 정체성을 지키기 위해, 통혼에 대항하여 싸우는 것이 필수적이었다.

In order to preserve the Judean identity guard against the serious threat to the Judean community's existence, it was most imperative to fight against intermarriages.

---

[185] K. Luke, "The Nephilim were on the Earth (Gen. 6:4)", *Bible Bhashyam*, 9(1983), 293-294.

4-2. 유대 공동체의 회복 Restoration of Judean community

에스라와 느헤미야가 통혼 문제에 강력하게 대응하므로 이방인과 하나가 되는 일과는 호의적이지 않는 유대 공동체 전통을 세우는 데 도움이 되었다. 그러한 전통이 없이는 유대 공동체가 페르샤 시대에 살아남기 어려웠을 것이다.[186]

Ezra and Nehemiah's strong stood on the matter of intermarriages helped Judah to establish a community tradition unfavourable to such unions, and without such a tradition it was hard to see how Judean community would have survived in the Persian world.[186]

우선, 에스라와 느헤미야의 결혼 개혁은 유대 공동체 안에서 합법화되어야 했다. 유대 종교를 이방 오염으로부터 근본적으로 지키기 위해 유대인들을 분리시키는 것은 사회적 배타성의 형태처럼 외국 이웃들을 바라보게 만들었다. 그래서 이런 배타성이 당시 세계에서 유대인들에 대한 악한 감정으로 확실히 자리잡게 되었다.[187]

First of all, the marriage refom of Ezra and Nehemiah should have been legitimated within Judean community. The separateness of the Judeans, designed primarily to safeguard Judean religion from foreign contamination, must have looked to the foreign neighbors like a form of social exclusiveness, and it was undoubtedly a factor in creating animosity to the Judeans in

---

186) Cf. W. S. McCullough, *The History and Literature of the Palestinian Jews From Cyrus to Herod: 550 BC to 4 BC*, Toronto: University of Toronto Press, 1975, 49.
187) McCullough, 49.

the contemporary world.187)

본 항에서는 사회적 세계의 실체였던 에스라 개혁의 객관성의 과정을 다룬다.

In this section we deal with the process of objectivation of the Ezra's reform which was the reality of social world.

4-2-1. 사회 세계의 실재를 합법화함 The legitimation of the reality of social world

의미 있는 질서들에 의해 사회적으로 구성된 모든 세계들은 당연히 믿을 수 없이 취약하다. 인간들의 활동에 의해 지지를 받은 세계는 꾸준히 자기 이익과 우둔함의 인간적 사실들에 의해 협박을 받는다.188) 막스 웨버는 말하기를 사회적 관계의 가장 안정한 형태는 회원들의 주관적 태도가 합법적 질서를 믿는 믿음 안으로 향하고 있는 것이라고 했다. 웨버에 의하면 합법화는 그들을 주관하는 주권이 단순한 사실 뿐만 아니라, 도덕적 만족으로 기인한 사실임을 믿는 신념이다. 이 합법이 일어나는 과정은 합법화로 불리워지는 것으로 얻어진다.189)

All the worlds socially constructed by meaningful orders are ipso facto precarious. Supported by human activity, they are constantly threatened by the human facts of self-interest and stupidity.188) M. Weber said that the most stable forms of social relationship are those in which the subjective attitudes of the

---

188) Berger, 1967, 29.
189) Weber 1963:15, 47, 197, 111, 283.

participating individuals are directed towards the belief in a legitimate order. The legitimacy is, according to Weber, the belief held by people that the authority over them is not only a simple fact but is a fact charged with moral content. And the process by which this legitimacy is acquired is called legitimation.[189]

웨버의 이론을 받아들여 버거는 넓은 의미에서 합법화는 사회 질서를 설명하고 객관화하는 데 필요한 사회적으로 객관화된 지식으로 정의를 내린다. 모든 합법화의 형태들의 중요한 목적은 주관적이며 객관적인 수준에서 현실 유지로 묘사된다. 다시 말하면 객관화는 모든 수준들에 다양하게 나타나며 이론화가 꼭 필요하지 않는다. 버거는 인간의 역사 대부분을 살펴보면 사회를 유지하는 데 주요한 합법화가 종교에 의해 제공되어 왔다고 한다.[190]

Following Weber, Berger defines "legitimation" in a broader sense as socially objectivated "knowledge" that serves to explain and justify the social order. The essential purpose of all forms of legitimation is described as reality-maintenance, both on the objective and the subjective levels. That is, legitimation occurs on a variety of levels and it is not necessarily theoretical. He argues that through most of human history, the principal legitimations for the maintenance of society have been provided by religion.[190]

---

190) Berger, 1967:29ff; Berger & Luckmann, 1966:92-128.

4-2-1-1. 합법 규범 legitimate *nomoi*

사회에 참여하는 것은 그의 "지식"을 공유하는 것, 즉 합법화된 규범과 함께 사는 것이다. 객관적 규범은 이 당연히 여겨지는 특성이 내면화된 정도로 성공을 이루는 사회화의 과정 속에 내면화되어 있다.[191]

To participate in the society is to share its "knowledge," that is, to co-inhabit its *nomoi* which are legitimated. The objective *nomos* is internalized in the course of socialization which achieves success to the degree that this taken-for-granted quality is internalized.[191]

포수기 동안, 포로 공동체의 안과 밖 사이에 경계선이 엄격하게 그어져 버렸다. 예배의 거룩성, 인종 순결, 토라에 대한 열정, 할례, 안식일 준수, 코셔 음식 등이 중요한 경계 기준들이었다. 포로 공동체는 토라에 기초한 예배의 성격에 관심이 있었다. 그리고 제의화된 윤리성에 관심이 있었다.[192]

During the exilic period, a border line was strictly drawn between inside and outside the exile community. Cultic holiness, ethnic purity, zeal for Torah, circumcision, observance of Sabbath and kosher food were main border definers. The community of the exile was concerned with a ritual ethos based upon Torah; and it was concerned with a ritualized ethnicity.[192]

---

191) Berger, 1967:21-24.
192) Fishbane, 114.

유대 언약 공동체의 주요 원리는 외부인들로부터 분리하는 가장 중요한 언어가 순수성이었다. 하나님의 선택받은 민족으로서(암 3:2), 그들은 "나 여호와 너희 하나님이 거룩한 즉"(레 19:2) 그들도 거룩해야 한다. 그래서 거룩하지 못한, 경건하지 못한 행동들은 유대 언약 공동체에서 용납되지 않았다. 모든 내부자들은 할례를 행하고 음식법을 지키도 성전 예배에 매년 참여해야 했다. 그들은 지방민들(외부인)과 통혼하는 것이 금지되어 있다(신 7:3, 6; 스 9:1-2; 출 34:16; 참고. 수 23:12-13). 이들 이외에, 공동체 투쟁(레 19:17-18; 출 23:4-5; 신 22:1-4), 탐욕(출 20:17), 거짓과 중상모략(레 19:16; 출 20:16; 신 19:16-20), 부모 불효(출 20:12; 레 19:3, 20:9; 신 5:16, 21:18-21, 27:16), 교만(신 8:17-18, 9:4-5), 그리고 성적 문란(출 20:14; 레 18:1-30; 신 22:22-30, 27:20)은 거룩한 공동체에서 금지사항들이다.[193]

The main principle of life in the Judean covenant community was purity which was the most important language of separation from the outsiders. As the chosen people of God(Amos 3:2), they should be holy, "for I the LORD your God am holy"(Lev. 19:2). Thus unholy, ungodly conducts were not acceptable in the Judean covenant community. All insiders must practice circumcision, observe dietary laws and participate in the temple cult annually. They were prohibited to intermarry with the local(outsider) population(Deut.7:3, 6; Ezra 9:1-2; Ex. 34:16; cf. Josh. 23:12-13). Besides these, community strife(Lev. 19:17f; Ex. 23:4f; Dt. 22:1-4), covetousness(Ex. 20:17), deceit or slander(Lev. 19:16; Ex. 20:16; Dt. 19:16-20), disobedience to parents(Ex. 20:12; Lev. 19:3, 20:9; Dt. 5:16, 21:18-21,

---

193) Gunninghan, 49-52.

27:16), pride(Dt. 8:17-18, 9:4f) and sexual misconduct(Ex. 20:14; Lev. 18:1-30; Dt. 22:22-30, 27:20) are abominable to the holy community.[193]

거의 모든 종교 공동체는 배타와 포함 사이의 긴장을 알고 있다. 한편, 구별 없이 백성들을 포함하는 일은 위험하다. 왜냐하면 공동체의 기본 신념이나 규범들에 관심이 없는 사람을 받아들임으로 공동체 생활의 핵심이 제거되기 때문이다. 다른 한편으로는, 배타도 위험하다. 자주 배타나 출교를 하는 공동체들은 가혹해진다. "잘려진" 그룹들이 축출된 후에도 오랫동안 살아간다. 어떤 위험들에도 불구하고 한 공동체가 분리와 억제를 강조하게 된다.[194] 파멸적인 사람들을 거부하지 않는 공동체는 오래 지속될 수 없다.

Almost every religious community knows the tension of exclusion and inclusion. On the one hand, to include people without distinction is precarious because the very core of the community's life may be undercut by allowing people to enter who do not care about the basic beliefs or *nomoi* of the community. On the other hand, exclusion is also precarious. Communities given to exclusion frequently become harsh, "pinched" groups who continue to live long after they are dead. In spite of certain dangers, occasions do arise when a community may be forced to emphasize separation and restriction.[194] The community that does not say no to ruinous people cannot exist for long.

통혼은 에스라와 느헤미야가 주도한 언약 갱신 예배에서 뜨거운

---

194) Holmgren, 34.

이슈들 중 하나였다. 통혼은 가깝게 지내는 종교 공동체에 위험이 노출되지만, 영향력이 있는 사람들이 개입될 때는 항상 위험에 처해지게 된다. 느헤미야는 대제사장 집안의 한 젊은 이(제사장)가 느헤미야의 원수로 간주된 산발랏의 딸과 결혼했다는 소식에 분노했다(느 13:28-31). 그는 언약 공동체의 내부자와 외부자 사이에 경계선을 긋기를 원했다. 한 유대인 남성과 외국 여성과 결혼하면 외국 아내들과 자기들의 자녀들의 밀접한 관계성 때문에 느헤미야는 큰 근심을 하게 되었던 것이다. 아내가 외국인이기 때문에 자녀들에게 유대의 사회적이며 종교적 전통을 가르치지 않는다(참고. 느 13:23-24).

Intermarriage was one of the hot issues in the covenant renewal ceremony under Ezra and Nehemiah. Intermarriage always poses dangers to a close-knit, religious community, but it becomes especially threatening when it concerns influential peoples. Nehemiah was outraged to learn that a young man(a priest) from the family of the high priest has married the daughter of Nehemiah's determined foe, Sanballat(Neh. 13:28-31). He wanted to draw the border line between insider and outsider of the covenant community. The marriage of a Judean man to a foreign woman caused great anxiety in Nehemiah because of the close relationship the children in such a marriage would have to the non-Judean mother. Because she was a foreigner, she would not teach her children the Judean social and religious traditions(cf. Neh. 13:23-24).

다른 경우에, 느헤미야는 자기의 개혁을 반대한 공동체 밖의 사람들을 "기억해 달라"고 기도했다(느 6:14; 참고 4:3-5). 그들의 계속되는 반대의 짐이 무거웠다; 그러나 내부자들의 반발이 외부자들의 반대보다 더 아팠다. 거짓 대언자들과 이스라엘의 지도자들(사이비 내부자들)이 이스라엘 역사상 언약 공동체에 혐오스러웠다. 그들은 다른 상징적 세계를 가졌기 때문이었다. 에스라와 느헤미야의 사회적 역할은 내부자들을 합법적인 언약으로 하나가 되게 화합하는 것이었다.

On another occasion, Nehemiah called upon God to "remember" those outside the community who opposed him(Neh. 6:14; cf. 4:3-5). The burden of their continual opposition was heavy; however, more painful than the outside obstructionism was the rebellion of the "insiders." False prophets and leaders of Israel("quasi-insiders") had been hostile to the covenant community during the history of Israel. For they had different symbolic universe. The social role of Ezra and Nehemiah was to harmonize insiders into oneness with the legitimate covenant.

4-2-1-2. 갱신된 언약 공동체 The renewed covenant community

합법화는 제도권에서 생기는 "이유들"에 대한 질문에 대한 대답들이다. 합법화들은 사회적 객관화의 영역에 속한다. 즉 다른 말로 표현하자면 주어진 집합체에 존재하는 "지식"을 통과하는 것이다. 이것은 그들이 단순히 사회적 사건들의 "왜"와 "이유들"에 대한 개인적인 사고력과는 매우 다른 객관성의 상태를 가지고 있음을 암시하고 있다. 그래서 합법화들은 성격상 인지적이며 규범적일 수 있다.[195]

---
195) Berger, 1967:29.

Legitimations are answers to any questions about the "why" of institutional arrangements. Legitimations belong to the domain of social objectivations, that is, to what passes for "knowledge" in a given collectivity. This implies that they have a status of objectivity quite different from merely individual cogitations about the "why" and "wherefore" of social events. Thus legitimations can be both cognitive and normative in character.[195]

모든 사회적으로 객관화된 "지식"은 합법화된 것이다. 사회의 규범은 스스로 단순히 거기 있는 것으로도 합법화되고 있다. 제도들은 인간의 활동을 조직한다. 제도들의 의미가 과학적으로 결속되기에 제도들은 사실상 제도화된 행동들이 그것을 행한 자들에게 "명백해"지는 데까지 합법화되어진다.[196]

All socially objectivated "knowledge" is legitimating. The *nomos* of a society legitimates itself by simply being there. Institutions structure human activity. As the meanings of the institutions are nomically integrated, the institutions are in fact legitimated, to the point where the institutionalized actions appear "self-evident" to their performers.[196]

종교적인 제도들은 전통을 전수하는 것과 전수자의 경험의 사회적 영향을 길들이는 것의 이중 기능들을 가지고 있다. 만일 사회의 규범이 한 세대에서 다음 세대로 전수가 되어 새로운 세대가 같은 사회적 세계에 거주하게 될 것이라면, 새로운 세대의 마음속에서 일

---
196) Berger, 1967:30.

어나게 될 질문들에 대한 답변을 하는 형태를 합법화해야 할 것이다. 아이들뿐만 아니라 어른들도 합법화하는 답변들을 잊어버린다. 그들은 다시 "상기될 것이다." 다른 말로 표현하면, 합법화하는 형식들은 되풀이되어야 한다. 분명히 그러한 반복은 "망각"의 위험이 매우 예민할 때 특히 집단적 혹은 개인적 위기의 경우에 중요할 것이다.[197]

Religious institutions have their double functions of transmitting a tradition and of domesticating the social impact of the experience of the transcendent. If the *nomos* of a society is to be transmitted from one generation to another, so that the new generation will also come to "inhabit" the same social world, there will be have to be legitimating formulas to answer the questions that will arise in the minds of the new generation. Not only children but also adults as well "forget" the legitimating answers. They must ever again be "reminded." In other words, the legitimating formulas must be repeated. Clearly such repetition will be especially important on those occasions of collective or individual crisis when the danger of "forgetting" is most acute.[197]

언약 갱신 예식은 이런 관점에서 이해되어야 한다. 제2성전 봉헌 후 포로 생활에서 귀환한 이들을 포함한 유대인들은 그들의 종교적 전통들과 합법화한 대답들을 잊어버린 듯했다. 학사 에스라가 여호와께서 이스라엘에게 주신 모세의 율법서를 들고 와서 회중 앞에서

---

[197] Berger, 1967:30-31.

읽었을 때, 합법화한 대답들이 기억되어 모든 회중들이 "아멘, 아멘"으로 회답을 하였다(느 8:1-12).

The covenant renewal ceremony should be understood from this perspective. After dedication of the second temple, the Judeans including the group who returned from exile seemed to forget their religious traditions and their legitimating answers. When Ezra the scribe brought the book of the law of Moses which the Lord had given to Israel and read in front of the congregation, the legitimating answers were reminded: all the people answered, "Amen, Amen"(Neh. 8:1-12).

여기서 종교는 사회적으로 현실에 대해 정의를 내린다. 현실이 개인들의 의식 속에서 정의내려지고 유지되어지는 인지적이며 사회적인 장치를 제공한다. 토라는 개인의 생활을 부활시켰으며 그 마음을 즐거움을 회복시켰다(느 8:12). 느 9:13에서 여호와는 이스라엘에게 "정직한 규례와 진정한 율법과 선한 율례와 계명들"을 주신 분으로 축하를 받으셨다. 언약 갱신 예식 자체는 어떤 종류의 관계성을 회복함을 축하하는 의도였다.

Here religion provided a socially definition of reality; the cognitive and social mechanisms by which reality was defined and maintained in the consciousness of individuals. The Torah revived individual life and restored "rejoicing" to his heart(Neh. 8:12). In Neh. 9:13, the Lord was celebrated as the one who had given Israel "right ordinances and true laws, good statues and commandments." The covenant renewal ceremony itself intended to celebrate restoration of some sort of relationship.

진정한 축하는 우리로 하여금 매일 표현하는 자비로움의 종류를 상기시키는 예배적인 행동을 나누는 것을 의미했다(참고. 느 5:14-18):

"14 내가 유다 땅 총독으로 세움을 받은 때 곧 아닥사스다왕 이십 년 부터 삼십이 년까지 십이 년 동안은 나와 내 형제가 총독의 녹을 먹지 아니하였느니라 15 이전 총독들은 백성에게 토색하여 양식과 포도주와 또 은 사십 세겔을 취하였고 그 종자들도 백성을 압제하였으나 나는 하나님을 경외하므로 이같이 행치 아니하고 16 도리어 이 성 역사에 힘을 다하며 땅을 사지 아니하였고 나의 모든 종자도 모여서 역사를 하였으며 17 또 내 상에는 유다 사람들과 민장들 일백오십 인이 있고 그 외에도 우리 사면 이방인 중에서 우리에게 나아온 자들이 있었는데 18 매일 나를 위하여 소 하나와 살진 양 여섯을 준비하며 닭도 많이 준비하고 열흘에 한 번씩은 각종 포도주를 갖추었나니 비록 이같이 하였을지라도 내가 총독의 녹을 요구하지 아니하였음은 백성의 부역이 중함이니라."

True celebration meant sharing which was a "ritual" act that reminded us of the kind of generosity we were to express in everyday life(cf. Neh. 5:14-18): "14 Moreover from the time that I was appointed to be their governor in the land of Judah, from the twentieth year even unto the two and thirtieth year of Artaxerxes the king, that is, twelve years, I and my brethren have not eaten the bread of the governor. 15 But the former governors that had been before me were chargeable unto the people, and had taken of them bread and wine, beside forty shekels of silver; yea, even their servants bare rule over the people: but so did not I, because of the fear of God. 16 Yea, also I continued in the work of this wall, neither bought we any land: and all my servants were gathered thither unto the work. 17 Moreover there were at my table an hundred and fifty of the Jews and rulers, beside those that came unto us from among the heathen that are about us. 18 Now that which was prepared for me daily was one ox and six choice sheep; also fowls were prepared for me, and once in ten days store of all sorts of wine: yet for all this required not I the bread of the governor, because the bondage was heavy upon this people."

4-2-2. 한 사회적 제도로의 포수기 이후 언약 공동체 The post-exilic covenant community as a social institution

페르샤 시대의 유대 언약 공동체는 버거의 이론에 의하면,[198] 인간의 산물뿐만 아니라 이를 만든 이들을 지속적으로 행동하는 변증적 현상이었다. 유대 공동체는 인간의 의식이 기초된 터 위에 유대인들이 세운 산물이었다. 그러나 그 공동체는 유대인들이 세운 언약 공동체였는데 이 공동체 안에서 개인들은 사회적 과정들의 결과가 낳은 인간이 되었다.

The Judean covenant community in the Persian period was a dialectic phenomena in that it was a human product as well as

---

198) Berger 1967:3.

that yet continuously acted back its producer, according to the theory of Berger.198) The Judean community was a product of the Judeans upon which the human consciousness was based. Yet it may also be said that the Judean people was a product of the covenant community within which individual became a person as a result of social processes.

언약 공동체는 개인의 의식 없이는 흐르지 않는다. 개인의 의식은 현실의 사회적 구성 없이는 소멸되지 않는다. 언약 공동체의 각 회원은 사회 속에서 자기 정체성을 찾는다. 그래서 그는 언약 공동체로부터 떠나 존재할 수 없다. 이것은 사회적 현상의 변증적 성격을 반영한다.199)

The covenant community stagnates without the consciousness of the individual; and the consciousness of individual dies away without the social construction of reality. Each member of the covenant community finds his identity within the society, so he cannot exist apart from the covenant community. This reflects the dialectic character of the societal phenomenon.199)

언약 공동체는 사회적으로 구성된 의미 위에 기초되어 있다. 그 공동체는 전통적 언약으로부터 사회적으로 기인한 당연시 하는 세계관을 가지고 있다. 우선, 인지적 소수는 제도적 순서와 개인적 전기를 포함하는 일종의 상징적 세계를 가지고 있다. 사회적 객관화를 통해 상징적 세계는 합법화되어지고 독특한 현실 그 자체가 된다.

The covenant community is grounded on the socially

---

199) *Ibid.*

constructed meaning. It has a taken-for-granted world view which is socially derived from the traditional covenant. First of all, the cognitive minority has a sort of symbolic universe that overarches the institutional order and individual biography. Through the social objectivation, the symbolic universe is legitimated and becomes a reality *sui generis*.

언약 공동체는 거룩한 우주가 경험적 현상으로 세워지는 인간의 기업이다.[200] 그 공동체는 의미 있는 질서를 가지고 있는 거룩한 형태 속에서 사회적 우주화 자체이다.[201] 이 형태는 사회의 세속적인 공동체와는 다르다. 혼돈으로부터 벗어나와 거룩한 우주는 현실의 질서를 나타내고 제공한다. 배교로부터 벗어나, 언약 공동체는 혼돈 속에서 혼합되어지지 않고, 거룩한 율법이 의미 없게 되지 않는다. 언약에 충실하다는 것은 거룩한 질서와 관계성을 회복하는 것이다: "나는 너희들의 하나님이며, 너희들은 나의 백성이다."

The covenant community is the human enterprise by which a sacred cosmos is established as an empirical phenomenon.[200] It is a social cosmization in a sacred mode with a meaningful order.[201] This is different from the profane community of society. Out of chaos, the sacred cosmos emerges and provides an order of reality. Out of apostasy, the covenant community gets mixed up in a chaos and the sacred laws become meaningless. To be faithful to covenant is to restore the sacred order and relationship: "I am your God and you are my people."

---

200) *Ibid.*, 25.
201) *Ibid.*, 25-26.

이스라엘이 반복적으로 언약의 관계성을 깨뜨려도 여호와께서는 스스로 그 언약에 매여 있다. 이스라엘 백성들은 그들이 "좋았던 옛 시절"을 기억하며 그들의 하나님과 신실한 관계성을 회복하는 언약 갱신 예배가 필요했다.

Even though Israel repeatedly broke the covenant relationship, the Lord considered Himself bound to it. The Israelite people, *ad hoc*, needed the covenant renewal ceremony in which they remembered "good old days" and restored faithful relationship to their God.

4-3. 개혁 그룹의 상징적 세계 The symbolic universe of the reform group

4-3-1. 지식의 사회적 형태로서의 언약 Covenant as the social form of knowledge

본 항에서 우리는 상징적 우주의 핵심인 언약의 개념을 통하여 포수기 이후의 유대 사회의 가장 중요한 현실[202]을 살펴볼 것이다.

---

[202] 슈츠에 의하면 현실은 하나의 통일된 전체로서 경험되지 않는다. The reality, according to A. Schutz, is not experienced as one unified whole; 다른 말로 하면 사람의 일상 세계는 다양한 현실들로 이뤄진다. that is, man's life-world consists of "multiple realities." 다양한 현실들 가운데 의식속에 한 특권적 성격을 가진 현실이 있는데 일상적인 매일의 생활 속에 만연된 현실이 있다. Among the multiple realities, there is one reality that has a privileged character in consciousness, and it is precisely the reality of being wide awake in ordinary, every life. 슈츠는 이를 "가장 중요한 현실"이라고 부른다. Schutz calls it the "paramount reality." 다른 한편, 다른 현실들은 의식이 들어와서 그곳으로부터 매일의 생활의 실제 세상으로 돌아가는 일종의 영토처럼 보인다. on the other hand, the other realities appear as some sort of enclaves into which

In this section, we will examine the paramount reality[202] of the post-exilic Judean society through the term of covenant which was the core of the symbolic universe.

지식 사회학적인 관점에서, 한 상징적 우주는 알려진 "세계"여서 알려진 것으로부터 멀리 떨어진 것이 아니라 누구나 체험하는 지식의 형식을 갖추고 있다. 그리고 상징적 우주는 보여지는 "세계"이지, 볼 수 없는데 존재하는 세계는 아니다.

From the perspective of the sociology of knowledge, a symbolic universe is the "world" as it is known and therefore as the knowledge of it shapes one's experience of it, not as something that exists apart from what is known. And a symbolic universe is the "world" as it is viewed, not as something that exists apart from the way we view it.

다른 한편에서 신학은 상징적 우주에 대한 조직적인 성찰의 산물인 일종의 지시이다. 상징적 우주를 구성하는 지식을 변호하고 유지하는 데 생산된 일종의 지식인 것이다. 그러므로 우리는 상징적 세계가 지식의 원초적(성찰 이전의) 형태로 말할 수 있고, 신학은 거기에

---

consciousness moves and from which it returns to the "real world" of everyday life. 슈츠는 이런 다른 현실들을 "의미의 유한한 영토"라고 부른다. Schutz calls these other realities "finite provinces of meaning." 일상 생활의 평범한 현실인 "가장 중요한 현실"은 다른 현실들보다 더욱 실제여서 중요하다. The paramount reality, which is the mundane reality of everyday life, is important because it is more real than the other realities. 이 현실은 사회적으로 확증되어 가장 강한 타당성 구조를 가지고 있다. It is socially confirmed and has the strongest plausibility structure. 그러나 가장 중요한 현실의 다른 측면은 그것의 위험성에 의해 이뤄진다. But the other aspect of the paramount reality is characterized by its precariousness. 다른 말로 표현하면 그 현실은 본래 부숴지기 쉽고 쉽게 방해받는다 In another words, it is inherently fragile and easily interrupted(Schutz, 207ff).

의존하는 이차적(성찰적) 형태라고 할 수 있다.203)

Theology, on the other hand, is a kind of knowledge that is the product of systematic reflection upon a symbolic universe, and a kind of knowledge that is produced to defend and maintain the knowledge comprising a symbolic universe. Therefore, we can speak of a symbolic universe as a primary(pre-reflective) form of knowledge and theology as a secondary(reflective) form that is dependent on it.203)

에스라와 느헤미야 당시의 개혁 집단이 가진 상징적 우주를 살피면서, 우리는 어떤 신학을 논하지 않지만 그들이 신학화한 우주에 대해 관심이 있다. 에스라가 가진 신학 보다는 그가 신학화한 과정이 우리에게는 더 중요하다. 왜냐하면 그의 신학화 과정이 그 자신과 그의 사회적 우주에 동조하는 공동체 사이의 사회적 관계의 형태로서 일어났기 때문이다.

In exploring the symbolic universe of the reform group(in the time of Ezra and Nehemiah), we are not be concerned on any theology but on the universe about which they theologized. Ezra's theologizing is more important for us than his theology because his theologizing took place as a form of social relations between himself and his support group in the sphere of their social universe.

그래서 우리는 그의 개혁 속에 있던 사회적 관계들의 우주를 살펴봄으로써 그의 신학화 과정을 고찰할 수 있다. 또한 그의 상징적

---

203) Petersen, 29-30.

세계를 살피기 위해 그의 신학을 관철할 수 있는 것이다.

Thus we can consider Ezra's theologizing in our exploration of the universe of social relations in his reform, and we can seek to penetrate through his theology in order to explore his symbolic universe.

개혁 그룹의 상징적 우주는 회중들이 듣고 수용한 모세의 율법 중심으로 형성되었다(느 8:1-12). 에스라는 "너는 네 손에 있는 네 하나님의 율법을 따라"(스 7:14) 유대 공동체 안에 질서를 회복하기 위해 귀환했다. 모세 율법에 기초한 개혁의 정신은 레위인들, 제사장들, 평신도들(참고. 스 10:18-43; 느 9:38-10:39)로 구성된 다양한 사회적 계층들을 한 사회 조직으로 통합했다.

The symbolic universe of the reform group was crystallized around the law of Moses which the congregation heard and accepted(Neh. 8:1-12). Ezra returned to restore order in the Judean community "according to the law of your God, which is in your hand"(Ezra 7:14). The spirit of reform based on the law of Moses integrated into one social system diverse social classes which included Levites, priests, and the laypersons(cf. Ezra 10:18-43; Neh. 9:38-10:39).

개혁을 통하여 유대 공동체의 회원들은 하나의 제의적이며 민족적인 순수한 세계를 만드는 데 합의했다. 만약 어떤 사람이 이 상징적 우주를 반대했다면 그는 사회제도에서 파문을 당했을 것이다. 그래서 이 상징적 우주는 귀환한 유대 공동체의 정체성을 당시 경쟁자인 이방민족들과 그들의 신앙에 맞서 세웠다.

Through the reform, the insiders of Judean community agreed

to construct a pure world, cultic and ethnic. If anyone opposed this symbolic universe, he/she might be excommunicated from the social system. Thus this symbolic universe served to establish the identity of the returned Judean community in relation to rival foreign peoples and to their faith.

"언약"의 개념은 고대 이스라엘 사회에서 사회적으로 유래된 것이다. 오늘날로 말하자면 상호의 책임을 포함한 두 사람 혹은 두 단체 사이에 이뤄지는 "준엄한 합의" 같은 것을 말하는데 예를 들면 혼인 서약, 종교 단체의 교인들 사이의 합의문, 통치적 정치 세력들 사이의 조약 같은 것이다. 계약은 세계가 통합되고 유지되게 만드는 사회적 연대이다.

The term "covenant" was socially derived in the ancient Israelite society. Today the term refers to "a binding and solemn agreement" made by two or more parties which involves mutual responsibilities, as for instance, a marriage covenant, an agreement among members of a religious body, or a treaty between sovereign political powers. Covenant is a social bond with which the world is consolidated and maintained.

구약성경에서 언약이란 단어는 약속과 의무가 수반된 헌신에 기초하여 지속성과 일관성을 가진 연관성을 묘사할 때 사용된다.[204]

In the Hebrew Bible, the word is used to describe a binding relationship that is based on commitment, that carries with it promises and obligations, and that has the quality of constancy or

---

204) Cf. D. J. McCarthy, *Treaty and Covenant*, Rome:Bbilical Institute Press, 1981; J. Bright, *Covenant & Promise*, London: SCM Press, LTD, 1977.

durability.204)

가족 대표들이나 사회적-정치적 그룹들 사이의 언약들이 있다. 예를 들면 야곱과 라반 사이의 언약(창 31:44-50), 정복한 이스라엘과 기브온 사람들 사이의 언약(수 9:3-27), 혹은 다윗과 이스라엘의 장로들 사이의 언약(삼하 5:3) 등이다.205)

There are various examples of covenants between heads of families or socio-political groups, such as Jacob and Laban(Gen. 31:44-50), the conquering Israelites and the Gibeonites(Josh. 9:3-27), or David and the elders of Israel (II Sam. 5:3).205)

다른 표현으로, 성경적 언약은 지식의 사회적 형태이다. 하나님께서 언약을 통해 알려지셨고 이스라엘 공동체는 언약을 통하여 사회적 질서를 확립했다.

In other word, the biblical covenant is the social form of knowledge. God was known through covenant and the Israelite community could build a social order through covenant.

최초 이스라엘 공동체가 형성되었을 때 모세의 언약은 히브리 사람들과 어중이떠중이들을(출 12:38) 사회적으로 결속시키는 데 중요한 역할을 하였다. 모세는 이집트에서 나올 때 조직이 엉성한 그룹들을 법적인 관할로 조직화하여 그들 자신의 사회적 법을 만드는 곳으로 인도했다. 다윗은 언약을 통하여 이스라엘 전체를 다스리는 합법적인 왕이 되었다(삼하 7:5-16).206)

When the first Israelite community was organized, the Mosaic covenant played a central role to bind Hebrew people and a

---

205) Anderson, 89.
206) Weber, 76.

mixed multitude socially(Ex. 12:38). Moses led an unorganized group from out of Egyptian into the legal jurisdiction in a region where they had to make their own social laws. David became a legitimate king over whole Israel through covenant(2 Sam. 7:5-16).[206]

긴 왕정시대 동안 옛 언약 전통이 새로운 사회적, 법적, 종교적 사고틀과 조직에 양보한 후, 예루살렘 성전 안에 있는 신명기 법전에 발견되어 옛 전통의 부활이 있었다(주전 621년). 요시야 왕은 자기 백성들과 언약 갱신을 하면서 이 책에 기록된 언약의 말씀들을 따르기로 약속하였다(왕하 23:3). 이 사건은 여러 가지 면에서 포수기 후기에 일어난 랍비적 유대교의 기초를 제공하였다.[207]

After the long period of monarchy, in which the old covenant traditions gave way to new social, legal, and religious patterns of thought and organization, there was a resurgence of the older traditions, initiated by the discovery of a lawbook(the Deuteronomic Code) in the Jerusalem temple(621 BC). King Josiah made a covenant renewal with his people, promising to follow the "words of this covenant that were written in this book"(II Kings 23:3). This event furnished in many important respects the foundations of the rabbinical Judaism which arose in the post-exilic period.[207]

언약 갱신의식의 사회적 제도가 여호수아 고별 설교에 처음 나타났는데(수 24장) 이스라엘에서 종교적-사회적 제도를 합법화하는 데 매우 중요했다.[208]

---
207) Mendenhall, 721.
208) cf. Weber, 77.

The social institution of the covenant renewal ceremony, first appeared in the Bible at the covenant Joshua(Josh. 24), was very important in legitimating a religious-social organization in Israel.208)

에스라의 지도하에 모세 언약이 갱신되는 거룩한 성회가 열렸다(느 9-10장). 학사 겸 제사장인 에스라의 기도 형식으로 그는 언약을 파기한 이스라엘의 죄들을 지적했다. 언약 공동체의 개연성 구조를 파괴하는 원인이 하나님의 율법을 불순종하는 데 있었던 것이다.

Under Ezra, a sacred convocation took place in which the Mosaic covenant was renewed(Neh. 9-10). In the form of a prayer of Ezra the priest and scribe, he pointed out the sins of Israel which broke the covenant. The destruction of the plausibility structure of the covenant community attributed to their failure to obey the divine law.

그러므로 왕족들, 레위인들, 제사장들, 일반 백성들이 견고하며 신실한 언약 합의에 참여하도록 해서 인봉하게 하였다(느 9:38). 웨버는 주장하기를 "포수기 후기에 언약(Berit)이란 '연맹' 뿐만 아니라 제의적으로 합당한 전체 유대인들에게 의미심장했다."209)

Therefore, the princes, Levites, and priests and people were called to enter a firm or faithful covenant agreement and set a seal to it(Neh. 9:38). Weber wrote, "In post-exilic times this term ("covenant") signifies the "ritually correct full Jews" as well as "confederation.""209)

---

209) Weber, *Ancient Judaism*, 75.

언약은 당시 유대 공동체에서 중요한 사회적 근거가 되었는데, 왜 냐하면 이스라엘의 고대 사회 제도는 부분적으로 정착한 전사 가족들과 법적으로 보호를 받은 이들로서의 손님 부족들 - 순회하는 유목민들과 손님 전사들, 상인들, 그리고 제사장들 - 사이의 영원한 관계성을 계약적으로 규정한 것 위에 있기 때문이다.[210]

The covenant was the major social basis in that Judean community, for the ancient social structure of Israel in part rested essentially upon a contractually regulated, permanent relationship of landed warrior sibs with guest tribes as legally protected metics: itinerant herdsmen and guest artisans, merchants and priests.[210]

4-3-2. 인지적 소수자로서의 개혁 그룹 The reform group as the cognitive minority

칼 막스에 의하면, 하부구조와 상부구조는 변증적으로 사회에서 연관이 있다. 여기서 하부구조는 경제적인 "기초" 뿐만 아니라 일반적인 일상생활을 뜻한다.[211] 막스 베버는 칼빈주의와 현대 자본주의 활동의 경제적 윤리 사이에 선택적인 밀접한 관계가 있다고 제시한다. "선택적인 밀접한 관계"란 어떤 종교적 이념들과 그들의 사회적인 제도가 역사상 상호 변증적이라는 뜻이다.[212]

According to K. Marx, substructure and superstructure are dialectically related in a society. Substructure here is identified

---
210) Ibid., 79.
211) See Berger, 1967:192.
212) Weber, 1958.

not only with an economic "base" but with praxis in general.²¹¹⁾ And M. Weber suggests that there is an elective affinity between Calvinism and the economic ethics of modern capitalist activity. By the concept of "elective affinity" Weber means that certain religious ideas and their social "carriers" seek each other out in history.²¹²⁾

그러나 피터 버거에게는 개연성 구조가 종교의 현실 유지를 이해하는 데 중요하다.²¹³⁾ 세계들이 사회적으로 형성되었고 사회적으로 유지되고 있다. 그들의 지속적인 현실은 당연시 되는 사실성과 개인적 의식에 부여된 사실성으로 특별한 사회적 과정들 – 즉 지속적으로 재구성되며 의문의 특수 세계들을 유지하는 과정들 – 위에 의존해 있다.

For Berger, however, the plausibility structure is important in understanding the reality-maintaining task of religion.²¹³⁾ Worlds are socially constructed and socially maintained. Their continuing reality, both taken-for-granted facticity and facticity imposing itself on individual consciousness, depends upon specific social processes, namely those processes that ongoingly reconstruct and maintain the particular worlds in question.

그래서 서로 서로의 세계는 실제적인 인간들에 진실한 세계로서 지속적인 존재의 사회적 근거를 요구하고 있다. 피터 버그는 이러한 사회적 기초를 "개연성 구조"라고 부른다.²¹⁴⁾ 다른 말로 표현하자면,

---

213) Berger, 1967:45.
214) Ibid.

현실의 특별한 정의가 사람들에게 그럴듯하게(개연성) 남아있는 사회적 조건들이다.

Thus each world requires a social "base" for its continuing existence as a world that is real to actual human beings. Berger calls this social "base" its plausibility structure.[214] In other words, it is the social conditions under which a particular definition of reality remains plausible to people.

웨버는 언약 공동체에 대해 다음과 같이 정의한다:[215]

> 특별히 종교적인 관점에서 부르는 "공동체" 혹은 "회중"이란 특별한 관점에서 예언과 연관된 모임만을 지칭하지 않는다. 종교적 공동체가 예언 운동을 일상화의 결과로 연관시키는 데에서 생기지 않는다. 일상화란 예언자 자신 혹은 그의 제자들이 그의 설교의 우월성을 주장하여 은혜를 회중들에게 나눠주는 과정을 말한다. 또한 일상화는 한 기업과 인간의 경제적 존재를 안전하게 하며, 종교적 기능들로 부여받은 자들을 위해 예비된 권리를 독점한다.

Weber wrote about the covenant community as follows:[215]

A "community" or "congregation" in the specifically religious sense does not solely mean in connection with prophecy in the particular sense. Nor does religious community arises in connection with a prophetic movement as a result of ro utinization(Veralltaeglichung), i.e., as a result of the process whereby either the prophet himself or his disciples secure

---

215) Max Weber, *The Sociology of Religion*, 60-61.

the premanence of his preaching and the congregation's distribution of grace, hence insuring the economic existence of the enterprise and those who man it, and thereby monopolizing as well the privileges reserved for those charged with religious functions.

사회적으로 구성되어 유지되는 공동체는 실제 세계로서 계속 존재할 수 있는 사회적 기초를 가지고 있다. 예배가 반복됨으로 그 개연성 구조를 강화시킨다. 예배는 포로기 후의 유대인들을 하나님의 백성으로 정체성을 가지게 할 뿐만 아니라. 이스라엘을 세상을 향한 하나님의 목적의 도구로 만들 수 있는 추진력을 제공한다.[216] 예배 중에 하나님의 실재가 세속과 만난다. 성과 속이 만나는 예배 중의 언약 갱신이 일어난다. 종교적인 전통들은 종교적인 언약 갱신 의식에서 기억된다.

The socially constructed and maintained community has its social base for its continuing existence as a real world. The repeated worship consolidates its plausibility structure. Not only does worship identify the post-exilic Judeans as the people of God, it also provides a generative force capable of molding Israel into an agent of God's purpose in the world.[216] In worship, God's reality reaches in the profane area. The covenant renewal enacts during worship in which sacred and profane meet. The religious traditions are remembered at the covenant renewal rite.

---

216) Hanson, 73-75.

모든 종교적 세계는 그 자체가 인간의 활동의 결과인 개연성 구조에 기초하기에, 모든 종교적 세계는 본래 그 자체로는 위태롭다.217) 이 가능성이 의문의 개연성 구조의 불일치 혹은 불안정의 도가 더할수록 높아진다. 혼돈으로부터 그들의 공동체를 지키기 위해, 유대 공동체는 위에 살핀 경계선을 기준으로 회원들을 제한했다. 거룩한 우주는 항존하는 혼돈에서 그의 견고성을 유지하듯이, 언약 공동체는 낯선 환경 속에서 그의 신실성을 지켜나간다.

Since every religious world is based on a plausibility structure that is itself the product of human activity, every religious world is inherently precarious in its reality.217) This possibility increases with the degree of instability or discontinuity of the plausibility structure in question. In order to keep their community from the chaos, the Judean community delineated membership by the border lines which we examined above. As a sacred cosmos is able to maintain its solidarity in the ever-present face of chaos, so the covenant community keeps its credibility in the alien surroundings.

위기의 때에는 한 공동체의 반응이 항상 규범적이지는 않는다. 가끔씩 생존하기 위해서 한 공동체는 자신을 상충하는 정책 속에 참여시킬 수 있다. 바벨론 포로에서 돌아온 그룹은 588 BC의 재앙을 그들의 조상들의 불신에 대한 하나님의 심판으로 여겨서, 그들이 유다와 예루살렘으로 귀환한 것은 하나님의 은총으로 간주했다(슥 1:1-6).218) 에스라와 느헤미야가 인도한 개혁 집단은 그들의 정체성의

---

217) Berger, 1967:50.
218) 슥 1:1 다리오 왕 제이년 여덟째 달에 여호와의 말씀이 잇도의 손자 베레갸의 아들 대언자 스가랴에게 임하니라 이르시되 In the eighth month, in the second year of Dar-

위기를 알고 있었다.

In time of crisis a community's response is not always a normative one. Sometimes, in order to survive, a community may involve itself in contradictory policies. The group that returned from the Babylonian exile considered catastrophe of 588 BC as God's punishment for their faithlessness of their fathers, so that they considered their return to Judah and Jerusalem as God's grace (Zech. 1:1-6).[218] The reform group led by Ezra and Nehemiah knew the crisis of their identity.

한편으로는, 모든 이방적인 요소로부터 분리하는 일이 강조되었으며; 다른 한편으로는, 페르샤 정부와 연합하여 감사하였다. 이 두

---

ius, came the word of the LORD unto Zechariah, the son of Berechiah, the son of Iddo the prophet, saying, 2 여호와가 너희의 조상들에게 심히 진노하였느니라. The LORD hath been sore displeased with your fathers. 3 그러므로 너는 그들에게 말하기를 만군의 여호와께서 이처럼 이르시되 너희는 내게로 돌아오라 만군의 여호와의 말이니라 그리하면 내가 너희에게로 돌아가리라 만군의 여호와의 말이니라 Therefore say thou unto them, Thus saith the LORD of hosts; Turn ye unto me, saith the LORD of hosts, and I will turn unto you, saith the LORD of hosts. 4 너희 조상들을 본받지 말라 옛적 대언자들이 그들에게 외쳐 이르되 만군의 여호와께서 이같이 말씀하시기를 너희가 악한 길, 악한 행위를 떠나서 돌아오라 하셨다 하나 그들이 듣지 아니하고 내게 귀를 기울이지 아니하였느니라 여호와의 말이니라 Be ye not as your fathers, unto whom the former prophets have cried, saying, Thus saith the LORD of hosts; Turn ye now from your evil ways, and from your evil doings: but they did not hear, nor hearken unto me, saith the LORD. 5 너희 조상들이 어디 있느냐? 또 대언자들이 영원히 살겠느냐? Your fathers, where are they? and the prophets, do they live for ever? 6 내가 나의 종 대언자들에게 명령한 내 말과 내 법도들이 어찌 너희 조상들에게 임하지 아니하였느냐? 그러므로 그들이 돌이켜 이르기를 만군의 여호와께서 우리 길대로, 우리 행위대로 우리에게 행하시려고 뜻하신 것을 우리에게 행하셨도다 하였느니라 But my words and my statutes, which I commanded my servants the prophets, did they not take hold of your fathers? and they returned and said, Like as the LORD of hosts thought to do unto us, according to our ways, and according to our doings, so hath he dealt with us.

가지 강조점은 공동체의 주요 문제인 "생존"을 대면하는 시도였다. 왜냐하면 타 종교 전통을 가진 사람들과 동화되는 일이 중단되고 공동체 지도력이 페르샤 정부와 협력할 때만 공동체가 살아남을 수 있음을 인지했기 때문이다.[219]

On the one hand, separation from all the foreign elements was emphasized; on the other hand, there was appreciation for, and cooperation with, the Persian government. This twofold emphasis was an attempt to confront the community's chief problem: survival. For it was recognized that the community would survive only if assimilation with peoples of other religious traditions was halted and the community leadership cooperated with the Persian government.[219]

평상시에는 공동체 지도력이 다르게 행동했을 것이나 공동체가 위협을 당하고 있을 때에는 생존을 위한 일은 무엇이든지 행해졌다. 이처럼, 에스라와 느헤미야가 이끄는 개혁 그룹은 다른 방식으로 행동했다. 그들은 현실에 대한 사회적 현상을 인식하여 통혼을 지지한 일부 동료 유대인들의 잘못된 지식을 까발리려고 노력했다.

In normal times the community leadership might have acted differently, but in a time when the life of the community was threatened, whatever promoted survival was done. Likewise, the reform group led by Ezra and Nehemiah acted in a different way. They recognized the social phenomena of reality and tried to rebunk the false "knowledge" of some fellow Judeans who

---

[219] Holmgren, 5.

supported intermarriage.

버거와 러커만에 의하면 "지식"이란 현상이 사실인 것과 그들이 특징을 가지고 있다는 확실성이다[220]: "그것 없이는 어떤 사회도 존재할 수 없는 의미의 체계를 구성하는 것이 정확히 말하면 '지식'이다."[221] 개혁 그룹은 자기 자신들이 모세 율법을 전수한 자라고 여겼다. 종교 전통에 대한 바른 지식을 가졌다고 여겼다. 그들은 당분간 소수자로 살아야 했다.

For Berger and Luckmann, "knowledge" is the certainty that phenomena are real and that they possess specific characteristics:[220] "it is precisely this 'knowledge' that constitutes the fabric of meanings without which no society could exist."[221] The reform group identified themselves as the true bearers of the law of Moses; that is, those who had a right knowledge about their religious tradition. They had to live as a minority group for a while.

그들 자신의 전통을 수호하면서 그들은 또한 외부자들을 공격하지 않는 정책을 발전시켰다. 이 정책에는 되도록 갈등을 최소화하면서 다른 생각을 가진 사람들과 함께 살면서 소수 그룹의 염원을 반영했다.

While in the main holding to their own traditions, they have also developed the policy of not offending the outsiders. This policy reflected the desire of a minority group to live among others with as little conflict as possible.

---

220) Berger & Luckmann, 1966:1.
221) Ibid., 15.

4-4. 요약 Summary

에스라와 느헤미야가 이끌었던 결혼 개혁은 이스라엘 역사상 의미심장했다. 비록 유대 공동체 안에서 통혼한 모든 가족들이 그들의 이방 배우자들과 이혼하지 않았을지라도, 개혁은 큰 성공으로 평가를 받을 수 있었다. 왜냐하면 개혁이 유대 공동체의 회원과 외부자 사이에 튼튼한 경계선을 그어서, 유다의 개연성 구조를 강화시켰기 때문이다.

The marriage reform led by Ezra and Nehemiah was significant in the history of Israel. Even though not all the intermarried families of Judean community were divorced from their foreign spouses, the reform could be evaluated as a great success. For the reform drew a strong border line between inside and outside of Judean community, consolidating the plausibility structure of Judah.

통혼이 퍼져서 귀환한 유대 공동체의 제의적이며 인종적 순결과 국가의 정체성을 분해하려는 위협이 만연했던 것이다. 초기 페르샤 시대에는 통혼이 생존을 위해 필요했을지도 모른다. 그러나 에스라와 느헤미야가 귀환했을 때는 공동체의 전체 특징을 협박하고 있었다.

The spread of intermarriage threatened to disintegrate the national identity and the purity, cultic and ethnic, of the returned Judean community. In the early Persian period, intermarriage might have been necessary for survival. In the time of Ezra and Nehemiah, however, it was threatening the whole character of the community.

에스라의 관점에서 보면 포로는 우상 숭배 죄에 대한 심판이었고, 통혼이 퍼지면 비슷한 심판이 다시 있게 된다는 것이다.

The exile was, from Ezra's point of view, the punishment for the sin of idolatry, and, with the spread of intermarriages, the similar punishment might happen again.

통혼은 문화적이고 인종적인 동화로 귀결될 수 있다. 이방 여인들과 결혼함으로 유대인과 이방인 사이의 경계선, 유대인과 사마리아 사람들 사이의 경계선이 모호하게 되었다. 이리하여 유대 공동체의 개연 구조가 붕괴되거나 해체되기 시작했던 것이다. 그들 공동체의 개연 구조를 지키기 위해, 귀환한 그룹의 지도자들은 정치적이며(아닥사스다 황제의 친서를 가짐), 종교적이며(편집된 토라를 가지고 옴), 경제적인 힘(황제로부터 재정 지원을 받음)을 가지고 돌아온 에스라에게 통혼의 현상들을 보고했던 것이다. 유대 공동체의 존재에 심각한 협박을 막아내고 유대인의 정체성을 지키기 위해서, 통혼과 싸우는 것은 필수적이었다.

Intermarriage can result in the cultural and ethnic assimilation. By marrying foreign women, the border line between Judean and gentile, and between Judean and Samaritans became vague. Thus the plausibility structure of the Judean community began to be deconstructed or disintegrated. In order to keep the plausibility structure of their community, the leaders of the returned group made report of the facts about intermarriage to Ezra who had the political(with Letters of Artaxerxes), religious(with the written Torah), economic(with the financial support from the king's treasury) power. In order to preserve the Judean identity guard against the serious threat to the Judean community's existence, it was most imperative to fight against intermarriages.

언약 공동체 생활에서 중요한 원칙은 순결인데, 외부인과 구별하는 데 가장 중요한 언어이다. 통혼은 에스라와 느헤미야가 주도한 언약 갱신 의식에서 뜨거운 논점들 중 하나였다. 왜냐하면 통혼은 항상 가깝게 지내는 종교 공동체에 위험을 야기하며 특히 영향력 있는 지도자들이 관여되어 있으면 특히 위협적이 될 수 있기 때문이다. 에스라와 느헤미야의 사회적 역할은 내부인들을 합법적인 언약과 하나님을 중화하는 것이었다.

The main principle of life in the covenant community was purity which was the most important language of separation from the outsiders. Intermarriage was one of the hot issues in the covenant renewal ceremony under Ezra and Nehemiah. For intermarriage always poses dangers to a close-knit, religious community, but it becomes especially threatening when it concerns influential peoples. The social role of Ezra and Nehemiah was to harmonize insiders into oneness with the legitimate covenant.

합법화는 사회적 객관화의 영역에 속한다. 다시 말하면 객관화란 주어진 집합체 속에 내재한 "지식"을 통과하는 것을 말한다. 사회적 사건들의 "이유들(왜, 그런 이유로)"에 대한 개인적인 사고력과는 많이 다른 객관성의 상태를 유지함을 함축하고 있다. 사회적으로 객관화된 "지식"은 모두 합법화의 과정을 거친다. 사회의 규범은 단순히 거기 존재한다는 것으로도 스스로를 합법화한다. 제도들이 인간의 활동을 구성한다. 제도들의 의미가 명목상 통합되어지듯이 제도들은 제도적인 행동들이 행하는 자들에게 자명하게 나타나는 데까지 사실상 합법화되어진다.

Legitimations belong to the domain of social objectivations, that is, to what passes for "knowledge" in a given collectivity. This implies that they have a status of objectivity quite different from merely individual cogitations about the "why" and "wherefore" of social events. All socially objectivated "knowledge" is legitimating. The *nomos* of a society legitimates itself by simply being there. Institutions structure human activity. As the meanings of the institutions are nomically integrated, so the institutions are in fact legitimated, to the point where the institutionalized actions appear "self-evident" to their performers.

이런 관점에서 언약갱신의식을 이해해야 한다. 제2성전이 봉헌되고 나서, 포로에서 귀환한 그룹을 포함한 유대인들은 그들의 종교 전통들과 합리적인 대답들을 잊어버린 듯했다. 서기관 에스라가 여호와께서 이스라엘에게 주신 모세의 율법책을 가지고 와서 회중들 앞에 읽었을 때, 백성들은 아멘 아멘 하며 합법적인 응답이 들려졌다(느 8:1-12).

The covenant renewal ceremony should be understood from this perspective. After dedication of the second temple, the Judeans including the group who returned from exile seemed to forget their religious traditions and their legitimating answers. When Ezra the scribe brought the book of the law of Moses which the Lord had given to Israel and read in front of the congregation, the legitimating answers were heard: all the people answered, "Amen, Amen"(Neh. 8:1-12).

(에스라와 느헤미야 시대에) 개혁 그룹의 상징적 우주를 탐구해 보면,

우리는 어떤 신학에 관심있지 않고 그들이 신학화한 우주에 대해 관심이 있다. 에스라의 신학화는 그의 신학보다 더 우리에게 중요하다. 그 이유는 그의 신학화가 그들의 사회적 우주의 영적에서 그 자신과 그를 지지하는 그룹 사이의 사회적 관계들의 형태로 일어났기 때문이다. 그래서 우리는 그의 개혁 속에 있었던 사회적 관계들의 우주를 탐구한 에스라의 신학화를 살펴볼 수 있으며, 그의 상징적 우주를 탐구하기 위해 그의 신학을 통해 침투한 것을 찾을 수 있다.

In exploring the symbolic universe of the reform group(in the time of Ezra and Nehemiah), we are not be concerned on any theology but on the universe about which they theologized. Ezra's theologizing is more important for us than his theology because his theologizing took place as a form of social relations between himself and his support group in the sphere of their social universe. Thus we can consider Ezra's theologizing in our exploration of the universe of social relations in his reform, and we can seek to penetrate through his theology in order to explore his symbolic universe.

폴 핸슨 교수는 다음과 같이 저술한다:[222]

> 한 새로운 상징적 우주(혹 대체적인 의미 우주)가 고립의 체험에 책임 있는 사회제도에 지배적인 것과 교체되어야 한다. 이 세상의 구조의 중요한 의미성을 부정하고, 더 높은 현실의 비전으로 들어가 미래를 창출해야 새로운 상징 우주가 생겨난다.

---

[222] Hanson, 1984:30.

Hanson writes as follows:[222]

> If the life of a community is to be sustained, a new symbolic universe(or an alternative universe of meaning) must replace that which was dominant in the social system responsible for the experience of alienation... The creation of a new symbolic universe begins by denial of the ultimate significance of this world's structures and by a retreat into a vision of the "higher" reality and of what that reality implies for the future.

개혁 그룹의 상징적 우주는 회중들이 듣고 받아들인 모세의 율법 중심으로 형성되었다(느 8:1-12). 개혁의 정신은 모세의 율법 위에 기초되어졌다. 이 율법이 레위인들, 제사장들 및 평신도들로 구성된 다양한 사회적 계층들을 하나의 사회적 제도로 통합시켰다(참고. 에스라 10:18-43, 느헤미야 9:38-10:39).

The symbolic universe of the reform group crystallized around the law of Moses which the congregation heard and accepted (Neh. 8:1-12). The spirit of reform based on the law of Moses integrated into one social system diverse social classes which included Levites, priests, and the laypersons (cf. Ezra 10:18-43, Neh. 9:38-10:39).

개혁을 통하여 유대 공동체의 일원들은 제의적이며 인종적인 하나의 순결한 세계를 만들기로 합의했다. 그래서 이 상징적 우주는 이방인들과 그들의 신앙과 맞서서 귀환한 유대 공동체의 정체성을 세우는 데 사용되었다.

Through the reform, the insiders of Judean community agreed to construct a pure world, cultic and ethnic. Thus this symbolic universe served to establish the identity of the returned Judean community in relation to rival foreign peoples and to their faith.

에스라의 지도력 아래, 거룩한 성회가 열려 모세 언약이 새롭게 체결이 되었다(느 9-10장). 언약 공동체의 개연 구조기 무너져서 하나님의 율법을 순종하지 못했다. 사회적으로 구성되고 유지되는 언약 공동체의 실제 세계로서 계속 존속하기 위해 사회적인 기초를 가지게 되었다.

Under Ezra, a sacred convocation took place in which the Mosaic covenant was renewed (Neh. 9-10). The destruction of the plausibility structure of the covenant community attributed to their failure to obey the divine law. The covenant community socially constructed and maintained had its social base for its continuing existence as a real world.

반복적인 예배가 개연 구조를 공고히 한다. 예배는 포수기 후의 유대인들의 정체성을 하나님의 백성으로 확인시켜 줄 뿐만 아니라, 이스라엘을 이 세상에서 하나님의 목적을 이룰 도구로 만들 수 있는 설계력을 제공한다. 예배 속에서 하나님의 실재가 세속 영역과 만난다. 언약 갱신은 성(聖)과 속(俗)이 만나는 예배 동안에 재연된다. 종교적인 전통은 언약 갱신 제의 속에서 기억된다.

The repeated worship consolidates its plausibility structure. Not only does worship identify the postexilic Judeans as the people of God, it also provides a generative force capable of molding Israel into an agent of God's purpose in the world. In worship, God's reality reaches in the profane area. The covenant renewal enacts during worship in which sacred and profane meet. The religious traditions are remembered at the covenant renewal rite.

모든 종교 세계는 그 자체가 인간 활동의 생산인 개연 구조 위에 기초하기에 종교 세계는 모두 그 실존 자체가 불안하다. 이런 가능성은 의문의 개연 구조가 불안하거나 불연속의 도가 높을수록 증가한다. 신성한 우주가 끊임없는 혼돈 속에서 그 견고함을 유지할 수 있듯이, 언약 공동체는 이방적 요소들이 있는 곳에도 그 진정성을 유지할 수 있다.

Since every religious world is based on a plausibility structure that is itself the product of human activity, every religious world is inherently precarious in its reality. This possibility increases with the degree of instability or discontinuity of the plausibility structure in question. As a sacred cosmos is able to maintain its solidarity in the ever-present face of chaos, so the covenant community can keep its credibility in the alien surroundings.

다음 장에서 우리는 요약, 평가, 남기는 연구과제를 통해 본 연구의 결론을 도출한다.

In the following chapter, we conclude our study with summary, evaluation, and implications.

V

결론

CONCLUSION

5-1. 전체 요약과 맺는말 General summary and concluding remark

본 연구에서 지식사회학의 합법화 이론을 페르샤 시대의 포수기 후의 공동체의 사회적 재구성의 문제에 적용을 해 보았다. 본 연구에서 밝힌 것은 에스라와 느헤미야가 인도한 결혼 개혁이 사이비 유대 공동체 회원들과 외부인들로부터 오는 위협들을 극복하고 유대 공동체를 재구성하는 데 결정적인 역할을 했다는 것이다.

We have so far applied a legitimation theory of the sociology of knowledge to the problem of the social re-construction of the post-exilic Judean community in the Persian period. Our study has shown that the marriage reform led by Ezra and Nehemiah played on a decisive role in re-forming Judean community, overcoming the threats from the quasi-insiders and outsiders.

본 연구에서 이스라엘 사람들과 이스라엘 사람이 아닌 이방인들 사이의 통혼은 그들이 가나안 땅에 거주하기 시작한 이후부터 특별히 만연되었다는 것을 살폈다. 성경내의 대부분 통혼은 요셉, 모세, 에스더의 통혼은 예외였지만 비참한 결과 즉 가족 내의 갈등과 투쟁, 수치심, 우상 숭배 등을 가져왔기에, 바벨론 포로로부터 귀환한 개혁 그룹은 페르샤의 통치 아래에서 그들 자신의 정체성을 지키기 위해 통혼을 금지했어야 했다.

Our survey revealed that intermarriages between Israelite people and non-Israelite people became especially popular after the Israelites settled in Canaan. Since most intermarriages in the Bible led to disastrous results(strife within the family, shame, idolatry, etc.), except those of Joseph, Moses, and Esther, the reform group that returned from the Babylonian exile had to prohibit against intermarriage in order to keep their own identity under the Persian rule.

우리는 에스라와 느헤미야 이전에 통혼을 금지한 몇 가지 성경 구절들을 고찰해 보았다. 연구결과 가나안인들과 통혼한 것이 문화적-종교적 이유로 금지가 되었고(창 24:2이하, 27:46-28:4, 34:14이하), 사회적-종교적 이유들로 금지되었음을 구약성경을 통해 알았다(출 34:11-16; 신 7:2이하, 23:4이하; 수 23:7이하; 참고. 민 25:1이하; 삿 3:6).

We examined some biblical passages which strictly forbid intermarriage prior to Ezra and Nehemiah. Our investigation has shown that intermarriage with Canaanites was banned for cultural-religious reason(Gen. 24:2ff., 27:46-28:4, 34:14ff.) and for socio-religious reason(Ex. 34:11-16.; Deut. 7:2ff. 23:4ff.; Josh. 23:7ff.; cf. Num. 25:1ff.; Jud. 3:6) in the Hebrew Bible.

암몬인들과 모압인들과의 통혼은 역사적인 이유(신 23:4이하)로 금지되었다. 창세기 설화에서는 통혼에 대해 부정적인 태도(24:1-4, 27:46-28:4, 34:1-25)를 가진 주요 이유는 순수 혈통을 지키는 것과 여호와 신앙의 독특성을 유지하는 것이다. 통혼에 대해 율법 문서(출 34:11-16; 신 7:1-4, 23:3-8)에서 강력하게 금지하는 또 다른 이유는 이스라엘 공동체의 사회적-종교적 구조를 해체하도록 위협하는 배교를 금지하기 위함이었다.

And intermarriage with Ammonites and Moabites was prohibited for historical reasons(Deut. 23:4ff.). The main reason for the negative attitude towards intermarriage in the Genesis narratives(24:1-4, 27:46-28:4, 34:1-25) was to keep pure blood and to maintain distinctiveness of Yahwism. Another important reason for strong interdictions against intermarriage in the legal texts (Ex. 34:11-16; Deut. 7:1-4, 23:3-8) was to ban apostasy which threatened to disintegrate the social-religious structure of the Israelite community.

이스라엘 사람들과 이방인들 사이의 통혼은 왕조 시대에는 논쟁이 되지 않았던 것 같다. 구약성경에서는 왕정시대에 통혼한 경우를 몇 가지만 보고하고 있다. 비록 포로기 이전의 대언자들이 통혼 문제에 대해서는 침묵을 지켰지만 통혼에 대한 더욱 비판적인 견해가 왕정시대 후기와 포로시기에 발전되었던 것 같다. 그러나 통혼이 퍼지면 국가의 정체성을 해체하며 귀환한 유대 공동체의 제의적이고 인종적인 순수성이 무너질 수 있는 위협이 있었다.

We assume that intermarriage between Israelites and non-Israelites was not an issue in the monarchial period. The Hebrew Bible reports only some cases of intermarriage during the monarchial period. Even though all pre-exilic prophets were silent on the problem of intermarriage, a more critical view toward intermarriage seemed to develop during the late monarchial and exilic periods. The spread of intermarriage threatened to disintegrate the national identity and the purity, cultic and ethnic, of the returned Judean community.

비록 유대 공동체 일원 중 통혼한 가족들 모두가 이방인 배우자들로부터 이혼하지 않았어도 결혼 개혁은 큰 성공할 수 있었다.

Even though not all the intermarried families of Judean community were divorced from their foreign spouses, the reform could be evaluated as a great success.

에스라와 그를 지지한 그룹들은 에스라 9-10장에서 이방 아내들과 이혼을 주장하였으나, 느헤미야는 과격한 행동으로 통혼한 평신도들에게 초기 맹세를 상기시켜 주면서, 대제사장 손자 가운데 통혼한 자를 유대 공동체로부터 추방했다. 명백하게 이 결혼 개혁은 유대공동체의 가족들과 외부자들 사이에 두꺼운 경계선을 제공해서 유대의 개연 구조를 강화시켰다.

While Ezra and his support group insisted upon the divorce of foreign wives in Ezra 9-10, Nehemiah reminded the guilty laypersons of the earlier pledge with violent action, and he expelled the guilty grandson of the high priest from Judean community. Evidently this marriage reform contributed to make a thick border line between insiders and outsiders of Judean community, consolidating the plausibility structure of Judah.

결혼 개혁의 합법화 과정을 다음과 같이 요약한다:

(1) 사회적으로 객관화된 모든 "지식"이 설명되고 정당화되어져야 한다. 합법화들은 사회적 객관화들의 영역에 속한다. 즉 주어진 집합체에 당연하다고 간주하는 "지식"을 말한다. 이것은 사회적 사건들의 이유에 대한 개인적 인식과는 다소 차이가 나는 객관성의 상

태를 자기고 있음을 함축한다.

We summarize the process of legitimation of the marriage reform as follows:

> All socially objectivated "knowledge" is to be explained and justified. Legitimations belong to the domain of social objectivations, that is, to what passes for "knowledge" in a given collectivity. This implies that they have a status of objectivity quite different from merely individual cogitations about the "why" and "wherefore" of social events.

"합법화는 인식의 타당성을 객관화된 의미로 돌림으로 제도적인 질서를 설명한다. 합법화는 실제적인 정언에 규범적인 품위를 줌으로써 제도적인 질서를 정당화시킨다."[223] 에스라의 결혼 개혁 전에 실시된 언약 갱신 의식은 이런 관점에서 이해될 수 있다.

"Legitimation explains the institutional order by ascribing cognitive validity to its objectivated meanings. And legitimation justifies the institutional order by giving a normative dignity to its practical imperatives".[223] The covenant renewal ceremony done before the marriage reform of Ezra can be understood from this perspective.

제2성전 봉헌 후 포로에서 귀환한 그룹을 포함한 유대인들은 그들의 종교적 전통들과 합리적인 대답들을 잊어버린 것 같았다. 서기

---

[223] Berger & Luckmann, 93.

관 에스라가 여호와께서 이스라엘에 주신 모세의 율법책을 가져와서 회중들 앞에서 낭독했을 때, 합법적인 대답들이 나오기를 모든 백성들이 "아멘, 아멘"으로 화답했다(느 8:1-12).

After dedication of the second temple, the Judeans including the group who returned from exile seemed to forget their religious traditions and their legitimating answers. When Ezra the scribe brought the book of the law of Moses which the Lord had given to Israel and read in front of the congregation, the legitimating answers were responded: all the people answered, "Amen, Amen"(Neh. 8:1-12).

(2) 개연 구조가 확실하게 자리를 잡게 된다. 에스라의 주도하여 소집된 거룩한 성회가 열렸고 모세의 언약이 갱신되었다(느 9-10장). 언약 공동체의 옛 개연 구조가 파괴된 것은 그들이 하나님의 율법을 순종하지 못했기 때문이었다. 사회적으로 구성되고 유지된 언약 공동체는 진정한 세계로서 계속 존재할 수 있도록 사회적 기초를 가지게 되었다.

The plausibility structure is to be firmly constructed. Under Ezra, a sacred convocation took place in which the Mosaic covenant was renewed(Neh. 9-10). The destruction of the old plausibility structure of the covenant community attributed to their failure to obey the divine law. The covenant community socially constructed and maintained had its social base for its continuing existence as a real world.

예배가 반복됨으로 개연 구조가 공고화되었다. 예배는 이스라엘을 이 세상에서 하나님의 목적을 실현시키는 도구가 될 수 있도록 생성력을 제공하기 때문이었다. 언약 갱신은 성과 속이 만나는 예배시간에 체결되었다. 언약 갱신 예배 동안 종교적 전통들이 기억된다.

The repeated worship consolidated its plausibility structure. For the worship provided a generative force capable of molding Israel into an agent of God's purpose in the world. The covenant renewal rite can be enacted during worship in which sacred and profane met. The religious traditions were remembered at the covenant renewal worship.

(3) 상징적 우주는 지도자들에 의해 만들어지고 승인된다. 개혁 그룹의 상징적 우주는 모든 회중들이 듣고 수용한 모세의 율법 중심으로 구성되었다(느 8:1-12). 모세 율법에 기초한 개혁의 정신으로 다양한 사회적 계층의 사람들로 하나의 사회적 계층으로 통합되었다(참고. 에스라 10:18-43; 느 9:38-10:39). 변증적 개혁을 통하여 유대 공동체 내부자들은 제의적이고 인종적인 순수한 세계를 구성하는 데 합의했다. 그래서 상징적 우주는 귀환한 유대 공동체의 정체성을 이방인들과 그들의 신앙들로부터 차별을 두게 한 것이다.

The symbolic universe is to be crystallized and approved by leadership. The symbolic universe of the reform group was crystallized around the law of Moses which the congregation heard and accepted(Neh. 8:1-12). The spirit of reform based on the law of Moses integrated into one social system diverse social classes(cf. Ezra 10:18-43; Neh. 9:38-10:39). Through the dialectic reform, the insiders of Judean community agreed to construct a pure world, cultic and ethnic. Thus this symbolic universe can serve to establish the identity of the returned Judean community in relation to rival foreign peoples and to their faiths.

그러므로 우리는 포로로부터 귀환한 그룹의 "상징적 우주"가 에스라의 결혼 개혁을 합법화했으며 포로 후기 유대의 종교적이고 인종적 공동체를 재구성하고 유지하였다고 결론을 내릴 수 있다.

Therefore, we conclude that the "symbolic universe" of the group that returned from exile legitimated Ezra's marriage reform and reinforced the re-formation and maintenance of the post-exilic Judean religious and ethnic community.

5-2. 본 연구의 평가 Evaluation of the study

본 연구를 통해 지식 사회학이 성경 본문을 해석하는 데 여러 가지로 공헌할 수 있음을 알게 되었다.

Through this study, we find that the sociology of knowledge will be able to contribute to interpretation of the biblical texts in several ways.

첫째, 지식사회학은 성경에 나오는 공동체의 합법화 과정을 이해하는 데 도움을 준다. 지금까지 어떤 성경 연구도, 예배 공동체든, 언약 공동체든, 신앙 공동체든, 회당 혹은 교회든, 종교적 공동체의 합법화 문제를 취급하지 않았다. 이제 합법화 이론을 가지고 공동체의 사회적 구성에 대해 충분히 확실하게 살필 수 있다.

First of all, it helps us to understand the legitimating process of the community in the Bible. Until now, no biblical study has treated the problem of legitimation of the religious community, whether it is a worship community, or a covenant community, or a believing community, or a synagogue, or a Church. Now we can examine clearly enough the social construction of the community with a legitimation theory.

    두 번째로, "거룩한 상징적 세계"는 성경 해석학에 있어서 모든 사회적으로 객관화된 것과 주관적으로 실제 의미들이 신학적으로 포괄하는 모체를 제공할 수 있다. 이 방법은 성경 해석의 분석적 방법에서 종합적 방법으로 가는 길에 방해되는 것을 극복하는 데 기여할 수 있다.

    Secondly, the term "sacred symbolic universe" can provide a theological overarching matrix of all socially objectivated and subjectively real meanings for the biblical interpretation. This method can contribute to overcome the analytical way of biblical interpretation toward the synthetical ways.

    셋째로, 합법적인 규범들을 탐구함으로써 언약 갱신 예배에 대한 신선한 이해를 할 수 있다. 경계선에 대해 연구함으로 우리는 구약과 신약에 나오는 공동체의 일원과 외부인 사이에 있는 사회적 관계들을 이해한다.

    Thirdly, we can have a fresh understanding about the covenant renewal ceremony by exploring the legitimate *nomoi*. By studying the border languages, we understand the social relations between insider and outsider of the community in both Testaments.

    마지막으로 본 연구를 통하여 어떤 공동체의 재구성과 유지에 대한 이해를 향상시킬 수 있다. 제한된 자료들로 인해 포수기 이후의 유대공동체에 대한 최근 몇 십년간 연구가 진전을 이루어오지 못했다. 본 연구에서 시도한 새로운 방법론을 통해 페르샤 시대의 유대의 종교적이고 인종적 공동체를 회복하는 과정을 심층적으로 이해하게 되기를 희망한다.

Finally, our study can enhance the understanding of the reconstruction and maintenance of any community. Because of the limited sources, there has been little progress in the study of the post-exilic Judean community in recent decades. Through the new methodological approach of this study, we hope to understand more deeply the process of the restoration of the Judean religious and ethnic community during the Persian period.

5-3. 연구과제로 남기는 문제들 Implications of the study

구약성경에 나오는 결혼 개혁의 연구는 미국에 사는 유대인들 사이에 통혼에 대한 최근 논의에 공헌할 것이다. 다민족과 자유 사회에서 통혼은 인종과 민족을 무시하고 무서운 속도로 급증하고 있다. 지금까지 통혼문제는 어떤 유대인 사회에서 뜨거운 논쟁이 되어 왔다.

Our study of the marriage reform in the Hebrew Bible will contribute to the recent discussion of intermarriage among the American Jews. In our multiracial and free society, intermarriage is increasing at alarming rates regardless of race or people. Until now, the problem of intermarriage has been at hot issue in the any Jewish society.

미국인 유대인 남성들과 비유대인들 사이의 통혼 사례가 늘어가고 있다. 1955년에 7%가 1983-87년에 37% 늘어났다는 연구가 있다. 유대인의 여성인 경우는 2%에서 25%로 증가했다. 남성과 여성 모두

재혼인 경우에 타민족과 혼인하는 경우가 55%라고 한다.[224] 이러한 추세는 유대인들의 생물학적 통일성에 심각한 타격을 미치는데, 이런 통혼으로 태어난 자녀들은 유대인의 법상 유대인이 아니라고 한다(할라카 원리).

There has been a vast increased rate of intermarriage between American Jews and non-Jews. A study reveals that "intermarriage rates for Jewish men in a first marriage have gone from 7 percent in 1955 to 37 percent in the period 1983-87. For Jewish women, the rates have gone from 2 percent to 25 percent. For second marriage rates for both men and women are over 55 percent."[224] This fact has posed severe problems to the continued biological unity of the Jewish people, since the offspring of many of these marriages are not considered as Jewish by Jewish law (halakhic principle).

이런 문제의 해결책 중에 하나는 부계 후손의 입양원리이다. 이 원리 조차도 정통 유대인과 보수 랍비들은 거부하고 있다고 한다.[225]

One proposed solution to this problem is the adoption of the principle of patrilineal descent. But this solution founders on its rejection by the Orthodox and Concervative rabbinates.[225]

보수와 개혁 유대인들은 비 유대인들과 결혼하는 문제에 대한 전통적 신념들과 그들의 랍비들로부터 깊이 분열되어 있다. 신앙이 다

---

224) The New York Times, Tuesday, Sep. 18, 1990, p. A25.
225) 미국 유대인들의 통혼에 대한 최근 연구에 따르면, 신앙이 다른 결혼 문제를 해결하려고 여전히 투쟁중이라고 한다 According to a recent study concerning intermarriage of the American Jews, they still struggle to solve the problem of Jewish interfaith unions The New York Times , "Jews found split on mixed marriage," Sep. 18, 1990, p. A25. & Oct. 18, 1992.

른 결혼식을 랍비가 주례하였는데, 여기서 태어난 자녀들을 유대인으로 인정하는가 하는 문제에 의견이 있다. 유대인 엄마의 자녀들은 전통적으로 유대인으로 여겨지나, 엄마가 유대인이 아닌 경우의 자녀들은 개종을 해야 한다.

Conservative and Reform Jews are deeply divided from their rabbis and from traditional beliefs about crucial issues arising from marriages to non-Jews... The differences emerged over willingness to recognize the children of a the propriety of a rabbi's officiating at an interfaith wedding. Children of a Jewish mother have traditionally been considered Jews, while children of a non-Jewish mother must undergo conversion to be considered Jews.

유대인의 법은 통혼을 정죄하기 때문에 대다수 랍비들은 이런 결혼 주례하기를 거부한다. 정통 유대인들과 랍비들은 통혼을 반대했다. 또한 랍비들이 통혼 주례를 거부하고 비유대인들이 유대인 조직에 들어오는 것도 불허하고, 비유대인 여성들로부터 태어난 자녀들을 유대인으로 받아들이지 않는다.

Because Jewish law condemns intermarriage, the vast majority of rabbis refuse to officiate at such ceremonies. Orthodox laity and Orthodox rabbis opposed intermarriage, rabbinic officiation, acceptance of non-Jews into Jewish organizations and recognition of the child of a non-Jewish mother as Jewish.

심카 코헨은 완전히 새로운 해법을 제시하는데, 할라카와 탈무드 자료에 근거하여 다음과 같다.[226]

---

[226] A. Dashefsky and H. Shapiro, *Ethnic Identification Among American Jews*, Lexington, MA: D. C. Heath, 1974, 21.

아빠는 유대인이고 엄마는 유대이 아닌 자녀들은 합당한 법정(랍비 법정)인 벳 딘(*bet din*)에서 유아기 때 개종되어야 한다. 그래서 통혼의 유아 자녀를 벳 딘으로 데려와 개종시키는 아빠를 거부해서는 안 된다. 이에 더하여, 유대인 부모는 자녀의 가정환경이 율법 준수가 없다 하더라도 이방인 자녀를 입양해서 개종시켜야 한다.

J. Simcha Cohen proposes a totally new solution, based exclusively on halakhic and Talmudic sources, as follows:[226]

> ··· we see that children born to Jewish fathers and gentile mothers may be converted during infancy by a proper *bet din* ("Rabbinic court"). Thus, Jewish fathers of such marriages who bring their infant children to *bet din* for conversion purposes should not be rejected. In addition, Jewish parents may adopt gentile children and have them converted even though the familial milieu lacks observance of commandments.

그는 이 제안을 매우 논쟁적인 댓글에서 했는데, 많은 동의를 얻고 있다. 유효한 할라카 대화에서 네 가지 일반적 과정을 거쳐야 한다: 계명 준수의 의지와 의무를 가르치는 카빠랏 미쯔보트(*kabbalat mitzvot*), 남성 개종자에게 할례를 요구하는 밀라(*milah*), 침례의식인 테빌라(*tevilah*), 랍비 법정에 출두하는 벳 딘(*bet din*)이다.[227] 만약 개종 절차가 합법화 이론으로 연구가 된다면, 우리는 최근 통혼의 경향을 해결하는 돌파구를 찾아낼 수 있다.

---

227) J. S. Cohen, 8.

He lays out this proposal in a closely argued responsum, which has gained increasing general approval. A valid halakhic conversion requires four integral elements: *kabbalat mitzvot* ["the awareness of and commitment to observe commandments"], *milah* ["circumcision for a male convert"], *tevilah* ["immersion in a ritualarium"] and *bet din* ["the presence of a Rabbinical court"].[227] If the process of conversion is to be studied by the legitimation theory, we can find any breakthrough to solve the recent trend of intermarriage.

몇 가지 사회학적 수사적인 질문을 할 수 있다: 미국의 정통 유대인들과 보수 유대인들이 가지고 있는 상징적 우주란 무엇인가? 각 미국-유대인이 가지고 있는 객관화된 지식이란 무엇인가? 왜 많은 유대인들이 비유대인들과 결혼을 하는가? 신앙이 다른 결혼이 과연 흩어진 유대인 공동체를 해체하려는 위협이 있는가? 유대인 지도자들은 통혼을 어떻게 방지할 수 있는가? 현대 유대인들은 제2의 결혼개혁이 필요한가?

We may raise some sociological rhetorical questions: What are the symbolic universes of American Orthodox and Conservative Jews? What is the objectivated knowledge of each American Jewish community? Why do many Jews marry non-Jews? Do these interfaith unions threaten to disintegrate the diaspora Jewish community? How can Jewish leaders stop further intermarriages? Do they need a second marriage reform?

본 연구는 이런 종류의 연구에 한층 더 공헌할 것이다. 통혼은 교회에서도 마찬가지 문제이다. 우리는 이 주제에 대해 예수님으로

부터 받은 말씀은 없다.228) 바울은 성도가 아닌 자와의 혼인을 금지하고 있다(고후 6:14-18):

Our study will enhance this kind of investigation. Intermarriage is an important issue for the Church as well. We have no word from Jesus on this subject,228) while a non-Pauline material mentions prohibition against marriage with unbelievers(2 Cor. 6:14-18):

고후 6:14 너희는 믿지 않는 자와 멍에를 함께 메지 말라 의와 불법이 어찌 함께 하며 빛과 어둠이 어찌 사귀며 Be ye not unequally yoked together with unbelievers: for what fellowship hath righteousness with unrighteousness? and what communion hath light with darkness?

15 그리스도와 벨리알이 어찌 조화되며 믿는 자와 믿지 않는 자가 어찌 상관하며 And what concord hath Christ with Belial? or what part hath he that believeth with an infidel?

16 하나님의 성전과 우상이 어찌 일치가 되리요? 우리는 살아 계신 하나님의 성전이라. 이와 같이 하나님께서 이르시되 내가 그들 가운데 거하며 두루 행하여 나는 그들의 하나님이 되고 그들은 나의 백성이 되리라 And what agreement hath the temple of God with idols? for ye are the temple of the living God; as God hath said, I will dwell in them, and walk in them; and I will be their God, and they shall be my people.

---

228) Holmgren, 74-75.

17 그러므로 너희는 그들 중에서 나와서 따로 있고 부정한 것을 만지지 말라 내가 너희를 영접하여 Wherefore come out from among them, and be ye separate, saith the Lord, and touch not the unclean thing; and I will receive you,

18 너희에게 아버지가 되고 너희는 내게 자녀가 되리라 전능하신 주의 말씀이니라 하셨느니라 And will be a Father unto you, and ye shall be my sons and daughters, saith the Lord Almighty.

교단이 다른 결혼(가톨릭과 기독교인 사이를 포함), 불신자와의 결혼, 같은 기독교인인데 인종이 다른 결혼, 혹은 이단 종교인과의 결혼이 앞으로 사회학적인 관점에서 연구되어져야 한다.

Interdenominational unions (including between Catholic and Protestant believer), marriage with unbeliever, Christian interracial marriage, or marriage with heretical religious person are also to be studied from a sociological perspective in the future.

미주에 사는 대부분 한인 1세대는 자녀들이 타 인종과 결혼하는데 부정적인 시각을 가지고 있다. 그들은 미국에 이민 온 다른 미국인들처럼,[229] 한인 종족의 후손을 원하고 이민 공동체를 지키고 싶

---

229) Cf. L. Dinnerstein and D. Reimers, *Ethnic Americans: A History of Immigration and Assimilation*, New York: Dodd, Mead, 1975; M. L. Hansen, *The Immigrant in American History*, Cambridge, MA : Harvard University Press, 1940; Won M. Hurh, Hei C. Kim, and Kwang C. Kim, *Assimilation Patterns of Immigrants in the Chicago Area*, Washington, D.C.: University Press of America, 1978; R. Adams, *Interracial Marriage in Hawaii*, Montclair, NJ: Patterson Smith Press, 1937; Bok L. Kim, "Asian wives of U.S. servicemen: women in shadows," *Amerasia Journal* 4 (1977), 91-115; Bok L. Kim, "Pioneers in intermarriage: Korean women in the United States," pp. 59-95 in H.H. Sunoo and D. S. Kim (eds.), *Korean Women in a Struggle for Humanization*, Memphis, Tenn.: Association for Korean Christian Scholars in North America, 1978;

어 한다.

Most first-generation Korean immigrant families in America take a negative attitude toward intermarriage of their children, for they want to keep their ethnic identity and immigrant community, like many immigrants in America.[229]

그러나 더욱 미국화된 이민 자녀들은 그들 부모들의 상징 세계에 안주하기보다는, 다양한 문화와 차원의 사회에서 남기를 원한다. 미래 이민 공동체의 문제, 국제 결혼, 이민 2세대와 차세대를 위한 교육방법이 앞으로 합법화 이론과 더불어 계속 연구되기를 바란다.

But the more Americanized immigrant children want to remain in the multi-cultural, dimensional society, rather than in their parents' symbolic universes. The problem of the future immigrant communities, the international marriage, the method of education for second or further generation of immigrant family, are to be studies with the legitimation theory in the future.

Hyung C. Kim, "Ethnic enterprises among Korean emigrants in America," *Journal of Korean Affairs* 6 (1976), 40-58; J. Leon, "Sex-ethnic marriage in Hawaii: a non-metric multi-dimensional analysis," *Journal of Marriage and Family* 37 (1975), 775-781.

> 참고 문헌   The Selective Bibliography

1. 에스라-느헤미야와 통혼 연구 자료들
Studies of Ezra-Nehemiah and Intermarriage

Ackroyd, Peter R. *I & II Chronicles, Ezra, Nehemiah*. Torch Bible Paperbacks. London: SCM Press LTD. 1973

_____. "The Jewish community in Palestine in the period. " *The Cambridge History of Judaism*. eds. W. Davies and L. Findelstein. New York: Cambridge University. 130-161. 1984.

Alexander, P. S. "Remarks on Aramaic Epistolography in the Persian Period." *Journal of Semitic Studies* 23, 1978. 155-170.

Allan, N. "The Jerusalem Priesthood During the Exile." *Heythrop Journal* 23, 1982, 259-269.

Allen, Leslie C. "'For He Is Good…' Worship in Ezra-Nehemiah." In *Worship and the Hebrew Bible*. Edited by M. Patrick Graham, Rick R. Marrs, and Steven L. McKenzie. Sheffield: Sheffield Academic Press, 1999.

Allen, L, and T. Laniak, "Ezra, Nehemiah, Esther." *New International Biblical Commentary*. Peabody, MA: Hendrickson Press. 2003.

Allgeier, A. "Beobachtungen am LXX-Text der Bücher Esdras und Nehemias." *Biblica* 22, 1941, 227-251.

Allrik, H. L. "The Lists of Zerubbabel (Nehemiah 7 and Ezra 2) and the Hebrew Numeral Notation." *BASOR* 136 (1954): 21-27.

Alt, A. "Judas Nachbarn zur Zeit Nehemias." Palästina-Jahrbuch 27, 1931, 58-74.

_____. "Die Rolle Samarias bei der Entstehung des Judentums." *Festschrift Otto Procksch zum 60 Geburtstag*, Leipzig, 1934, 5-28.

Batten, L. W. *The Books of Ezra and Nehemiah*. The International Critical Commentary. Edinburgh: T. & T. Clark Ltd. 1913.

Bayer, E. *Das dritte Buch Esdras und sein Verhältnis zu den Büchern Esra-Nehemia*, Freiburg-im-Breisgau: Herdersche Verlagshandlung, 1911.

Becking, Bob. "Ezra's Re-enactment of the Exile." In *Leading Captivity Captive: 'The Exile' as History and Ideology*. Edited by Lester L. Grabbe. Sheffield: Sheffield Academic Press, 1998.

_____. "Ezra on the Move···Trends and Perspectives on the Character and His Book." In *Perspectives in the Study of the Old Testament & Early Judaism*. Edited by Florentino Garca Martnez and Ed Noort. Leiden: E. J. Brill, 1998.

_____. "Continuity and Community: The Belief System of the Book of Ezra." In *The Crisis of Israelite Religion: Transformation of Religious Tradition in Exilic and Posy Exilic Times*. Edited by Bob Becking and Marjo C. A. Korpel. Leiden: E. J. Brill, 1999.

Bennet, J. K. "Aliens in Israel." *Bibliotheca Sacra* 13, 1856, 564-574.

Bertholet, A. *Die Bücher Esra und Nehemia*, KHAT. Tübingen: Mohr. 1902

Bewer, J.A. *Der Text des Buches Esra*. Göttingen: Vandenhoeck & Ruprecht. 1922

Bickermann, Elias J. "The Edict of Cyrus in Ezra 1." *JBL* 65 (1946): 249-275.

Bleich, J.D. "The Prohibition Against Intermarriage." *Journal of Halacha and Contemporary Society* 1. 1981, 5-27.

Blenkinsopp, J. "The Mission of Udjahorresnet and Those of Ezra and Nehemiah." *Journal of Biblical Literature* 106. 1987, 409-421.

_____. *Ezra-Nehemiah: A Commentary*. The Old Testament Library. Philadelphia: The Westminster Press. 1988.

_____. "A Jewish Sect of the Persian Period." *CBQ* 52, 1990, 5-20.

Bliese, Loren F. "Chiastic Structures, Peaks and Cohesion in Neh. 9:6-37." *The Bible Translator* 39. 1988, 208-215.

Bossard, J.H.S. & E.S. Boll. "One Marriage, Two Faiths: Guidance on Interfaith Marriage." New York: The Ronald Press Company. 1957

Bossman, David. "Ezra's Marriage Reform: Israel Redefined." *Biblical Theology Bulletin* 9. 1979, 32-38.

Bowman, R. A. "The Book of Ezra and the Book of Nehemiah." in *The Interpreter's Bible*. Nashville,Tenn.: Abingdon. 1954, 549-819.

Braun, R. L. "A Reconsideration of the Chronicler's Attitude toward the North." *Journal of Biblical Liturature* 96/1, 1977, 59-62.

_____. "Chronicles, Ezra and Nehemiah: Theology and Literary History." In Studies in the *Historical Books of the Old Testament*. Edited by J. A. Emerton. *VTSup* 30. Leiden: E. J. Brill, 1979. 52-64.

Breneman, Mervin. *Ezra, Nehemiah, Esther*. The New American Commentary. Edited by E. Ray Clendenen. Nashville: Broadman &

Holman Publishers, 1993.

Brockington, L.H. *Ezra, Nehemiah and Esther*. New Century Bible. London: Nelson. 1969.

Brown, Philip II. *Hope Amidst Ruin*. Greenville, SC: Bob Jones University Press, 2009.

_____. "A Literary and Theological Analysis of the Book of Ezra," Ph.D. dissertation, 2002.

Clines, D.J. *Ezra, Nehemiah, Esther*. The New Century Bible Commentary. Grand Rapids, MI.: Wm. B. Eerdmans Pub. Co. 1984.

Coggins, R.J. *Ezra and Nehemiah*, Cambridge Bible Commentary on NEB, Cambridge: Cambridge University Press. 1976.

Coggins, R. J. and M. A., Knibb, *The First and Second Books of Esdras*, New York and London. 1979.

Cohen, Shaye J. D. "From the Bible to the Talmud: The Prohibition of Intermarriage." *Hebrew Annual Review* 7 (1983): 23-29.

Cohen, J. Simcha. "Intermarriage and Conversion: A Halakhic Solution." Hoboken, NJ: KTAV Pub. House, Inc. 1987.

Cohen, S.J.D. "From the Bible to the Talmud : The Prohibition of Intermarriage." *Hebrew Annual Review* 7. 1983, 23-39.

_____. "Solomon and the Daughter of Pharaoh: Intermarriage, Conversion, and the impurity of Women." *The Journal of the Ancient Near Eastern Society* 16/17. 1984/5, 23-37.

Coogan, M. D. "Patterns in Jewish Personal Names in the Diaspora." *Journal for the Study of Judaism in the Persian* 4, 1973, 184-191.

Cowley, A. "Ezra's Recension of the Law." *Journal of Theological Studies* 11, 1910, 542-545.

Cross, Frank Moore. "Geshem the Arabian, Enemy of Nehemiah, *BA* 18,

1955, 46-47.

_____. *Canaanite Myth and Hebrew Epic*, Cambridge, MA:Harvard University Press. 1973.

_____. "A Reconstruction of the Judean Restoration." *JBL* 94. 1975, 4-18.

Cundall, A. E. "Ezra and Nehemiah." In *The Eerdmans Bible Commentary*. 3d ed. Edited by D. Guthrie and J. A. Motyer. Grand Rapids: William B. Eerdmans Publishing Company, 1987.

de Vaux, R. *Ancient Israel : Its Life and Institutions*. New York: McGraw-Hill book Company, Inc. 1961.

Demsky, Aaron. "Who Came First, Ezra or Nehemiah? The Synchronistic Approach." *HUCA* 65 (1994): 1-19.

Dulin, Rachel. "Leaders in the Restoration." *The Bible Today* 24. 1986, 287-291.

Dumbrell, W.J. "The Tell el-Maskhuta Bowls and the 'Kingdom' of Qedar in the Persian Period." *BASOR* 203, 1971, 33-44.

_____. "Malachi and the Ezra-Nehemiah Reforms." *RTR* 35 no. 2 (1976): 42-52.

_____. "The Purpose of the Books of Chronicles." *JETS* 27 (1983): 257-266.

_____. "The Theological Intention of Ezra-Nehemiah." *RTR* 45 no. 3 (1986): 65-72.

Dyck, Jonathan E. "Ezra 2 in Ideological Critical Perspective." In *Rethinking Contexts, Rereading Texts: Contributions from the Social Sciences to Biblical Interpretation*. Edited by M. Daniel Carroll R. Sheffield: Sheffield Academic Press, 2000.

Eichhorst, W. R. "Ezra's Ethics on Intermarriage and Divorce." *Grace*

Journal 10. 1969, #3. 16-29.

Ellison, H. L. "The Importance of Ezra." *Evangelical Quarterly* 53, 1981, 48-53.

Emerton, J. A. "Did Ezra Go to Jerusalem in 428 B.C.?" *JTS* 17 (1966): 1-19.

Emery, D. L. "Ezra 4: is Josephus Right After All?" *JNSL* 13 (1987): 33-44.

Epstein, K. K. "Sexual Purity and Redemption." *Judaism* 17. 1968 65-57.

Epstein, L. M. *Marriage Laws in the Bible and the Talmud*. Cambridge, MA : Harvard University Press. 1942

Eskenazi, T. C. "The Chronicler and the Composition of 1 Esdras." *CBQ* 48, 1986, 39-61.

_____. "In An Age of Prose: A Literary Approach to Ezra-Nehemiah" Ph.D. diss., Illiff School of Theology and The University of Denver [Colorado Seminary], 1986.

_____. "Current Perspectives on Ezra-Nehemiah and the Persian Period." *Currents in Research: Biblical Studies* 1 (1993): 59-86.

_____. "Torah and Narrative and Narrative as Torah." In Old Testament Interpretation: Past, Present, and Future: Essays in Honor of Gene M. Tucker. Edited by James Luther Mays, David L. Petersen, and Kent Harold Richards. Nashville: Abingdon Press, 1995.

Eskenazi, Tamara C. and Eleanore P. Judd. "Marriage to a Stranger in Ezra 9-10." In *Second Temple Studies: 2. Temple Community in the Persian Period*. Edited by Tamara C. Eskenazi and Kent H. Richards. Sheffield: Sheffield Academic Press, 1994. 266-285.

Feldman, Ephraim, "Intermarriage Historically Considered." *Yearbook* of the Central Conference of American Rabbis 19. 1909, 271-301.

Fensham, F. Charles. "The Books of Ezra and Nehemiah." *NICOT*. Grand Rapids: Wm. Eerdmans. 1982.

_____. "The Books of Ezra and Nehemiah." *The New International Commentary on the Old Testament*. Edited by R. K. Harrison. Grand Rapids, MI: Wm B Eerdmans. 1982.

_____. "Some Theological and Religious Aspects in Ezra and Nehemiah." *Journal of Northwest Semitic Languages* 11, 1983, 59-68.

_____. "Medina in Ezra and Nehemiah." *VT* 25 (1975): 795-797.

Finkelstein, J. J. "Sex Offenses in Sumerian Laws." *Journal of the American Oriental Society* 86. 1966, 355-372.

Fishbane, Michael. *Biblical Interpretation in Ancient Israel*. Oxford: Clarendon Press. 1985.

Galling, Kurt. *Die Bücher der Chronik, Esra, Nehemia*. ATD. Göttingen: Vandenhoeck & Ruprecht. 1954.

_____. "The 'Gola-List' According to Ezra 2 & Nehemiah 7." *JBL* 70 (1951): 149-158.

Ginsberg, Harold Louis. "Ezra 1:4." *JBL* 79 (1960): 167-169.

Glazier-McDonald, B. "Intermarriage, Divorce, and the daughter of Priest." *JBL* 106. 1987, 603-611.

Gordon, A. I. "Intermarriage: Interfaith, Interracial, Interethnic." Boston, MA: Beacon Press. 1964.

Grabbe, Lester L. *Ezra-Nehemiah*. Old Testament Readings. London: Routledge, 1998.

_____. "Reconstructing History from the Book of Ezra."

In *Second Temple Studies: 1. Persian Period*. Edited by Philip R. Davies. Sheffield: Sheffield Academic Press, 1991.

_____. "What Was Ezra's Mission?" In *Second Temple Studies: 2. Temple Community in the Persian Period*. Edited by Tamara C. Eskenazi and Kent H. Richards. Sheffield: Sheffield Academic Press, 1994.

_____. "Triumph of the Pious or Failure of the Xenophobes? The Ezra-Nehemiah Reforms and their Nachgeschichte." In *Jewish Local Patriotism and Self-Identification in the Graeco-Roman Period*. Edited by Sin Jones & Sarah Pearce. Sheffield: Sheffield Academic Press, 1998.

_____. "Israel's Historical Reality After the Exile." In *The Crisis of Israelite Religion: Transformation of Religious Tradition in Exilic and Post Exilic Times*. Edited by Bob Becking and Marjo C. A. Korpel. Leiden: E. J. Brill, 1999.

Graham, M. P. "A Connection Proposed Between 2 Chron.24:26 and Ezra 9-10." *ZAW* 97, 1985, 256-258.

Gruenthaner, M. J. "Hebrew Tribal Intermarriage." *The American Ecclesiastical Review* 113. 1945, 149.

Halpern, Baruch. "A Historiographic Commentary on Ezra 1-6: A Chronological Narrative and Dual Chronology in Israelite Historiography." In *The Hebrew Bible and Its Interpreters*. Edited by William Henry Propp, Baruch Halpern, and David Noel Freedman. Winona Lake: Eisenbrauns, 1990.

Hanson, P. D. *The Dawn of Apocalyptic*. Philadelphia: Fortress Press. 1975.

_____. "Apocalypticism." *IDB Supplementary Volume*, 1984,

28-34.

_____. *The People Called: The Growth of Community in the Bible*. San Francisco: Harper & Row, Pub. 1986.

Haran, Menahem, "Explaining the Identical Lines at the End of Chronicles and the Beginning of Ezra." *Bible Review* 2. 1986, 18-20.

Hawley, C. A. *A Critical Examination of the Peshitta Version of the Book of Ezra*. New York. 1922.

Hayes, Christine. "Intermarriage and Impurity in Ancient Jewish Sources." *HTR* 92 (1999): 3-36.

Heichelheim, F. M. "Ezra's Palestine and Periclean Athens."*Zeitschrift für Religions-und Geistesgeschichte* 3, 1951, 251-253.

Hensley, L. V. "The Official Persian Documents in the Book of Ezra." Unpub. diss. of Ph.D., University of Liverpool. 1977.

Holmgren, F. C. *A Commentary on the Books of Ezra & Nehemiah: Israel Alive Again*. International Theological Commentary. Edited by George A. F. Knight and Fredrick Carlson Holmgren. Grand Rapids, MI: Wm. B. Eerdmans Pub. Co. 1987.

Hoppe, Leslie J. "The Restoration of Judah." *The Bible Today* 24.1986, 281-286.

Horn, S. H., and L. H. W. *The Chronology of Ezra* 7. 2d. ed. Washington, D.C.: Review and Herald Publishing Association, 1970.

Houtman, C. "Ezra and the Law: Observations on the SupposedRelation Between Ezra and the Pentateuch." in A.S. van der Woude(ed.), *Remembering All the Way*. OTS 21, Leiden. 1981.

Hunt, Harry B. "Attitudes Toward Divorce in Post-Exilic Judaism."

Biblical Illustrator (Summer 1996): 62-65.

Japhet, Sara. "The Supposed Common Authorship of Chronicles and Ezra-Nehemiah Investigated Anew." VT 18, 1968, 330-371.

_____. "People and Land in the Restoration Period." *Das Land Israel in biblischer Zeit*, ed. G. Strecker, 1983, 103-125.

_____. "Law and 'the Law' in Ezra-Nehemiah." *Proceedings of the Ninth World Congress of Jewish Studies*. 1985, 99-115.

_____. "The Ideology of the Book of Chronicles and Its Place in Biblical Thought." Frankfurt: Verlag Peter Lang. 1989.

_____. "Sheshbazzar and Zerubbabel Against the Background of the Historical and Religious Tendencies of Ezra-Nehemiah." Part 1. *ZAW* 94 (1982): 66-98. Part 2. *ZAW* 95 (1983): 218-229.

_____. "The Relationship Between Chronicles and Ezra-Nehemiah." In *Congress Volume: Leuven 1989*. Edited by J. A. Emerton. Leiden: E. J. Brill, 1991.

_____. "The Temple in the Restoration Period: Reality and Ideology." *USQR* 44 (1991): 195-251.

_____. "Composition and Chronology in the Book of Ezra-Nehemiah." In *Second Temple Studies: 2. Temple Community in the Persian Period*. Edited by Tamara C. Eskenazi and Kent H. Richards. Sheffield: Sheffield Academic Press, 1994.

Johnson, Marshall D. The Purpose of the Biblical Genealogies. 2d ed. Cambridge: Cambridge University Press, 1988.

Jellicoe, Sidney. "Ezra-Nehemiah: A Reconstruction." *The Expository Times* 59 (1947/8): 54.

Johnstone, William. "Guilt and Atonement: The Theme of 1 and 2 Chronicles." In *A Word in Season: Essays in Honour of William*

McKane. Edited by James D. Martin and Philip R. Davies. Sheffield: JSOT Press, 1986.

Kellermann, Von Ulrich. "Erwgungen zum Problem der Esradatierung." *ZAW* 80 (1968): 55-87.

Kapelrud, Arvid S. *The Question of Authorship in the Ezra-Narrative: A Lexical Investigation*. Oslo: I Kommisjon Jacob Dybwad, 1944.

Keil, C. F. *Ezra*. Translated by Sophia Taylor. Edinburgh: T. & T. Clark, 1866-91; reprint, Peabody, MA: Hendrikson Publishers, Inc., 1996.

Kellermann, U. "Nehemia: Quellen, Überlieferung und Geschichte." *BZAW* 102. Berlin: T pelmann. 1967.

Kidner, F. D. *Ezra and Nehemiah: An Introduction and Commentary* The Tyndale Old Testament Commentaries. Edited by D. J. Wiseman. Downers Grove: Inter-Varsity Press, Leicester, Ill.: IVP. 1979.

Kirshenbaum, D. *Mixed Marriage and the Jewish Future*. New York : Bloch Publishing Company. 1958

Klein, R. W. "Ezra and Nehemiah in Recent Studies." *Magnalia Dei. Essays on the Bible and Archaeology in Memory of G. Ernest Wright*, eds. F. M. Cross, W. E. Lemke and P.D. Miller, Jr. Garden City, NY: Doubleday & Company, Inc. 1976, 361-376.

Koch, K. "Ezra and the Origins of Judaism." *Journal of Semitic Study* Vol. xix, no.2, 1974, 173-197.

König, E. "Israel's Attitude Respecting Alien-Right and Usages War in Antiquity." *Homiletic Review* 72. 1916, 184-189.

Kraemer, David. "On the Relationship of the Books of Ezra and Nehemiah." *JSOT* 59 (1993): 73-92.

Leeseberg, M. W. "Ezra and Nehemiah: A Review of the Return and

Reform." *Concordia Theological Monthly* 33, 1962, 79-90.

Maccoby, Hyam. "Holiness and Purity: The Holy People in Leviticus and Ezra-Nehemiah." In *Reading Leviticus: A Conversation with Mary Douglas*. Edited by John F. A. Sawyer. Sheffield: Sheffield Academic Press, 1996.

Mace, D. R. *Hebrew Marriage: A Sociological Study*. New York : Philosophical Library, Inc. 1953.

Macmillan, K. D. "Marriage Among the Early Babylonians and Hebrew." *Princeton Theological Review* 6, 1908, 211-245.

Margalith, Othniel. "The Political Role of Ezra as Persian Governor." *ZAW* 98 (1986): 110-112.

Marmorstein, A. and S. Zeitlin, "The Takkanot of Ezra." *Jewish Quarterly Review* 10, 1919/20, 367-371.

McCarthy, Dennis J. "Covenant and Law in Chronicles-Nehemiah." *CBQ* 44 (1982): 25-44.

McConville, J. G. *Ezra, Nehemiah, and Esther*. The Daily Study Bible Series. Philadelphia, PA: Westminster Press, 1985.

_____. "Ezra-Nehemiah and the Fulfillment of Prophecy." *VT* 36 (1986): 203-224.

McFall, Leslie. "Was Nehemiah Contemporary with Ezra in 458 BC?" *WTJ* 53 (1991): 263-293.

Merrill, Eugene, H. "A Theology of Ezra-Nehemiah and Esther." In *A Biblical Theology of the Old Testament*. Edited by Roy B. Zuck. Chicago: Moody Press, 1991.

Mendenhall, G. E. "Law and Covenant in Israel and the Ancient Near East." *The Biblical Colloquium*. Pittsburgh, PA, 1955.

Mowinckel, Sigmund. *Studien zu dem Buche Ezra-Nehemia 1*. Oslo:

Universitetsforlaget, 1964.

Myers, Jacob M. *Ezra. Nehemiah.* Vol. 14 of The Anchor Bible. Edited by William Foxwell Albright and David Noel Freedman. Garden City, NY: Doubleday & Company, Inc. 1965.

Neusner, J. *The Idea of Purity in Ancient Judaism.* Leiden: E. J. Brill. 1973.

_____. *From Testament to Torah: an Introduction to Judaism in its Formative age.* Englewood Cliffs, NJ: Prentice Hall. 1988

Newton, M. *The Concept of Purity at Qumran and in the Letters of Paul.* Cambridge: Cambridge Univeristy Press. 1985.

Niditch, S. "Legends of Wise Heroes and Heroines." in *The Servant of the Lord and other essays on the Old Testament* London: Lutterworth Press. 1952. 454.

North, R. "Ezra and Nehemiah." Jerome Biblical Commentary, ed. R.E. Brown, J.A. Fitzmyer, and R.E. Murphy, London: Chapman, 1968, 402-438.

_____. "Civil Authority in Ezra." *Studi in onore di Edoardo Volterra*, Vol. 6. Milan:Giuffr , 1971, 377-404.

Noth, M. *The Chronicler's History.* ET by H. G. M. Williamson. Sheffield, England : Sheffield Academic Press. 1987

Nykolaishen, Doug. "The Use of Jeremiah 31 in the Book of Ezra." M.A. thesis, Trinity Evangelical Divinity School, 1991.

Ogden, Graham S. "The Use of Figurative Language in Malachi 2.10-16." *The Bible Translator* 39, 1988, 223-230.

Pope, W. B. "Ezra." In Vol. 2 of Ellicott's *Commentary on the Whole Bible.* Edited by Charles John Ellicott. Grand Rapids: Zondervan Publishing House, 1959.

Rabinowitz, Yosef. *The Book of Ezra*. New York: Mesorah, 1984.

Rawlinson, G. "Ezra." In Vol. 7 of *The Pulpit Commentary*. Edited by H. D. M. Spence and Joseph S. Exell. New York: Funk & Wagnalls Co., n.d.; reprint, Grand Rapids: William B. Eerdmans Publishing Co., 1950.

_____. *Ezra and Nehemiah: Their Lives and Times*. New York: Fleming H. Revell Company, 1890.

Richards, Kent Harold. "Reshaping Chronicles and Ezra-Nehemiah Interpretation." In *Old Testament Interpretation: Past, Present, and Future: Essays in Honor of Gene M. Tucker*. Edited by James Luther Mays, David L. Petersen, and Kent Harold Richards. Nashville: Abingdon Press, 1995.

Rothschild, M. M. "Aliens and Israelites." *Dor le Dor* 9 (196-202), 10 (118-121), 11(35-39), 12(245-248), 13 (220-224). 1981-1985.

Rudolph, Wilhelm. *Esra und Nehemia* samt 3. Esra, Handbuch zum Alten Testament. T bingen: J. C. B. Mohr, 1949.

Ryle, Herbert Edward. "The Books of Ezra and Nehemiah." In *The Cambridge Bible for Schools and Colleges*. Edited by A. F. Kirkpatrick. Cambridge: Cambridge University Press, 1923.

Scherman, Nosson, and Meir Zlotowitz, eds. *Ezra*. New York: Mesorah Publications, Ltd., 1984.

Schneider, H. *Die Bücher Esra und Nehemia* (2nd ed.). HSAT IV/2. Bonn: Peter Hanstein. 1959.

Schultz, C. "The Political Tensions Reflected in Ezra-Nehemiah," in C.D. Evans et al. (eds.), *Scripture in Context: Essays on the Comparative Method*, Pittsburg, 1980, 221-244.

Schultz, F. U. "The Books of Ezra and Nehemiah." Translated and edited by Charles A. Briggs. In vol. 7 of Lange's *Commentary on the Holy Scriptures*. Edited by Philip Schaff. 1871; reprint, Grand Rapids: Zondervan Publishing House, n.d.

Seters, J. V. "Jacob's Marriages and Ancient Near East Customs: A Re-examination." *Harvard Theological Review* 62. 1969, 377-395.

Shaver, Judson R. "Ezra and Nehemiah: On the Theological Significance of Making them Contemporaries." In *Priests, Prophets and Scribes: Essays on the Formation and Heritage of Second Temple Judaism in Honour of Joseph Blenkinsopp*. Edited by Eugene Ulrich, et al. Sheffield: Sheffield Academic Press, 1992.

Smith, M. *Palestinian Parties and Politics that Shaped the Old Testament*. New York: Columbia University Press. 1971.

Smith-Christopher, Daniel L. "The Mixed Marriage Crisis in Ezra 9-10 and Nehemiah 13: A Study of the Sociology of the Post-Exilic Judaean Community." In Second Temple Studies: 2. Temple Community in the Persian Period. Edited by Tamara C. Eskenazi and Kent H. Richards. Sheffield: Sheffield Academic Press, 1994.

Snaith, N. H. "The Date of Ezra's Arrival in Jerusalem." *ZAW* 63 (1951): 53-66.

_____. "Note on Ezra 8:35" *JTS* 22 (1971): 150-152.

Sorgwe, Felisi. "The Canonical Shape of Ezra-Nehemiah and Its Theological and Hermeneutical Implications." Ph.D. diss., Baylor University, 1991.

Sperling, S. D. "Rethinking Covenant in Late Biblical Books." *Biblica* 70. 1989 50-72.

Sprinkle, Joe M. "Old Testament Perspectives on Divorce and Remarriage." *JETS* 40 (1997): 529-550.

Stern, E. *Material Culture of the Land of the Bible in the Persian Period 538-332 B.C.*, Jerusalem: Israel Exploration Society. 1982.

Suiter, David Eugene. "The Contribution of Chronological Studies for Understanding Ezra-Nehemiah." Ph.D. diss., The Iliff School of Theology and University of Denver, 1992.

Talmon, S. "Ezra and Nehemiah." *IDB Supplementary Volume*, 1984, 317-328.

Thomson, A. "An Inquiry Concerning the Books of Ezra and Nehemiah." *AJLLiterature* (1931-32): 99-132.

Throntveit, Mark A. "Ezra-Nehemiah." *Interpretation*. Atlanta: John Knox Press. 1989. Louisville: John Knox Press, 1992.

Torrey, C. C. *Ezra Studies*, Chicago: University Press. 1910.

Ulrich, Eugene. "Ezra and Qoheleth Manuscripts from Qumran." In *Priests, Prophets and Scribes: Essays on the Formation and Heritage of Second Temple Judaism in Honour of Joseph Blenkinsopp*. Edited by Eugene Ulrich, et al. Sheffield: Sheffield Academic Press, 1992.

van Grol, Harm W. M. "Exegesis of the Exile Exegesis of Scripture? Ezra 9:6-9." In *Intertextuality in Ugarit and Israel*. Edited by Johannes C. de Moor. Leiden: E. J. Brill, 1998.

_____. "Indeed, Servants We Are: Ezra 9, Neh. 9 and 2 Chron. 12 Compared." In *The Crisis of Israelite Religion: Transformation of Religious Tradition in Exilic and Post-Exilic Times*. Edited by Bob Becking and Marjo C. A. Korpel. Leiden: E. J. Brill, 1999.

van Wyk, W. C. "The Enemies in Ezra 1-6: Interaction Between Text and Reader." *Journal for Semitics* 8 (1996): 34-48.

VanderKam, James C. "EzraNehemiah or Ezra and Nehemiah?" In *Priests, Prophets and Scribes: Essays on the Formation and Heritage of Second Temple Judaism in Honour of Joseph Blenkinsopp.* Edited by Eugene Ulrich, et al. Sheffield: Sheffield Academic Press, 1992.

Vasholz, Robert I. "A Note on Ezra 10:34." *Presbyterian* 25 (1999): 54.

Vos, Howard F. *Ezra, Nehemiah, and Esther.* Bible Study Commentary. Grand Rapids, MI: Zondervan Pub. House. 1987.

Washington, Harold C. "The Strange Woman (hyrkn/hrz hva) of Proverbs 1-9 and Post-Exilic Judaean Society." In *Second Temple Studies: 2. Temple Community in the Persian Period.* Edited by Tamara C. Eskenazi and Kent H. Richards. Sheffield: Sheffield Academic Press, 1994.

Weinberg, Joel. *The Citizen-Temple Community.* Translated by Daniel L. Smith-Christopher. Sheffield: Sheffield Academic Press, 1992.

Welch, A. *Post-Exilic Judaism.* London: W. Blackwood & Sons. 1935.

Williamson, H.G.M. *Ezra, Nehemiah.* Vol. 16 of Word Biblical Commentary, Edited by David A. Hubbard and Glenn W. Barker. Waco, TX: Word Books, Pub., 1985.

_____. "The Composition of Ezra i-vi." *JTS* 34 (1983): 30.

Wood, C. T. "Nehemiah-Ezra." *Expository Times* 59, 1947/48, 53-54.

Wright, J. Stafford. *The Date of Ezra's Coming to Jerusalem.* London: The Tyndale Press, 1958.

Yamauchi, Edwin. M. "Two Reformers Compared: Solon of Athens and Nehemiah of Jerusalem." in *The Bible World: Essays in Honor.* C. H. Gordon, G. Rendsburg, R. Adler(eds.), New York: KTAV. Pub. House, Inc., 1980, 269-292.

_____. "Was Nehemiah the Cupbearer a Eunuch?" *ZAW* 92, 1980, 132-141.

_____. "Ezra-Nehemiah." In Vol. 4 of *The Expositor's Bible Commentary*. Edited by Frank E. Gaebelein. Grand Rapids: Zondervan Publishing House, 1985.

_____. "The Reverse Order of Ezra/Nehemiah Reconsidered." *Themelios* 5 no. 3 (1980): 7-13.

_____. "The Archaeological Background of Ezra." *BS* 137 (1980): 195-211.

Yaron, R. "The Restoration of Marriage." *Journal of Jewish Studies* 17. 1966, 1-11.

Zadok, R. "Remarks on Ezra and Nehemiah." *ZAW* 94, 1982 296-298.

2. 역사적 연구들 Historical Studies

Ackroyd, P. R. *Exile and Restoration*. Philadelphia: The Westminster Press. 1968. London: SCM Press Ltd, 1968.

_____. "The History of Israel in the Exilic and Post-Exilic Periods." in *Tradition and Interpretation*, ed. G. W. Anderson, Oxford: Clarendon. 1979, 320-350.

Albright, W. F. *The Biblical Period From Abraham to Ezra*. New York : Harper & Row Publishers. 1963.

Andersen, F. I. "Who Built the Second Temple?" *Australian Biblical Review* 6 (1958): 1-35.

Avigad, N. *Bullae and Seals from a Post-exilic Judean Archive*, Qedem: Monographs of the Institute of Archaeology 4, Jerusalem. 1976,

Avi-Yonah, M. *The Holy Land from the Persian to the Arab Conquest.* Grand Rapids, MI: Esp. 1966, 11-31.

_____. "The Newly-Found Wall of Jerusalem and Its Topographical Significance." *Israel Exploration Journal* 21, 1971, 168-169.

Barstad, Hans M. *The Myth of the Empty Land: A Study in the History and Archaeology of Judah During the "Exilic" Period.* Oslo: Scandinavian University Press, 1996.

Benzinger, I. *Hebräische Archäologie*, Freiburg i. B.: J.C.B. Mohr. 1894

Bickerman, E. *From Ezra to the Last of the Maccabees: Foundations of Post-Biblical Judaism.* New York : Schocken Books. 1962.

Blenkinsopp, Joseph. "A Jewish Sect of the Persian Period." *CBQ* 52 (1990): 5-20.

_____. "Temple and Society in Achaemenid Judah." In *Second Temple Studies: 1. Persian Period.* Edited by Philip R. Davies. Sheffield: Sheffield Academic Press, 1991.

Bright, John. *A History of Israel.* Fourth Edition. Philadelphia: The Westminster Press. 2000.

Carroll, Robert P. "Textual Strategies and Ideology in the Second Temple Period." In *Second Temple Studies: 1. Persian Period.* Edited by Philip R. Davies. Sheffield: Sheffield Academic Press, 1991.

Cross, Frank Moore. Jr. "A Reconstruction of the Judean Restoration" *JBL* 94 (1975): 4-18.

de Vaux, Roland. *The Bible and the Ancient Near East.* Translated by Damian McHugh. Garden City: Doubleday & Company, Inc., 1971.

Galling, K. *Studien zur Geschichte Israels im persischen Zeitalter.* T bingen. 1964

Hanson, Paul D. "Israelite Religion in the Early Postexilic Period." In *Ancient Israelite Religion*. Edited by Patrick D. Miller, Jr., Paul D. Hanson, and S. Dean McBride. Philadelphia: Fortress Press, 1987.

Hogg, W. E. "The Founding of the Second Temple." *PTR* 25 (1927): 457-461.

Hoglund, Kenneth G. *Achaemenid Imperial Administration in Syria-Palestine and the Missions of Ezra and Nehemiah*. Atlanta: Scholars Press, 1992.

_____. "The Achaemenid Context." In *Second Temple Studies: 1. Persian Period*. Edited by Philip R. Davies. Sheffield: Sheffield Academic Press, 1991.

Horsley, Richard A. "Empire, Temple and Community—But No Bourgeoisie!" In *Second Temple Studies: 1. Persian Period*. Edited by Philip R. Davies. Sheffield: Sheffield Academic Press, 1991.

Hulstaert, L. "Some Problems of Achaemenid History." *Orientalia Lovaniensia Periodica* 8. 1977, 75-79.

Japhet, S. "Sheshbazzar and Zerubbabel: Against the Background of the Historical and Religious Tendencies of Ezra - Nehemiah." in *Zeitschrift für die alttestamentliche Wissenschaft* 94: 66-98. 1982.

_____. "Biblical Historiography in the Persian Period." *World History of the Jewish People*, VI, 176-202, 1983, 295-303(Hebrew)

Kaiser, Walter C. Jr. *A History of Israel*. Nashville: Broadman & Holman Publishers, 1998.

_____. *Hard Sayings of the Old Testament*. Downers Grove: Inter-Varsity Press, 1988.

Kaufmann, Y. *History of the Religion of Israel IV: From the Babylonian Captivity to the End of Prophecy*. ET by C. W. Efroymson. New

York: Ktav Publishing House, Inc. 1977.

_____. "From the Babylonian Captivity to the End of Prophecy." Translated by C. W. Efroymson. *Vol. 4 of History of the Religion of Israel*. New York: Ktav Publishing House, Inc., 1977.

Kuhrt, Amlie. "The Cyrus Cylinder and Achaemenid Imperial Policy." *JSOT* 25 (1983): 83-97.

_____. "Babylonia from Cyrus to Xerxes." In *The Cambridge Ancient History*. Edited by John Boardman, et al. 2d ed. Cambridge: Cambridge University Press, 1988.

McEvenue, S. E. "The Political Structure in Judah from Cyrus to Nehemiah," *Catholic Biblical Quarterly* 43: 353-364. 1981.

Meyers, Eric M. "The Persian Period and the Judean Restoration: From Zerubbabel to Nehemiah." In *Ancient Israelite Religion*. Edited by Patrick D. Miller, Jr., Paul D. Hanson, and S. Dean McBride. Philadelphia: Fortress Press, 1987.

Niehr, Herbert. "Religio-Historical Aspects of the 'Early Post-Exilic' Period." In *The Crisis of Israelite Religion: Transformation of Religious Tradition in Exilic and Post Exilic Times*. Edited by Bob Becking and Marjo C. A. Korpel. Leiden: E. J. Brill, 1999.

Oesterley, W. O. E., and Theodore H. Robinson. *A History of Israel*. Oxford: Clarendon Press, 1932.

Smith, M. "Jewish religious life in the Persian period." *The Cambridge History of Judaism*. eds. W. Davies and L. Findelstein. New York: Cambridge University. 1984, 219-278.

Stern, E. "The Persian empire and the political and social history of Palestine in the Persian period." *The Cambridge History of Judaism*. eds. W. Davies and L. Findelstein. New York:Cambridge

University. 1984, 70-87.

_____. "Religion in Palestine in the Assyrian and Persian Periods." In *The Crisis of Israelite Religion: Transformation of Religious Tradition in Exilic and Post Exilic Times*. Edited by Bob Becking and Marjo C. A. Korpel. Leiden: E. J. Brill, 1999.

Talmon, Shemaryahu. "The Emergence of Jewish Sectarianism in the Early Second Temple Period." In *Ancient Israelite Religion*. Edited by P. D. Miller Jr., Paul D. Hanson, and S. Dean McBride. Philadelphia: Fortress Press, 1987.

Tuland, C. G. "Josephus, Antiquities Book XI: Correction of Confirmation of Biblical Post-Exilic Records?" *Andrews University Seminary Studies* 4 (1966): 176-192.

Widengren, G. "The Persian Period." in *Israelite and Judean History*. ed. J. H. Hayes and J. M. Miller, Philadelphia. 1977, 489-538.

Williamson, H. G. M. "Post-Exilic Historiography." In *The Future of Biblical Studies*. Edited by Richard Elliott Friedman and H. G. M. Williamson. Atlanta: Scholars Press, 1987.

_____. "The Origin of the Twenty-Four Priestly Courses: A Study of 1 Chronicles xiii-xxviii." In *Studies in the Historical Books of the Old Testament*, Edited by J. A. Emerton. Leiden: E. J. Brill, 1979.

_____. "The Historical Value of Josephus' Jewish Antiquities XI. 297-301." *JTS* 28 (1977): 49-66. Wood, Leon. *A Survey of Israel's History*. Grand Rapids: Zondervan Publishing House, 1970.

Young, T. Cuyler, Jr. "The Early History of the Medes and the Persians and the Achaemenid Empire to the Death of Cambyses." In Vol. 4

of *The Cambridge Ancient History*. Edited by John Boardman, et al. 2d ed. Cambridge: Cambridge University Press, 1988.

3. 사회학과 구약성경 연구 Sociology and Old Testament Studies

Aharoni, Y. "New Aspects of the Israelite Occupation of the North." in *Near Eastern Archaeology in the Twentieth Century*. ed. J. A. Sanders. Garden City, NY: Doubleday. 1970, 254-267.

Albright, W. F. "The Names 'Israel' and 'Judah' with an Excursus on the Etymology of todah and torah." Journal of Biblical Literature 46:151-85. 1927.

_____. *From the Stone Age to Christianity*. New York: Doubleday. 1957.

_____. *The Biblical Period from Abraham to Ezra*. New York: Harper & Row. 1963.

Alt, A. *Essays on Old Testament History and Religion*. ET R.A. Wilson. Oxford: Basil Blackwell. 1966.

Anderson, B.W. & Walter Harrelson(eds.). *Israel's Prophetic Heritage: Essays in Honor of James Muilenburg*. New York : Harper & Row, Pub. 1962.

Anderson, G. W.(ed.) *Tradition and Interpretation*. Oxford: Clarendon. 1979.

Astour, M. C. "Habiru." in *The Interpreter's Dictionary of the Bible*, Supplementary Volume. ed. K. Crim. Nashville : Abingdon. 1976, 382-385.

Bagnall, R. S. *The Administration of the Ptolemaic Possessions Outside Egypt*. Leiden: Brill. 1976.

Bess, S. H. "Systems of Land Tenure in Ancient Israel." Ph.D. Dissertation, The University of Michigan. 1963.

Brueggemann, Walter. "Trajectories in Old Testament Literature and the Sociology of Ancient Israel." *Journal of Biblical Literature* 98: 161-185. 1979.

_____. *The Creative Word: Canon as a Model for Biblical Education*. Philadelphia: Fortress Press. 1982

_____. *The Message of the Psalms*. Minneapolis: Augsburg. 1984.

_____. *Hopeful Imagination: Prophetic Voices in Exile*. Philadelphia: Fortress Press. 1986.

_____. *Israel's Praise: Doxology against Idolatry and Ideology*. Philadelphia: Fortress Press. 1988.

Chaney, Marvin L. "Ancient Palestinian Peasant Movements and the Formation of Premonarchic Israel." in *Palestine in Transition: The Emergence of Ancient Israel*. eds. D.N. Freedman and D. F. Graf. Sheffield: The Almond Press. 1983, 39-90.

Cook, J. M. *The Persian Empire*. London : J.M. Dent & Sons. 1983.

Cross, Frank Moore. "The Divine Warrior in Israel's Early Cult." in *Studies and Texts 3: Biblical Motifs*, ed. A. Altmann. Cambridge, MA: Harvard University. 1966, 11-30.

Diakonoff, I. M. "The Rural Community in the Ancient Near East." *Journal of the Economic and Social History of the Orient*. 17:121-33. 1975.

Freedman, D. N. "Deuteronomic History." in *IDB Supplementary*. 1976,

226-228.

Geus, C. H. J. de. "The Importance of Agricultural Terraces, with an Excursus on the Hebrew word gbi." *Palestine Exploration Quarterly* 107: 65-74. 1975.

_____. "The Tribes of Israel." *Studia semitica Neerlandica* 18. Assen: Van Gorcum. 1976

Gottwald, Norman K. "Were the Early Israelites Pastoral Nomads?." in *Rhetorical Criticism: Essays in Honor of James Muilenburg*. eds. J. Jackson & M. Kessler. Pittsburg: Pickwick Press. 1974. 228-260.

_____. "Domain Assumptions and Societal Models in the Study of Pre-Monarchic Israel." in *Supplements to VT* 18. Leiden: Brill. 1975, 89-100.

_____. "Israel, Social and Economic Development of." in *IDB Supplementary*. 1976, 465-466.

_____. "Were the Early Israelites Pastoral Nomads?" *Biblical Archaeological Review* 4:2-7. 1978.

_____. *The Tribes of Yahweh: A Sociology of the Religion of Liberated Israel, 1250-1050 B.C.E.* Maryknoll, NY: Orbis Books. 1979.

_____. "Sociological Criticism of the Old Testament." *The Christian Century* 99: 474-477. 1982.

_____. *The Bible and Liberation : Political and Social Hermeneutics*. Maryknoll, NY:Orbis Books. 1983(ed.).

_____. "Early Israel and the Canaanite Socio-economic System." in *Palestine in Transition: The Emergence of Ancient Israel*, eds. D. N. Freedman and D. F. Graf. Sheffield: The Almond Press. 1983.

_____. *The Hebrew Bible : A Socio-Literary Introduction*. Philadelphia: Fortress Press. 1985 (본 서는 편집 혹은 혼합적 의미의 역사를 다루고 있다. 문학적 논쟁들과 사회학적인 관점에 집중한 성경 개론서임. Pursues either the history of composition or synchronic meaning. An introduction to the Bible concentrated on literary issues and sociological perspectives.)

Greenberg, M. "The Hab/piru." *American Oriental Series* 39. New Haven: American Oriental Society. 1955.

Hahn, Herbert F. "The Sociological Approach to the Old Testament." in *The Old Testament in Modern Research*. Philadelphia : Fortress Press. (1954 by Muhlenberg Press). 1966, 157-184.

Halligan, John M. "The Role of the Peasant in the Amarna Period." in *Palestine in Transition: The Emergence of Ancient Israel*, eds. D. N. Freedman and D. F. Graf. Sheffield: The Almond Press. 1983, 15-24.

Halpern, B. "Gibeon: Israelite Diplomacy in the Conquest Era." *The Catholic Biblical Quarterly* 37: 303-316. 1975.

Hanson, Paul D. *The Dawn of Apocalyptic*. Philadelphia: Fortress Press, 1975.

Hauser, A. J. "Israel's Conquest of Palestine: A Peasants' Rebellion?" *Journal for the Study of the Old Testament* 7: 2-19. 1978.

_____. "Response to Thompson and Mendenhall." *Journal for the Study of the Old Testament* 7: 35-36. 1978.

Heltzer, M. *The Rural Community in Ancient Ugarit*. Wiesbaden: Reichert.1976.

Holladay, W. L. "The Kingdom of Yahweh." *Interpretation* 27:269-274. 1973.

Holmgren, Fredrick Carlson. "Israel Alive Again." *International Theological Commentary*. Grand Rapids, MI: Wm B Eerdmans. 1987.

Kemp, K. A. & Norman Yoffee, "Ethnicity in Ancient Western Asia During the Early Second Millennium B.C.: Archaeological Assessments and Ethnoarchaeological Prospectives." *Bulletin of the American Schools of Oriental Research* 237: 85-104. 1980.

Long, Burke O. "The Social World of Ancient Israel." Interpretation 36: 243-255. 1982.

_____. "The Problem of Etiological Narrative in the Old Testament." *Beihefte zur Zeitschrift fuer die Alttestamentliche Wissenschaft* 108. Berlin: Toepelmann. 1968.

Luke, J. T. "Pastoralism and Politics in the Mari Period: A Re-examination of the Character and Political Significance of the Major West Semitic Tribal Groups of the Middle Euphrates." Ph.D. thesis, The University of Michigan. 1965.

Malamat, A. "Charismatic Leadership in the Book of Judges." *Magnalia Dei: Essays on the Bible and Archaeology in Memory of G. Ernest Wright*, eds. F. M. Cross, W. E. Lemke and P.D. Miller, Jr.. Garden City, N.Y.: Doubleday & Company, Inc.. 1976, 152-168.

_____. "Ancient Oriental and Biblical Law." *Biblical Archaeologist* 17:26-46. 1954.

_____. "The Hebrew Conquest of Palestine." *Biblical Archaeologist* 25: 66-87. 1962.

_____. *The Tenth Generation: The Origins of the Biblical Tradition*. Baltimore: Johns Hopkins University. 1973.

_____. "The Conflict Between Value Systems and Social

Control." in *Unity and Diversity: Essays in the History, Literature, and Religion of the Ancient Near East*, eds. H. Goedicke and J.J.M. Roberts. Baltimore: Johns Hopkins University. 1975, 169-180.

_____. "Social Organization in Early Israel." in *Magnalia Dei: Essays on the Bible and Archaeology in Memory of G. Ernest Wright*, eds. F. M. Cross, W. E. Lemke and P.D. Miller, Jr.. Garden City, N.Y.: Doubleday & Company, Inc.. 1976, 132-151.

_____. "Between Theology and Archaeology." *Journal for the Study of the Old Testament* 7:28-34. 1978.

_____. "Ancient Israel's Hyphenated History." in *Palestine in Transition: The Emergence of Ancient Israel*, eds. D. N. Freedman and D. F. Graf. Sheffield: The Almond Press. 1983, 95-103.

Miller, J. Maxwell. "The Israelite Occupation of Canaan." in *Israelite and Judaean History*, eds. J. H. Hays and J. M. Miller. Philadelphia : The Westminster Press. 1977, 213-284.

Miller, J. M. & John H. Hayes, *A History of Ancient Israel and Judah*. Philadelphia: The Westminster Press. 1986.

Miller, Patrick D., Jr. "Faith and Ideology in the Old Testament," in *Magnalia Dei: Essays on the Bible and Archaeology in Memory of G. Ernest Wright*, eds. F. M. Cross, W. E. Lemke and P.D. Miller, Jr.. Garden City, N.Y.: Doubleday & Company, Inc.. 1976, 464-479.

Moran, W. L. "Habiru (Habiri)." in Vol. 6 of *New Catholic Encyclopedia*. Washington: Catholic University. 1967, 878-880.

Neusner, Jacob, *Formative Judaism: Religious, Historical, and Literary Studies*, Brown Judaic Studies 37, Chico, CA: Scholars Press. 1982.

Noth, M. *The History of Israel*. 2nd ed. ET. P. R. Ackroyd from German, 1958. New York: Harper & Row. 1960.

_____. "The Laws in the Pentateuch and Other Essays." ET. D. R. Ap-Thomas from German, 1940, 1957, 1960. Edinburgh: Oliver & Boyd. 1966. Paul, S. M. "Studies in the Book of the Covenant in the Light of Cuneiform and Biblical Law." *Supplements to Vetus Testamentum* 18. Leiden: Brill. 1970.

Parker, Simon B. "Possession Trance and Prophecy in Pre-exilic Israel." *Vetus Testamentum* 28: 271-285. 1978.

Riemann, P. A. "Desert and Return to Desert in the Pre-exilic Prophets." Ph.D. dissertation, Harvard University. 1963.

Rofé, Alexander. "The Onset of Sects in Postexilic Judaism: Neglected Evidence from the Septuagint, Trito-Isaiah, Ben Sira, and Malachi." in *The Social World of Formative Christianity and Judaism*, eds. Jacob Neusner, Peder Borgen, E.S. Frerichs and Richard Horsley. Philadelphia: Fortress. 1988, 39-49.

Rogerson, J. W., *Anthropology and the Old Testament*. Atlanta, GA: John Knox. 1979.

_____, "Anthropology and the Old Testament." *Proceedings of the Irish Biblical Association* 10: 90-102. 1986.

Rosenbloom, J. R., "Social Science Concepts of Modernization and Biblical History." *Journal of the American Academy of Religion* 40: 437-44. 1972.

Rowton, M. B. "The Topological Factor in the Hapiru Problem." in *Studies in Honor of Benno Landsberger*, eds. H. G. Gueterbock and T. Jacobsen. *Assyriological Studies* 16. University of Chicago. 1965, 375-387.

_____. "Dimorphic Structure and the Problem of the 'Apiru-'Ibrim." *Journal of Near Eastern Studies* 35: 13-20. 1976.

Sasson, J. M. "Review of The Tenth Generation: The Origins of the Biblical Tradition by G. E. Mendenhall." *Journal of Biblical Literature* 93: 294-296. 1974.

Smith, Daniel L. "The Politics of Ezra: Sociological Indicators of Postexilic Judaean Society." In *Second Temple Studies: 1. Persian Period*. Edited by Philip R. Davies. Sheffield: Sheffield Academic Press, 1991.

_____. *Religion of the Landless: The Social Context of the Babylonian Exile*. Bloomington: Meyer-Stone Books, 1989.

Stager, L. E. "Agriculture." in *The Interpreter's Dictionary of the Bible, Supplementary Volume*, ed. K. Crim. Nashville: Abingdon Press. 1976. 11-13.

Talmon, S. "The 'Desert Motif' in the Bible and in Qumran Literature." in *Biblical Motifs: Origins and Transformations*, ed. A. Altmann. Cambridge, MA: Harvard University. 1966, 31-63.

Thompson, T. L. "Historical Notes on Israel's Conquest of Palestine: A Peasants' Rebellion?" *Journal for the Study of the Old Testament* 7:20-27. 1978.

Van Rooy, Harry V. "Prophet and Society in the Persian Period According to Chronicles." In *Second Temple Studies: 2. Temple Community in the Persian Period*. Edited by Tamara C. Eskenazi and Kent H. Richards. Sheffield: Sheffield Academic Press, 1994.

Weippert, M. "The Settlement of the Israelite Tribes in Palestine Studies" in *Biblical Theology*, 2nd ser., 21. ET J. D. Martin from German, 1967; London: SCM. 1971.

_____. "Canaan, Conquest and Settlement of." in *The Interpreter's Dictionary of the Bible*, Supplementary Volume, ed. K. Crim.

Nashville: Abingdon Press. 125-130.

Widengren, G. "Methodological Aspects of Old Testament Study." in Congress Volume, *Oxford VTS*, VII 1959: 13-30. 1960.

Wilson, Robert R. "The Old Testament Genealogies in Recent Research." *Journal of Biblical Literature* 94: 169-89. 1975.

_____. "Genealogy and History in the Biblical World." Ph.D. Dissertation of Yale University in 1972, New Haven: Yale University Press. 1977.

_____. *Prophecy and Society in Ancient Israel*. Philadelphia : Fortress Press. 1980.

_____. *Sociological Approaches to the Old Testament*. Philadelphia : Fortress Press. 1984

_____. "Sociology of the Old Testament." in *Harper's Bible Dictionary*, eds. P. J. Achtemeier with SBL. San Francisco: Harper & Row, Publishers. 1985. 968-973.

Wright, G. Ernest. "God Who Acts : Biblical Theology as Recital." *Studies in Biblical Theology*, No. 8. London: SCM Press. 1952.

_____. *Biblical Archaeology*. Rev. ed. Philadelphia: Westminster. 1962.

_____. "Cult and History: A Study if a Current Problem in Old Testament Interpretation." *Interpretation* 16: 320. 1962.

4. 사회학과 신약성경 연구 Sociology and New Testament Studies

Andrews, D. K. "Yahweh the God of the Heavens." In *The Seed of Wisdom: Essays in Honour of T. J. Meek*. Edited by W. S. McCullough. Toronto: University of Toronto Press, 1964.

Balch, D.L. and J.E. Stambaugh. *The New Testament in Its Social Environment*. Philadelphia: The Westminster Press. 1986.

Banks, Robert. "Paul's Idea of Community: The Early House Churches in their Historical setting." Greenwood, S.C.: the Attic Press, Inc.. 1980.

Barton, S. "Paul and the Cross: A Sociological Approach." *Theology* 85: 13-19. 1982.

Berger, Klaus. "Wissenssoziologie und Exegese des Neuen Testaments." *Kairos* 19: 124-133. 1977.

Brown, R. E. *The Community of the Beloved Disciple: The Life, Loves, and Hates of an Individual Church in New Testament Times*. New York: Paulist Press. 1979.

Elliot, John H. *A Home for the Homeless: A Sociological Exegesis of 1 Peter. Its Situation and Strategy*. Philadelphia : Fortress Press. 1981.

_____. "Social Scientific Criticism of the New Testament: More on Methods and Models." *Semeia* 35: 1-33. 1986.

Gager, John G. "Kingdom and Community: The Social World of Early Christianity." Englewood Cliffs, NJ: Prentice-Hall. 1975.

_____. "Shall We Marry Our Enemies? Sociology and the New Testament." *Interpretation* 36: 256-265. 1982.

Grant, Robert M. *Early Christianity and Society*. New York: Harper & Row. 1977.

Hindson, E. E. "The Sociology of Knowledge and Biblical Interpretation." *Theologia Evangelica* 17:33-38. 1984.

Hock, Ronald F. *The Social Context of Paul's Ministry: Tentmaking and*

Apostleship. Philadelphia: Fortress Press. 1980.

Holmberg, Bengt. *Paul and Power: The Structure of Authority in the Primitive Church as Reflected in the Pauline Epistles*. Philadelphia: Fortress. 1980.

Jewett, Robert J. "Christian Tolerance: Paul's Message to the Modern Church." *Biblical Perspectives on Current Issues*. Philadelphia:Westminster. 1982. (이 글은 바울의 선교를 통해 세워진 교회들 내에서 상호 수용하고 환영하는 것에 대한 주석적-조직적 연구. 로마서 위주. An exegetical-systematic study of mutual acceptance and welcoming in the churches established through Paul's mission. Centers upon material from Romans.)

Judge, E. A. *The Social Pattern of the Christian Groups in the First Century: Some Prolegomena to the Study of New Testament Ideas of Social Obligation*. London: Tyndale. 1960.

Kaylor, R. David. *Paul's Covenant Community: Jew & Gentile in Romans*. Atlanta: John Knox Press. 1988.

Kee, Howard Clark. *Christian Origins in Sociological Perspective: Methods and Resources*. Philadelphia: Westminster Press. 1980.

_____. "Weber Revisited: Sociology of Knowledge and the Historical Reconstruction of Christianity." in *Meaning, Truth, and God*. ed. Leroy S. Rouner. Boston Uni. Studies in Philosophy and Religion 3. Notre Dame, Ind.: Uni. of Notre Dame Press. 1982. 112-134.

_____. *Miracle in the Early Christian World : A Study in Sociohistorical Method*. New Haven, CT : Yale University Press. 1983.

_____. *The New Testament in Context : Sources and

Documents. Englewood Cliffs, NJ: Prentice-Hall. 1984.

_____. "Sociology of the New Testament." in Harper's Bible Dictionary, eds. P. J. Achtemeier with SBL. San Francisco: Harper & Row, Pub. 1985. 961-968.

_____. "Christology and Ecclesiology: Titles of Christ and Models of Community." _Semeia_ 30: 171-192. 1985.

_____. _Knowing the Truth : A Social Approach to New Testament Interpretation_. Philadelphia : Fortress Press. 1989.

Klauck, H.-J. _Hausgemeinde und Hauskirche im fruehen Christentum_. Stuttgart: Verlag Katholisches Bibelwerk. 1981.

Koenig, John. _New Testament Hospitality: Partnership with Strangers as Promise and Mission_. Philadelphia: Fortress Press. 1985.

Kyrtatas, D. J. _The Social Structure of the Early Christian Communities_. London: Verso. 1987.

LaFargue, Michael. "Sociohistorical Research and the Contextualization of Biblical Theology." in _The Social World of Formative Christianity and Judaism_, eds. Jacob Neusner, Peder Borgen, E.S. Frerichs and Richard Horsley. Philadelphia: Fortress. 1988, 3-16.

MacMullen, Ramsay. _Enemies of the Roman Order_. Cambridge, MA : Harvard Uni. 1966.

_____. _Roman Social Relations: 50 B.C. to A.D. 284_. New Haven, CT : Yale University Press. 1974.

Malherbe, A. J. _Social Aspects of Early Christianity_, 2nd ed. Philadelphia : Fortress Press. 1983. (초대 교회에 있는 사회 현상으로 다음 논문이 게재됨. "Hospitality and Inhospitality in the Church")

_____. _Paul and the Thessalonians : The Philosophic Tradition of Pastoral Care_. Philadelphia: Fortress Press. 1987. (바

울의 신학 대신 바울의 실천을 다룸. 교회를 단순히 조직하는 대신 공동체를 세우고 형성하고 양성했다. Deals with Paul's practice rather than his theology. Rather than simply organize a church, Paul founded, shaped, and nurtured a community.)

Malina, B. "The Social Sciences and Biblical Interpretation." *Interpretation* 36: 229-242. 1982.

_____. *Christian Origins and Cultural Anthropology: Practical Models for Biblical Interpretation.* Atlanta: John Knox. 1986.

Mathews, J. B. "Hospitality and the New Testament Church." Th.D. dissertation. Princeton Theological Seminary. 1964.

Meeks, Wayne A. "The Man from Heaven in Johannine Sectarianism." *Journal of Biblical Literature* 91: 44-72. 1972.

_____. "The Social World of Early Christianity." The Council on the Study of Religion Bulletin 6: 4-5. 1975.

_____. "Since then you would need to go out of the world": Group Boundaries in Pauline Christianity. in ed. T. Ryan, *Critical History and Biblical Faith: New Testament Perspectives.* Villanova, Penn. 1979. 1-23.

_____. "The Social Context of Pauline Theology." *Interpretation* 36: 266-277. 1982.

_____. *The First Urban Christians : The Social World of the Apostle Paul.* Haven, CT: Yale University Press. 1983.

Nineham, D. "A Partner for Cinderella?" in What About the New Testament?: Essays in Honor of Christopher Evans. London, UK: SCM Press. 1975, 143-154.

_____. "The Use and Abuse of the Bible." *A Study of the Bible in an Age of Rapid Cultural Change.* New York: Barnes & Noble/

Harper & Row. 1977.

_____. "The Strangeness of the New Testament World." *Theology* 85:171-177, 247-255. 1982.

Petersen, Norman R., *Rediscovering Paul: Philemon and the Sociology of Paul's Narrative World*. Philadelphia : Fortress Press. 1985.

Remus, H.E. "Sociology of Knowledge and the Study of Early Christianity." Studies in Religion/Sciences religieuses 11:45-56. 1982.

Robbins, V. *Jesus the Teacher: A Socio-Rhetorical Interpretation of Mark*. Philadelphia: Fortress Press. 1984.

Rohrbaugh, R. L. "Social Location of Thought as a Heuristic Construct in New Testament Study." *Journal for the Study of the New Testament* 30: 103-119. 1987.

Sampley, J. Paul. *Pauline Partnership in Christ: Christian Community and Commitmen in Light of Roman Law*. Philadelphia : Fortress Press. 1980.

Sanders, E. P. *Paul and Palestinian Judaism*. Philadelphia: Fortress Press. 1977.

Sch tz, J. H. *Paul and the Anatomy of Apostolic Authroity*. Cambridge: CUP. 1978.

Theissen, G. *Sociology of Early Palestine Christianity*, ET J. Bowden. Philadelphia : Fortress Press. 1978.

_____. *The Social Setting of Pauline Christianity: Essays of Corinth*. ET J.H. Schuetz. Philadelphia: Fortress Press. 1982.

_____. *Psychological Aspects of Pauline Theology*. ET J. P. Galvin. Philadelphia: Fortress Press. 1985.

Verner, David C. *The Household of God: The Social World of the*

Pastoral Epistles, SBL Dissertation Series 71, Chico, CA: Scholars Press, 1983.

5. 일반적인 사회학 연구들 General Sociological Studies

Abu Lughod, J. "Migrant Adjustment to City Life: the Egyptian Case." in *Readings in Arab and Middle Eastern Society and Culture*. ed. A. M. Lutfiyya and C. W. Churchill. The Hague: Mouton. Ahmed, A. Gh. 1970. 664-667. Tribal and Sedentary Elites : a Bridge Between

_____. "Two Communities." in *the Desert and the Sown*, ed. C. Nelson. Berkeley, CA: Institute of International Studies. 1973, 75-96.

Alter, Robert and Frank Kermode. *The Literary Guide to the Bible*. Cambridge, MA: Belknap Press. 1987.

Awad, M. "Settlement of Nomadic and Semi-nomadic Tribal Groups in the Middle East." *International Labor Review* 79: 25-56. 1959.

Barth, F. "Introduction." in *Ethnic groups and boundaries*, ed. F. Barth. Boston, MA: Little, Brown and Co. 1969, 9-38.

Bates, D. G. "The Role of the State in Peasant-nomad Mutualism." *Anthropological Quarterly* 44: 109-131. 1971.

Berger, Peter L. *The Sacred Canopy: Elements of a Sociological Theory of Religion*. Garden City, NY: Doubleday & Company, Inc.. 1967.

_____. *A Rumor of Angels*. Garden City, NY : Doubleday & Company, Inc. 1969.

Berger, Peter L. & Thomas Luckmann. *The Social Construction of Reality*. Garden City, NY: Doubleday & Company, Inc. 1966.

Charsley, S. R. "The Formation of Ethnic Groups." in *Urban Ethnicity* ed. A. Cohen. New York: Tavistock. 1974. 337-368.

Douglas, Mary. *Purity and Danger*. London: Routledge and Kegan Paul. 1966/76.

_____. Essays in the Sociology of Perception. London and Boston: Routledge and Kegan Paul. 1982.

Durkheim, E. Rules of Sociological Method: The Elementary Forms of the Religious Life. New York: Free Press. 1947.

Harris, M. *The Rise of Anthropological Theory: A History of Theories of Culture*. New York: Crowell. 1968.

Hobsbawm, E. J. "Social Banditry." in *Rural Protest : Peasant Movements and Social Change*, ed. H. A. Landsberge. New York:Barnes & Nobel. 1973. 142-157.

Mannheim, K. "Das Problem einer Soziologie des Wissens." in *Archiv für Sozialwissenschaft und Sozialpolitik* 54: 577-652, 1925.

_____. *Ideology and Utopia : An Introduction to the Sociology of Knowledge*, ET L. Wirth and E. Shils. New York: Harcourt, Brace and World. 1936.

Moore, B. *Social Origins of Dictatorship and Democracy: Lord and Peasant in the Making of the Modern World*. Boston: Beacon. 1966.

Parsons, T. "An Approach to the Sociology of Knowledge." in *Transactions of the Fourth World Congress of Sociology*. International Sociological Association, IV. 1959, 25-49.

_____. *The Evolution of Societies*. ed. and with an introduction by J. Toby. Foundations of Modern Sociology Series. Englewood Cliffs, NJ: Prentice-Hall. 1977.

Scheler, M. "Versuche zu einer Soziologie des Wissens, Schriften des Ferschungsinstitutes fuer Sozialwissenschaften" in Koeln 2 Munich: Duncker und Humbolt. 1924(ed.), Revised and expanded version in *Die Wissensformen und die Gesellschaft*. Leipzig: Neue Geist-Verlag, 1926.

Schutz, Alfred. "The Stranger: An Essay in Social Psychology." in Collected Papers, Vol. 2: Studies in Social Theory. ed. A. Brodersen. The Hague: Nijhoff. 1964. 91-103.

_____. *On Phenomenology and Social Relations*. Chicago, Ill: University of Chicago Press. 1970.

Schutz, A. & T. Luckmann. *Structures of the Life World*. Evanston, Ill: Northwestern University Press. 1973.

Sjoberg, G. *The Preindustrial City: Past and Present*, New York: Free Press. 1960.

Weber, Max. *Ancient Judaism*. ET H. H. Gerth and D. Martindale from German, 1917-19, 1921. New York: Free Press. 1952.

Wolf, E. R. *Peasants*. Foundations of Modern Anthropology Series. Englewood Cliffs: Prentice-Hall. 1966.

Wuthnow, R., M. Douglas, M. Foucault, and J. Habermas. *Cultural Analysis*. London and Boston: Routledge and Kegan Paul. 1984.

6. 구약성경 신학 연구들

Anderson, B. W. *Understanding the Old Testament*. 5th ed. Englewood Cliffs, NJ: Prentice-Hall. 2007.

Barth, Christopher. *God With Us: A Theological Introduction to the*

    Old Testament. Edited by Geoffrey W. Bromiley. Grand Rapids: William B. Eerdmans Publishing Company, 1991.

Bruggemann, Walter. *Theology of the Old Testament: Testimony, Dispute, Advocacy*. Fortress Press, 2012.

Childs, Brevard. *Introduction to the Old Testament as Scripture*. Philadelphia: Fortress Press, 1979.

Cooper, Alan. "On Reading the Bible Critically and Otherwise." In *The Future of Biblical Studies*. Edited by Richard Elliott Friedman and H. G. M. Williamson. Atlanta: Scholars Press, 1987.

Craigie, Peter C. *The Old Testament: Its Background, Growth, and Content*. Nashville: Abingdon Press, 1986.

Deuel, David C. "An Old Testament Pattern for Expository Preaching." *Master's Seminary Journal* 2 (1991): 125-138.

Dumbrell, William J. *The Faith of Israel: Its Expression in the Books of the Old Testament*. Grand Rapids: Baker Book House, 1988.

Dyrness, William. *Themes in Old Testament Theology*. Downers Grove: Inter-Varsity Press, 1979.

Eichrodt, Walter. *Theology of the Old Testament*, The Old Testament Library, Westminster John Knox Press, 1961(vol. 1) 1967(Vol. 2).

Fishbane, Michael. *Biblical Interpretation in Ancient Israel*. Oxford: Clarendon Press, 1985.

Genneweg, A. H. J. *Understanding the Old Testament*. Translated by John Bowden. Philadelphia: Westminster Press, 1978.

Goldingay, John. *Old Testament Theology*. IVP Academic; Reprint edition, 2015.

Gottwald, Norman K. *The Hebrew Bible: A Socio-Literary Introduction*. Philadelphia: Fortress Press, 1985.

Gray, George Buchanan. *A Critical Introduction to the Old Testament*. New York: Charles Scribner's Sons, 1913.

Harrelson, Walter. *Interpreting the Old Testament*. New York: Holt, Rinehart, and Wiston, Inc., 1964.

Harrison, R. K. *Introduction to the Old Testament*. Grand Rapids: William B. Eerdmans Publishing Company, 1969.

Hasel, Gerhard F. *The Remnant: The History and Theology of the Remnant Idea from Genesis to Isaiah*. Berrien Springs: Andrews University Press, 1972.

House, Paul R. *Old Testament Theology*. Downers Grove: InterVarsity Press, 1998.

_____. *Old Testament Survey*. Nashville: Broadman Press, 1992.

Hubbard, David A. "Hope in the Old Testament." *Tyndale Bulletin* 34 (1983): 33-59.

Kaiser, Walter C., Jr. *Toward an Old Testament Theology*. Grand Rapids: Zondervan Publishing House, 1978.

Keegan, Terence J. *Interpreting the Bible: A Popular Introduction to Biblical Hermeneutics*. New York: Paulist Press, 1985.

Lehman, Chester K. *Biblical Theology: Old Testament*. Vol. 1. Scottdale, PA: Herald Press, 1971.

Martens, Elmer A. "Accessing Theological Readings of a Biblical Book." *Andrews University Seminary Studies* 34 (1996): 223-237.

Morgan, Donn F. "The Beginnings of Biblical Theology." In *The Psalms and Other Studies on the Old Testament*. Edited by Jack C. Knight and Lawrence A. Sinclair. Cincinnati: Forward Movement Publications, 1990.

Oehler, Gustav. *Theology of the Old Testament*. Edited by George E. Day. 1883; reprint ed., Grand Rapids: Zondervan Publishing House, n.d.

Payne, J. Barton. *The Theology of the Older Testament*. Grand Rapids: Zondervan Publishing House, 1962.

Pfeiffer, Robert H. *Introduction to the Old Testament*. New York: Harper & Brothers Publishers, 1941.

Preuss, Horst Dietrich. *Old Testament Theology*. Vol. 2. Translated by Leo G. Perdue. Louisville: Westminster John Knox Press, 1996.

Rowley, H. H. *The Servant of the Lord and Other Essays on the Old Testament*. London: Lutterworth, 1952.

_____. *Men of God: Studies in Old Testament History and Prophecy*. London: Thomas Nelson and Sons Ltd, 1963.

Sailhamer, John. *Introduction to Old Testament Theology: A Canonical Approach*. Grand Rapids: Zondervan Publishing House, 1995.

von Rad, Gerhard. *Old Testament Theology*. Vol. 1. Translated by D. M. G. Stalker. London: Oliver and Boyd, 1962.

Young, Edward J. *An Introduction to the Old Testament*. Grand Rapids: William B. Eerdmans Publishing, Co., 1950.

Zimmerli, Walther. *Old Testament Theology in Outline*. Translated by David E. Green. Edinburgh: T. & T. Clark, 1978.

7. 문학 비평 연구 Literary Analysis

1) 단권 서적들 Books and Monographs

Abrams, M. H. *A Glossary of Literary Terms*. 4th ed. New York: Holt, Rinehart and Winston, 1981.

Alter, Robert. *The Art of Biblical Narrative*. New York: Basic Books, 1983.

Auerbach, Erich. *Mimesis(모방, 재현): The Representation of Reality in Western Literature*. Translated by Willard R. Trask. Princeton, NJ: Princeton University Press, 1953.

Avishur, Yitzhak. *Studies in Biblical Narrative: Style, Structure, and the Ancient Near Eastern Literary Background*. Tel Aviv: Archaeological Center Publication, 1999.

Bal, Mieke. *Narratology: Introduction to the Theory of Narrative*. 2d ed. Toronto: University of Toronto Press, 1997.

Bar-Efrat, Shimon. *Narrative Art in the Bible*. Translated by Dorothea Shefer-Vanson. 2d ed. Sheffield: Sheffield Academic Press, 1989.

Berlin, Adele. *Poetics and Biblical Interpretation*. Sheffield: Almond Press, 1983; reprint, Winona Lake: Eisenbrauns, 1994.

Bloom, Edward A. *The Order of Fiction: An Introduction*. Indianapolis: The Odyssey Press, 1964.

Booth, Wayne C. *The Rhetoric of Fiction*. Chicago: The University of Chicago Press, 1961.

Brichto, Herbert Chanan. *Toward a Grammar of Biblical Poetics: Tales of the Prophets*. Oxford: Oxford University Press, 1992.

Brooks, Peter. *Reading for the Plot: Design and Intention in Narrative*.

New York: Alfred A. Knopf, 1984.

Chatman, Seymour. *Story and Discourse: Narrative Structure in Fiction and Film*. Ithaca: Cornell University Press, 1978.

Davies, Philip R. "Sociology and the Second Temple." In *Second Temple Studies: 1. Persian Period*. Edited by Philip R. Davies. Sheffield: Sheffield Academic Press, 1991.

_____. "The Society of Biblical Israel." In *Second Temple Studies: 2. Temple Community in the Persian Period*. Edited by Tamara C. Eskenazi and Kent H. Richards. Sheffield: Sheffield Academic Press, 1994.

Dillard, Raymond B. and Tremper Longman III. *An Introduction to the Old Testament*. Grand Rapids: Zondervan Publishing House, 1994.

Dorsey, David A. *The Literary Structure of the Old Testament*. Grand Rapids: Baker Book House, 1999.

Eskenazi, Tamara Cohn. *In an Age of Prose: A Literary Analysis of Ezra-Nehemiah*. Atlanta: Scholars Press, 1988.

Eslinger, Lyle. *Into the Hands of the Living God*. Sheffield: The Almond Press, 1989.

Exum, J. Cheryl, and David J. A. Clines, eds. *The New Literary Criticism and the Hebrew Bible*. Valley Forge, PA: Trinity Press International, 1993.

Fokkelman, J. P. *Narrative Art and Poetry in the Books of Samuel. Vol. 1: King David*. Translated by George van Driem, Roy Vreeland, and Judith Frishman. Assen, The Netherlands, 1981.

_____. *Reading Biblical Narrative: An Introductory Guide*. Translated by Ineke Smit. Louisville: Westminster John Knox Press, 1999.

Forster, E. M. *Aspects of the Novel*. New York: Harcourt, Brace, and Company, 1927.

Friedman, Norman. *Form and Meaning in Fiction*. Athens: The University of Georgia Press, 1975.

Genette, Grard. *Narrative Discourse: An Essay in Method*. Translated by Jane E. Lewin. Ithaca: Cornell University Press, 1980.

Gibson, Andrew. *Towards a Postmodern Theory of Narrative*. Edinburgh: Edinburgh University Press, 1996.

Golden, Leon and O. B. Hardison Jr., *Aristotle's Poetics: A Translation and Commentary for Students of Literature*. Englewood Cliffs, NJ: Prentice-Hall, Inc., 1968.

Good, Edwin M. *Irony in the Old Testament*. Philadelphia: The Westminster Press, 1965.

Gros Louis, Kenneth R. R. *Literary Interpretations of Biblical Narratives*. Vol. 2. Nashville: Abingdon Press, 1982.

Hengel, Martin. "The Scriptures and Their Interpretation in Second Temple Judaism." In *The Aramaic Bible: Targums in their Historical Context*. Edited by D. R. G. Beattie and M. J. McNamara. Sheffield: Sheffield Academic Press, 1994.

Hengstenberg, E. W. *History of the Kingdom of God*. Vol. 2. Edinburgh: T. & T. Clark, 1872.

Kermode, Frank. *The Sense of an Ending*. New York: Oxford University Press, 1967.

Kort, Wesley A. *Story, Text, and Scripture: Literary Interests in Biblical Narrative*. University Park: The Pennsylvania State University Press, 1988.

Lanser, Susan S. *The Narrative Act: Point of View in Prose Fiction*.

Princeton: Princeton University Press, 1981.

Lewis, C. S. *Reflections on the Psalms*. New York: Harcourt, Brace and Company, 1958.

Licht, Jacob. *Storytelling in the Bible*. Jerusalem: The Magnes Press, 1978.

Long, Philips V. "The Art of Biblical History." Vol. 5 in *Foundations of Contemporary Interpretation*. Grand Rapids: Zondervan Publishing House, 1994.

Longman, Tremper III. "Literary Approaches to Biblical Interpretation." In *Foundations of Contemporary Interpretation*. Vol. 3. Grand Rapids: Zondervan Publishing House, 1987.

Lotman, Jurij. *The Structure of the Artistic Text*. Translated by Gail Lenhoff and Ronald Vroon. Ann Arbor: University of Michigan Press, 1977.

Norton, David. *A History of the Bible as Literature. Vol. 2: From 1700 to the Present Day*. Cambridge: Cambridge University Press, 1993.

O'Connell, Robert H. "The Rhetoric of the Book of Judges." *VTSup* 63. Leiden: E. J. Brill, 1996.

Patrick, Dale and Allen Scult. *Rhetoric and Biblical Interpretation*. Sheffield: The Almond Press, 1990.

Pratt, Richard L. Jr. *He Gave Us Stories: The Bible Student's Guide to Interpreting Old Testament Narratives*. Phillipsburg, NJ: Presbyterian and Reformed Publishing, 1990.

Prickett, S. *Words and the Word: Language Poetics and Biblical Interpretation*. Cambridge: Cambridge University Press, 1986.

Prince, Gerald. *A Dictionary of Narratology*. Lincoln: University of Nebraska Press, 1987.

Rhoads, David and Donald Richie. *Mark as Story: An Introduction to the Narrative of a Gospel*. Philadelphia: Fortress Press, 1982.

Ryken, Leland. *How to Read the Bible as Literature*. Grand Rapids: Zondervan Publishing House, 1984.

_____. *Words of Delight: A Literary Introduction to the Bible*. Grand Rapids: Baker Book House, 1987.

Scholes, Robert. *Approaches to the Novel*. San Francisco: Chandler Publishing Company, 1961.

Scholes, Robert and Robert Kellogg. *The Nature of Narrative*. New York: Oxford University Press, 1966.

Ska, Jean Louis. *Our Fathers Have Told Us: Introduction to the Analysis of Hebrew Narratives*. Rome: Pontifical Biblical Institute, 1990.

Sternberg, Meir. *Expositional Modes and Temporal Ordering*. Bloomington: Indiana University Press, 1978.

_____. *The Poetics of Biblical Narrative: Ideological Literature and the Drama of Reading*. Bloomington: Indiana University Press, 1985.

Uspensky, Boris. *A Poetics of Composition*. Translated by Valentina Zavarin and Susan Wittig. Berkeley: University of California Press, 1973.

2) 단편 연구, 논술 Articles and Essays

Alter, Robert. "A Response to Critics." *JSOT* 27 (1983): 113-17.

_____. "Introduction to the Old Testament." In *The Literary Guide to the Bible*. Edited by Robert Alter and Frank Kermode. Cambridge: The Belknap Press of Harvard University Press, 1987.

_____. "Sodom as Nexus: The Web of Design in Biblical Narrative." In *The Book and the Text: The Bible and Literary Theory.* Edited by Regina Schwartz. Cambridge: Basil Blackwell, Inc., 1990.

Bar-Efrat, Shimon. "Some Observations on the Analysis of Structure in Biblical Narrative." *VT* 30 (1980): 154-173.

Berlin, Adele. "Literary Exegesis of Biblical Narrative: Between Poetics and Hermeneutics." In *Not In Heaven.* Edited by Jason P. Rosenblatt and Joseph C. Sitterson, Jr. Bloomington: Indiana University Press, 1991.

Berlin, Adele and James Kugel. "On the Bible as Literature." *Prooftexts* 2 (1982): 323-332.

Clines, D. J. A. "Story and Poem: The Old Testament as Literature and as Scripture." *Beyond Form Criticism: Essays in Old Testament Literary Criticism.* SBTS 2. Winona Lake: Eisenbrauns, 1992.

Crane, R. S. "The Concept of Plot and the Plot of 'Tom Jones.'" In *Critics and Criticism.* Edited by R. S. Crane. Chicago: University of Chicago Press, 1952.

Culler, Jonathan. "Defining Narrative Units." In *Style and Structure in Literature.* Edited by Roger Fowler. Ithaca: Cornell University Press, 1975.

Du Rand, J. A. "Plot and Point of View in the Gospel of John." In *A South African Perspective on the New Testament.* Edited by J. H. Petzer and P. J. Hartin. Leiden: E. J. Brill, 1986.

Duke, Rodney K. "A Model for a Theology of Biblical Historical Narratives Proposed and Demonstrated with the Books of Chronicles." In *History and Interpretation: Essays in Honour of John H. Hayes.*

Edited by M. Patrick Graham, William P. Brown, and Jeffrey K. Kuan. Sheffield: Sheffield Press, 1993.

Egan, Kieran. "What is a Plot?" *New Literary History* 9 (1978): 455-73.

Eslinger, Lyle. "Viewpoints and Point of View in 1 Samuel 8-12." *JSOT* 26 (1983): 61-76.

Fewel, Danna Nolan, and David M. Gunn. "Tipping the Balance: Sternberg's Reader and the Rape of Dinah." *JBL* 110 (1991): 193-211.

Fokkelman, J. P. "Genesis." In *The Literary Guide to the Bible*. Edited by Robert Alter and Frank Kermode. Cambridge: The Belknap Press of Harvard University Press, 1987.

Garbini, Giovanni. "Hebrew Literature in the Persian Period." In *Second Temple Studies: 2. Temple Community in the Persian Period*. Edited by Tamara C. Eskenazi and Kent H. Richards. Sheffield: Sheffield Academic Press, 1994.

Green, Barbara. "The Plot of the Biblical Story of Ruth." in *Beyond Form Criticism: Essays in Old Testament Literary Criticism*. SBTS 2. Winona Lake: Eisenbrauns, 1992.

Green, Douglas. "Ezra-Nehemiah." In *A Complete Literary Guide to the Bible*. Edited by Leland Ryken and Tremper Longman III. Grand Rapids: Zondervan Publishing House, 1993.

Greenstein, Edward L. "Biblical Narratology." *Prooftexts* 1 (1981): 201-208.

House, Paul R. "The Rise and Current Status of Literary Criticism of the Old Testament." In *Beyond Form Criticism: Essays in Old Testament Literary Criticism*. SBTS 2. Winona Lake: Eisenbrauns, 1992.

_____. "Plot, Prophecy and Jeremiah." *JETS* 36 (1993): 297-307.

Lanser, Susan S. "Plot." In *The New Princeton Encyclopedia of Poetry and Poetics*. Edited by Alex Preminger and T. V. F. Brogan. New York: MJF Books, 1993.

Long, Philips V. "Toward a Better Theory and Understanding of Old Testament Narrative." *Presbyterian* 13 (1987): 102-109.

Longman, Tremper III. "The Literary Approach to the Study of the Old Testament: Promise and Pitfalls." *JETS* 28 (1985): 385-398.

_____. "Biblical Narrative." In *A Complete Literary Guide to the Bible*. Edited by Leland Ryken and Tremper Longman III. Grand Rapids: Zondervan Publishing House, 1993.

_____. "Storytellers and Poets in the Bible: Can Literary Artifice Be True?" In *Inerrancy and Hermeneutics*. Edited by Harvie M. Conn. Grand Rapids: Baker Book House, 1994.

_____. "Literary Approaches to Old Testament Study." In *The Face of Old Testament Studies: A Survey of Contemporary Approaches*. Edited by David W. Baker and Bill T. Arnold. Grand Rapids: Baker Book House, 1999.

Magonet, Jonathan. "The Problem of Perspective in Biblical Narrative." In *Literary Structure and Rhetorical Strategies in the Hebrew Bible*. Edited by L. J. de Regt, J. de Waard, and J. P. Fokkelman. Winona Lake: Eisenbrauns, 1996.

Martin, W. J. "'Dischronologized' Narrative in the Old Testament." *VTSup* 17 (1968): 179-186.

Matera, Frank J. "The Plot of Matthew's Gospel." *CBQ* 49 (1987): 233-253.

Mathewson, Steven D. "Guidelines for Understanding and Proclaiming Old Testament Narratives." *Bibliotheca Sacra* 154 (1997): 410-435.

McKnight, Scot. "Literary Criticism of the Synoptic Gospels." *Trinity

Journal 8 (1987): 57-68.

Mills, Watson and Richard Wilson. *Mercer Commentary on the Bible.* Macon, GA: Mercer University Press, 1995.

Muilenburg, James. "Form Criticism and Beyond." *JBL* 88 (1969): 1-18.

Perry, Menakhem. "Literary Dynamics: How the Order of a Text Creates its Meaning." *Poetics Today* 1, no. 1-2 (1979): 35-64, 311-361.

Pratt, Richard L. Jr. "Pictures, Windows, and Mirrors in Old Testament Exegesis." *WTJ* 45 (1983): 156-167.

Ricoeur, Paul. "Interpretive Narrative." In *The Book and the Text: The Bible and Literary Theory.* Translated by David Pellauer. Edited by Regina Schwartz. Cambridge, ME: Basil Blackwell, Inc., 1990.

Ryken, Leland. "Literary Criticism of the Bible: Some Fallacies (속임수)." In *Literary Interpretations of Biblical Narratives.* Vol. 1. Edited by Kenneth R. R. Gros Louis. Nashville: Abingdon Press, 1974.

_____. "The Bible as Literature—Part 1" *Bibliotheca Sacra* 147 (1990): 3-15.

_____. "The Bible as Literature—Part 2" *Bibliotheca Sacra* 147 (1990): 131-142.

_____. "The Bible and Literary Study." In *The Discerning Reader: Christian Perspectives on Literature and Theory.* Edited by David Barratt, Roger Pooley, and Leland Ryken. Grand Rapids: Baker Book House, 1995.

Satterthwaite, Philip E. "Narrative Criticism: The Theological Implications of Narrative Techniques." In Vol. 1 of New International Dictionary of Old Testament Theology and Exegesis. Edited by Willem A. VanGemeren. Grand Rapids: Zondervan Publishing House, 1997.

Schultz, Richard. "Integrating Old Testament Theology and Exegesis:

Literary, Thematic, and Canonical Issues." In Vol. 1 of *New International Dictionary of Old Testament Theology and Exegesis*. Edited by Willem A. VanGemeren. Grand Rapids: Zondervan Publishing House, 1997.

Sternberg, Meir. "Ordering the Unordered: Time, Space, and Descriptive Coherence." *Yale French Studies* 61 (1981): 60-88.

_____. "Deictic Sequence: World, Language and Convention." In *Essays on Deixis(직시)*. Edited by Gisa Rauh. T bingen: Gunter Narr, 1983.

_____. "The Bible's Art of Persuasion: Ideology, Rhetoric, and Poetics in Saul's Fall." *HUCA* 54 (1983): 45-82.

_____. "Telling in Time (I): Chronology and Narrative Theory." *Poetics Today* 11 (1990): 901-948.

_____. "Time and Reader." In *The Uses of Adversity: Failure and Accommodation in Reader Response*. Edited by Ellen Spolsky. Cranbury, NJ: Associated University Presses, Inc., 1990.

_____. "Time and Space in Biblical History Telling: The Grand Chronology." In *The Book and the Text: The Bible and Literary Theory*. Edited by Regina Schwartz. Cambridge: Basil Blackwell, Inc., 1990.

_____. "Double Cave, Double Talk: The Indirections of Biblical Dialogue." In *Not In Heaven*. Edited by Jason P. Rosenblatt and Joseph C. Sitterson, Jr. Bloomington: Indiana University Press, 1991.

_____. "Telling in Time (II): Chronology, Teleology(목적론), Narrativity." *Poetics Today* 13 (1992): 463-541.

Talmon, Shemaryahu. "The Presentation of Synchroneity and

Simultaneity in Biblical Narrative." In *Studies in Hebrew Narrative Art Throughout the Ages*. Edited by Joseph Heinemann. Jerusalem: The Magnes Press, 1978.

_____. "Ezra and Nehemiah." In *The Literary Guide to the Bible*. Edited by Robert Alter and Frank Kermode. Cambridge: The Belknap Press of Harvard University Press, 1987.

Trawick, Buckner B. "Establishment of a Church State after the Exile." In *The Bible as Literature*. 2d ed. New York: Barnes & Noble Books, 1970.

Van Aarde, A. G. "Plot as Mediated Through Point of View. MT 22:1-14 A Case Study." In *A South African Perspective on the New Testament*. Edited by J. H. Petzer and P. J. Hartin. Leiden: E. J. Brill, 1986.

3) 미간행 논문 Unpublished Works

Lehman, Mark L. "The Literary Study of Esther Showing Contributions to the Book's Historicity and Theology." Ph.D. diss, Bob Jones University, 1992.

Linares, Jose. "A Methodology for Preaching Old Testament Narrative." D. Min. diss., Bob Jones University, 2000.

Reynolds, Steve L. "A Literary Analysis of Nehemiah." Ph.D. diss., Bob Jones University, 1994.

8. 기타 Others

Costas, O. E. *Christ Outside the Gate : Mission Beyond Christendom*. Maryknoll, NY: Orbis Books. 1983. (사회의 주변에 사는 자들에게 복음을 전할 때 필요한 상황적 선교적 통찰력을 제공함. Provides contextual missiological insights of the Gospels outreach to those who live on the periphery of society.)

Dobson, Edward. "Divorce in the Old Testament." *Fundamentalist Journal* 10 (1985): 28-29.

Epstein, Louis M. *Marriage Laws in the Bible and the Talmud*. Cambridge: Harvard University Press, 1942; reprint, New York: Johnson Reprint Corporation, 1968.

Heth, William A. and Gordon J. Wenham. *Jesus and Divorce: The Problem with the Evangelical Consensus*. Nashville: Thomas Nelson Publishers, 1984.

Jacques, A. *The Stranger Within Your Gates: Uprooted People in the World Today*, World Council of Churches, Geneva. 1986. (우리와 함께 살아가는 낯선 사람들은 그들이 이민자든지 도망자든지 뿌리 뽑힌 사람들이다. 본 서는 그들의 체험들과 그리스도인으로서 우리의 책임에 관한 내용을 담고 있다. Strangers within our gates are the uprooted people, whether they are migrants or refugees. This book is about their experiences and about our responsibility as Christians.)

Johnson, Luke T. *Sharing Possessions: Mandate and Symbol of Faith*. Overture to Biblical Theology. Philadelphia : Fortress Press. 1981. (기독교 공동체 생활의 경제적 차원을 고찰한 책이다. 부와 구제를 포기하는 신약성경의 견해와는 대조를 이루며 부와 구제에 대한 현대적 논증을 제시한다. Investigates the economic dimensions of Christian community life.

Contrasts New Testament views on renouncing wealth and almsgiving and presents a contemporary argument for the latter.)

Macleod, David. "The Problem of Divorce, Part 2." *The Emmaus Journal* 2 (1993): 23-44.

Nouwen, Henri. *Reaching Out: The Three Movements of the Spiritual Life*. New York: Doubleday & Co. 1975. ("적대에서 환대로" 논술을 다룬 목회적 글임. A pastoral essay in which the second movement treated is entitled "From Hostility to Hospitality.")

Ogletree, Thomas W. *Hospitality to the Stranger: Dimensions of Moral understanding*. Philadelphia: Fortress Press. 1985 (나그네에게 호의를 베푸는 것이 새롭고, 익숙하지 않으며 우리 생활세계에 알려지지 않는 것을 환영하는 것이라는 논지로 쓴 글이다. The thesis is that to offer hospitality to a stranger is to welcome something new, unfamiliar, and unknown into our life world.)

Osborne, Grant R. *The Hermeneutical Spiral*. Downers Grove: InterVarsity Press, 1991.

Palmer, Parker, *The Company of Strangers: Christians and the Renewal of America's Public Life*. New York: Crossroad. 1981 (현대 생활 속에서 "손님 가운데의 생활"과 "영적 가이드로서의 손님"에 대한 탁월한 논쟁을 담고 있다. Contains illuminating discussions of "Life among Strangers" and "The Stranger as Spiritual Guide" within contemporary society.)

Rusche, H., *Gastfreundschaft in der Verkuendgigung des Neuen Testaments und ihr Verhaeltnis zur Mission*. Muenster: Aschendorff. 1959.

Russell, Letty M. *The Future of Partnership*. Philadelphia: Westminster Press. 1979.

_____. *Growth in Partnership*. Philadelphia: Westminster

Press. 1981. (새로운 창조 속의 하나님과 인간의 협력관계에 대한 실천적이고 신학적 접근: 해방신학적 관점. A Practical-theological approach to human partnership with God in the New Creation; argues for a form of liberation theology.)

Schuessler Fiorenza, Elisabeth. *In Memory of Her: A Feminist Theological Reconstruction of Christian Origins*. New York: Crossroad. 1983.

Warren, Max, *Partnership: The Study of an Idea*. London: SCM Press. 1956.

에스라·느헤미야의 결혼 개혁
The Marriage Reforms of Ezra-Nehemiah

1판 1쇄 인쇄 _ 2025년 6월 20일
1판 1쇄 발행 _ 2025년 6월 25일

지은이 _ 윤사무엘
펴낸이 _ 이형규
펴낸곳 _ 쿰란출판사

주소 _ 서울특별시 종로구 이화장길 6
편집부 _ 745-1007, 745-1301~2, 747-1212, 743-1300
영업부 _ 747-1004, FAX 745-8490
본사평생전화번호 _ 0502-756-1004
홈페이지 _ http://www.qumran.co.kr
E-mail _ qrbooks@daum.net / qrbooks@gmail.com
한글인터넷주소 _ 쿰란, 쿰란출판사
페이스북 _ www.facebook.com/qumranpeople
인스타그램 _ www.instagram.com/qrbooks
등록 _ 제1-670호(1988.2.27)
책임교열 _ 최진희·김준표

© 윤사무엘 2025 ISBN 979-11-94464-68-6 93230

책값은 뒤표지에 있습니다.
이 출판물은 저작권법에 의해 보호를 받는 저작물이므로 무단 복제할 수 없습니다.
파본(破本)은 구입처에서 교환해 드립니다.